THE COST OF DEMOCRACY

Party funding has given rise to great controversy since 1997, and continues to do so. In recent years, row has followed row – from million-pound donations, to the so-called 'loans for peerages' affair. The question is now the subject of an official investigation by Sir Hayden Phillips, whose blueprint for reform is expected early in 2007. This book charts the evolution of the party funding problem in recent years and explores the weaknesses of the Political Parties, Elections and Referendums Act 2000, which was enacted in a vain attempt to clean up British politics.

The book sets out a number of core principles which should inform the development of public policy in this field, and examines the different strategies for the implementation of these principles. Having regard to the experience of other countries, including Canada, Germany and Sweden, a radical framework of reform is proposed, designed to address the emerging crisis of party government – with serious implications for democracy itself. The main concern is with the development of bold reform initiatives to encourage political parties to recruit and retain members, and give members rights in relation to the government and administration of these parties.

This thoughtful yet hard-hitting account by one of the leading scholars in the field will be of interest to constitutional lawyers and political scientists, as well as journalists and those with an interest in the way we are governed.

The Cost of Democracy
Party Funding in Modern British Politics

K D EWING

·HART·
PUBLISHING

OXFORD AND PORTLAND, OREGON
2007

Published in North America (US and Canada) by
Hart Publishing
c/o International Specialized Book Services
920 NE 58th Avenue, Suite 300
Portland, OR 97213-3786
USA
Tel: +1-503-287-3093 or toll-free: +1-800-944-6190
Fax: +1-503-280-8832
Email: orders@isbs.com
Website: www.isbs.com

Hart Publishing, 16C Worcester Place, Oxford, OX1 2JW
Telephone: +44 (0)1865 517530   Fax: +44 (0) 1865 510710
Email: mail@hartpub.co.uk
Website: http://www.hartpub.co.uk

British Library Cataloguing in Publication Data
Data Available

ISBN-13: 978-1-84113-716-2 (hardback)
ISBN-10: 1-84113-716-2 (hardback)

Typeset by Forewords, Oxford
Printed and bound in Great Britain by
Biddles Ltd, King's Lynn, Norfolk

For Alexander

Preface

The Labour government elected in May 1997 has many achievements, not least in the area of constitutional reform. But the premiership of Tony Blair has also been dogged from its very beginning by allegations of 'sleaze', 'cash for favours', and 'cash for coronets'. The allegations began in the earliest days of the administration with the controversy surrounding the donation of £1 million from Mr Bernie Ecclestone, and continue into the twilight of Mr Blair's period in office with the so-called 'loans for peerages' affair.

So far as the latter is concerned, *The Guardian* has written of the affair travelling over the course of 2006 'from the margins of politics to the very centre', speculating gravely about the Prime Minister being questioned by the police, and debating about when in such circumstances a Prime Minister should be required to resign, with 'Britain's elastic constitution' being stretched 'in new directions' (18 November 2006). Whatever the faults of the unwritten constitution, the seriousness with which this matter has been investigated by the police suggests that the rule of law at least remains a vibrant principle of great substance, though this is not to under-estimate the very real concerns expressed in some quarters about the political impact of a prolonged investigation of this kind. This may be of little comfort to the governing classes, but it provides some re-assurance to the rest of us.

At the time of writing, it is not known how the 'loans for peerages' affair will end. But regardless of whether the affair ends with a bang or a whimper, it has rekindled an acute interest in the funding of political parties. It has also forced a re-assessment of the legal regulation of party financing, and a re-examination of the statutory framework established in the wake of the Ecclestone affair. Despite being in force for only five years, the Political Parties, Elections and Referendums Act 2000 has already been found wanting, and a fresh statutory response is now required, to deal not only with so-called 'loans for peerages', but with a number of other problems which have emerged as well.

But what form should any new legal settlement take? This simple question lies at the heart of this book, which tracks the problem of party funding in the ten-year period since 1997. As will be revealed, there is no simple solution to the problem, though any package for reform must be based on a recognition of the central importance of political parties as constitutional players. Thereafter, the aim should be to seek a regulatory framework that (i) guards against the risk of corruption, (ii) promotes equality of electoral opportunity, (iii) ensures that political parties are adequately funded for the discharge of their constitutional duties, (iv) promotes citizen participation in the funding of political parties, (v) respects the diversity of party structure, and (vi) ensures that human rights obligations (such as freedom of association and expression) are fully respected. In promoting these regulatory objectives, there are a number of regulatory methods which can be adopted. These different regulatory methods are fully explored in chapter 3.

In terms of these regulatory objectives, however, there are two points that need to be addressed at this stage. The first relates to the prevention of corruption. It is perhaps remarkable that this now needs to be seen explicitly as a serious regulatory objective, Britain typically being regarded as a country free from the worst excesses of corruption. Indeed, it is with some reluctance that such a strong word is even used in the context of British government, for fear of gross exaggeration of the true state of affairs. But as is pointed out in chapter two, corruption is a word with many shades of meaning, and its use in this book is to raise questions about the corruption of principle, as a result of the way in which political parties generally are funded, whether in the United Kingdom or elsewhere. This is not to suggest or imply any corrupt motive or intent on the part of any donor, or any corrupt conduct on the part of any recipient. And certainly it is not to suggest any unlawful or improper conduct on the part of either.

The other issue to be emphasised here is the problem of diverse party structures and the asymmetrical nature of our political parties, which are quite unlike those operating in the United States or mainland Europe. Specifically, unlike the Conservative and Liberal Democrat parties, the Labour Party is an association of individuals and organisations (trade unions and socialist societies), the latter making financial contributions based to some extent on the number of members in the different organisations in question. Such a model of party organisation – which has counterparts in Commonwealth countries – presents peculiar challenges for the regulator. Insensitivity to diversity would lead to significant inroads on freedom of association if it meant that the State was to prescribe a template for party organisation. Over-sensitivity to diversity, on the other hand, would make it difficult to control large personal donations and the corruption of principle already alluded to.

In the course of preparing this book, I have accumulated debts to a large number of people, some of which I will never be able to repay. Navraj Ghaleigh kindly agreed to me including in chapter 6 material prepared by us jointly for several projects on which we have worked together. As well as thanking the editors of the *Election Law Journal* for permission to include in chapter 7 material first published in that journal, I should also like to acknowledge the support, advice and assistance of Tony Bradley, Yves-Marie Doublet, Barry Fitzpatrick, Andrew Geddis, Reuben Hasson, Éric Hébert, Samuel Issacharoff, Arnauld Miguet, Lewis Minkin, George Newlands, Graeme Orr, Joo-Cheong Tham and Stuart Weir. Tom Adams, Mel Hamill and Richard Hart have been superb, not only in their encouragement, but also in their speed and efficiency, turning an incomplete manuscript delivered in September 2006 into a book ready to go into the shops less than four months later. Thanks also to Steve Bell for permission to use the cartoon.

Finally, and most importantly, Gail, Kate, Lucy and Alexander have encouraged over many years my obsession with politics and the money that sustains it; while my colleagues at King's continue to provide a warm and hospitable academic environment in which to work.

KDE
24 November 2006

Contents

1

A Drama Unfolds

Introduction

On 12 July 2006, Lord Levy of Mill Hill was arrested in a London police station as part of investigations by the Specialist Crime Directorate into allegations about political party funding.[1] The arrest was made in connection with inquiries under the obscure Honours (Prevention of Abuses) Act 1925 and the more recent Political Parties, Elections and Referendums Act 2000 (PPERA).[2] This was a sensational development, as Lord Levy is widely reported as being 'Tony Blair's chief fund-raiser', as well as his Special Envoy to the Middle East, and his tennis partner. It was all the more sensational for the fact that no charges were brought, for the fact that the arrest was condemned as being 'wholly unnecessary' (with Lord Levy willing to co-operate with the police), and for the fact that Lord Levy vigorously denied any wrongdoing and denied having committed any offence. Nevertheless, opponents were not slow to see the political consequences, with the leader of the Scottish National Party (SNP) claiming that the 'water was now lapping around the Prime Minister's feet', others no doubt privately hoping that the police investigation would lead in due course to the water levels rising even higher. But whatever the final outcome of this unfolding constitutional drama, how could something as simple as the funding of political parties have such remarkable consequences?

The Conservative Funding Legacy

Although a long-standing problem, the question of party funding became more prominent in the 1990s as part of the overall question of the 'sleaze' that was affecting the British political system.[3] This is a matter brought to public attention by the so-called 'cash-for-questions affair', in which two Conservative MPs were

---

[1] See also *The Guardian*, 12 July 2006, *The Independent*, 12 July 2006, and *The Times*, 12 July 2006
[2] *The Independent*, 12 July 2006.
[3] See K D Ewing, 'The Funding of Political Parties in Britain: Prospects for Reform' (1998) 7 *Griffith Law Review* 185.

alleged to have taken money for asking questions in Parliament.[4] The affair led to the establishment of the Committee on Standards in Public Life, and a new Code of Conduct for MPs.[5] But concerns were also expressed about the funding of political parties, with the donation of £440,000 to the Conservative Party by the Polly Peck tycoon Asil Nadir being particularly controversial. Nadir subsequently fled to Northern Cyprus after having been accused of fraud following the collapse of Polly Peck, and questions were raised about whether the donation should be returned. Yet this was not the only concern about the funding of the governing party: another was that in an area when there was a growing demand for transparency, the funding arrangements of the Conservatives remained strangely secret; while yet another was the suspicion that large sums were being contributed to the Conservatives from foreign sources.

Secret Funding

By 1997, it was the practice of almost every democratic country in the world that political parties should be required to reveal the sources of their income. Not in Britain. The parties voluntarily published annual income and expenditure accounts, but they were under no legal obligation to provide even this basic information, and there was no one to vouch for the accuracy of the information that was provided. The Labour Party had since 1995 published annually the names of those who donated more than £5,000, but did not publish the amount. The Conservative Party refused to publish even the names of donors; this information was said to be 'one of the Party's most closely guarded secrets', locked in the Treasury Department at Conservative Central Office.[6] The information was concealed even from party members who complained about the inadequacy of membership rights, especially in the area of financial accountability.[7] The secrecy was justified by the then treasurer of the party on the ground that 'Conservative Central Office is not a charity dedicated to helping the sick and suffering', and that it would be 'the height of folly to expose how such a machine manages its resources or, indeed, how large, or how small these resources are at any one time'.[8]

The secrecy of party funding was one of the issues addressed by the House of Commons Home Affairs Committee which conducted an inquiry into *The Funding of Political Parties* in 1993. But the Conservative-dominated committee concluded that the case had not been made out 'for requiring disclosure of the identity of donors; where donations are made from identifiable and legitimate sources known to the party they should be allowed to remain private'.[9] In so

---

[4] HC 30 (1996–97).
[5] HC 688 (1996–97).
[6] *Sunday Times*, 27 September 1992.
[7] HC 726 (1992–93), pp 164–5.
[8] Lord McAlpine, *Once a Jolly Bagman* (1997), p 229.
[9] HC 726 (1992–93), para 80.

concluding, the Committee hid in a fog of arguments based on considerations of principle and overwhelming practical objections. The argument of principle had been provided in oral evidence to the Committee by Sir Norman Fowler, the Chairman of the Conservative Party. Drawing on Sir Norman, the Committee was of the view that

> Privacy in donations was as fundamental a right when giving to political parties as when giving to any other charitable organisation. What individuals did with their own money was entirely a matter for them and was not of legitimate interest to either inquisitive journalists, political opponents, or even the State. To reveal a name would be a breach of a donor's right to privacy, although of course if he wished to disclose his identity, he was at liberty to do so.[10]

So far as 'particular and substantial difficulties' were concerned,[11] these related to the threshold at which any donation would be subject to disclosure, in view of the widely different proposals made by the range of witnesses to the Committee. There was also concern about the administrative machinery that would be needed to ensure compliance with any such obligation, and reference to the experience in Germany where it was said by one of the academic witnesses to the Committee that 'the main parties had simply colluded to break the law'.[12]

Foreign Funding

Because the Conservative Party refused to publish adequate financial information, it was impossible to know exactly who was funding the party. But it was strongly suspected that significant sums were being contributed from overseas. Indeed, as one leading Tory MP said:

> In the 1990s, this party was a beacon for the rest of the world, leading from the front on privatisation and free enterprise. It's perfectly reasonable if businessmen anywhere want to see this government continue to set an example for the rest of the world. I don't want more openness. I think the party is too open about its affairs as things are.[13]

There were in fact a number of well-documented foreign donations, including £1m from Sir Y K Pao (Hong Kong), £1.5 m from John Latsis (Greek shipping millionaire), and £1m from C K Ma (Hong Kong).[14] There were also allegations that as much as £1.5m had been given by the family of an alleged drug smuggler who had been based in Hong Kong,[15] though it was hotly denied that the donor ever raised with the Party 'the fate of his father, a suspected drugs trafficker and

---

10 *Ibid*, para 73.
11 *Ibid*, para 74.
12 *Ibid*, para 79,.
13 *The Times*, 27 June 1993.
14 See *Daily Mirror*, 4 March 1997, *Daily Telegraph*, 20 January 1998, and *Daily Mail*, 21 January 1998.
15 *Daily Mail*, 21 January 1998.

fugitive'.[16] Substantial donations were reported from the United States, Australia and Macao,[17] while evidence also surfaced about fifty branches of Conservatives Abroad in eighteen countries. Official estimates of Tory funding from overseas put the total received in this period at £16.2m.[18] In more recent times, evidence has come to light that the Conservative Party had been bankrolled by an Australian entrepreneur during Mr Major's tenure as leader. The businessman in question is said to have paid an average of £4.5 m annually for six years into a Conservative Party account, and 'to have persuaded a string of Australian multinationals, including oil and gas companies, banks and property giants to join him in giving generously'. Senior Conservative Party officials were now said to acknowledge that without this money the 'party may not have survived the financial crisis it faced in the mid 1990s when it carried a £14m overdraft and needed millions to prepare for a general election campaign'.[19]

Again, the issue of foreign funding of British political parties was examined by the Home Affairs Committee in 1994. But the Committee saw 'no reason to propose that parties should refuse foreign donations',[20] the main obstacle being how to define whether someone was 'foreign' for this purpose. It had been suggested to the Committee that 'participation in . . . elections should be restricted to people and organisations that have a legitimate interest and stake in the future of the country'. But this was rejected on the ground that 'deciding who has a legitimate interest in British elections is, however, not particularly simple'. Referring again to the evidence of Sir Norman Fowler, the Committee pointed out that

> Britons living abroad, European Community citizens resident in the United Kingdom and entitled to vote in local and European elections, and businesses with interests in the United Kingdom were all legitimate donors. In their different ways, it could be argued that Bangladeshi citizens resident in Britain, residents of Hong Kong, citizens of the European Union resident anywhere in the Community, and businesses operating within the Single Market equally have a legitimate interest and stake in the future of the United Kingdom.[21]

It is true that there will be problems of scope at the margins. But it is not clear why anyone who does not have a right to vote in this country should have the right to influence the outcome of an election by financial donations, regardless of the nature of the interest they may have in its outcome. Nor is it clear why a company or any other legal person which does not have a base in this country should have the right to influence the outcome of an election by financial

---

[16] *The Times*, 21 January 1998.

[17] Details of other foreign donations emerged in the press from time to time. See *The Guardian*, 5 June 1994 (donation of £200,000 to the Conservative Party from a head of one of the most powerful companies in Hong Kong), and *The Guardian*, 22 May 1996 (donation of £100,000 to the Conservative Party from a businessman based in Macao).

[18] Cm 4057–I, 1998, para 3.12.

[19] *Sunday Times*, 17 November 2002.

[20] HC 726 (1992–93), para 90.

[21] *Ibid*, para 89.

donations. Indeed, in this latter case there are some who would question why even British-based legal persons should be entitled to influence electoral outcomes.

The 'Arms Race'

Apart from questions about the income of the parties, the other emerging concern in the 1990s related to expenditure. Although there were limits on the amount of permitted expenditure by candidates, there were no limits on party spending at election or at any other times. Spending levels had gradually increased at general elections in the late twentieth century, though even by 1992 they were comparatively modest. At the general election in that year, the Conservative Party spent £11m, and the Labour Party £10m, though these figures are to be treated with caution on the ground that they represent the untested claims of the parties themselves. It is also the case that these figures may be calculated on different bases, so that what one party considers to be an election expense, the other does not. But with these qualifications, it remains the case that there was extraordinary inflation in the period between 1992 and 1997 when the parties were reporting election expenses of £28m in the case of the Conservative Party and £26.8m in the case of the Labour Party. In the case of the Labour Party, this expenditure extended back to 1995 when £2.67m was spent, rising to £10.38m in 1996 and £13.75m in 1997. In the case of the Conservatives, however, the £28m is an assessment of what was spent only in the twelve months before the election.

Funding Pressures

The 1997 election spending puts into stark perspective what became known as the 'arms race' in British politics. In the case of the Labour Party, expenditure in 1997 was thought to be growing at around 10 per cent per annum compound in real terms, and to have been doing so for twenty years. This meant that the party was doubling its expenditure every seven years, at a time when trade union membership was in freefall. Trade unions historically had provided the bulk of party finances, and indeed in the 1970s had provided some 85 per cent of its income. But trade union membership in 1997 had fallen to only half its 1980 level of 13 million, and trade union affiliation levels were falling as a result. Trade unions thus could not sustain this level of activity, and for a number of reasons it was not appropriate that they should. This in any event suited the new party leadership, anxious to dilute trade union influence, including the financial influence of the trade unions. Fund-raising was developed and diversified, with the emergence of new techniques and the identification of new sources of income. The latter included large donors, euphemistically referred to as high-value donors, who quickly became a significant part of the Labour Party fund-raising enterprise. Those donating more than £1,000 accounted for 20 per cent of Labour Party income in 1997, in what was a sharp break with the past.

With the rise in income came a rise in expenditure, and although it was difficult to identify the areas of difference when comparing the 1970s with the 1990s, it was clear that election spending had risen dramatically. There was a concern that unless spending was capped in some way, it would grow larger and larger. These predictions were being made at a time when the parties were about to face even more spending demands, and consequently a need for even more money. Devolution for Scotland, Northern Ireland and Wales would add to election costs, as would the new Greater London Authority and the directly elected mayor. There were also proposed referendums in the wind on proportional representation and the single European currency, to add to the referendums that had taken place on Scottish and Welsh devolution. Although a referendum on proportional representation may not have been very expensive, the same could not be said about the euro if there were to be no limit on what could be spent. Much of the referendum spending would, of course, be spent by individuals and organisations in highly polarised referendum campaigns. But the political parties would still have been expected to play a prominent part, and indeed to take a lead in these campaigns.

State Abstention

So with the parties striving to keep up with each other at a time of increased obligations, where was the money to come from? The Home Affairs Committee had ruled out public funding for the parties in 1994, decisively rejecting even the modest proposals of the Houghton report less than twenty years earlier. The question of State funding was in fact the main issue examined by the Home Affairs Committee, the terms of reference of which included an examination of 'the case for and against State funding of political parties, excluding their work inside Parliament'.[22] But the main parties were split on the desirability of the State as a source of income, with the Labour Party and Liberal Democrats in favour and the Conservatives and SNP opposed. The Northern Irish parties were also split, with the Social Democratic and Labour Party (SDLP) being in favour and the Ulster Unionists against. With the parties conveniently split, it was 'unlikely that any proposal to introduce a substantial measure of State funding is practical politics'. Moreover, the Committee was not convinced that the parties were in such dire financial straits that they needed support by the taxpayer. According to the Committee, the cost of elections had fallen between 1929 and 1992, while the parties had managed to thrive despite the failure to implement Houghton's plans for State funding. In the words of the Committee, 'Houghton's 'direst warnings' about the collapse of party government 'have not proved well

[22] HC 301 (1993–94), para 1.

founded', and at a time when the public sector 'is facing severe budgetary restraint' the Committee was unable to 'endorse the case for a general extension of State funding along the lines proposed in previous reports'.[23]

The most that the Committee was able to offer was the recommendation that the government consider the feasibility of offering the main opposition parties one or two 'able' civil servants on a temporary attachment for an experimental period.[24] But this rather bizarre gesture was unlikely to stretch very far, even if able civil servants could be found to volunteer for work of this kind. In the absence of State funding or support, it would thus be left to the private sector to pick up the bill and to meet the increased costs. One way by which this could be done would be by the parties recruiting new members or by finding more small donors: mass movements to fund massive campaigns. But this was looking increasingly unlikely. The great Conservative growth had come to an end, and Labour Party membership would also soon collapse, as New Labour, like previous Labour governments, found that it was easier for parties of the Left to be elected than to meet the expectations of the faithful.[25] Indeed, it was recognised within the Labour Party as early as 1997 that although the party had a huge base of small donors, this was going to be increasingly difficult to expand. So if there was no reversal of the demand for political spending, it was inevitable that fund-raising would continue to concentrate heavily on high-value donations. This was not something about which anyone could be sanguine:

> Unlimited national expenditure creates an unlimited demand for funds to pay for the expenditure and the unlimited demand for funds causes . . . the parties, in practice, to turn for money to wealthy individual donors and wealthy organisations. Further, the fact that the parties turn to such individuals and organisations means that as in the United States, the suspicion arises that the money is not given without strings and that influence and money can be bought by means of large donations.[26]

The Labour Party's Response

The Labour Party responded to these developments by seeking to exploit the Conservative Party's discomfort and embarrassment about funding. The Labour Party submitted very full evidence to the Home Affairs Committee in 1993, in

---

[23] *Ibid*, para 56.

[24] *Ibid*, para 57.

[25] By 2004, Labour Party membership had fallen to 208,000 – from 405,000 in 1997: *The Guardian*, 3 August 2004.

[26] Fifth Report of the Committee on Standards in Public Life, *The Funding of Political Parties*, Cm 4057–1, para 10.25. Here the committee was reflecting arguments that had been made in evidence to it. For its part, the Committee thought that these concerns could be largely addressed by disclosure, but acknowledged that even with the disclosure of donations, 'the suspicion would still remain, as in the United States, that large cheques purchased large rewards' (*ibid*).

which it made a number of proposals for radical reform. These included the disclosure of financial information by the parties, such as annual accounts, donations by companies and trade unions (to include both the name of the donor and the amount of the donation), and large donations over an unspecified amount by individuals. It was also proposed that there should be full disclosure of income to election campaign funds (including donations in kind) and election expenditure. At the same time, the Labour Party renewed its commitment to State aid on the Houghton model, which updated for inflation would mean financial support for each qualifying party of 30p per vote based on the most recent general election. This would be funding for organisational needs of the parties, which the Labour Party proposed should be supplemented by the partial reimbursement of election expenses. But unlike the Houghton Committee, the Labour Party proposed that the reimbursement should apply not only to candidates' expenses, but also to the expenses of the parties themselves. It was made clear, however, that this proposal was tied to the additional recommendation that there should be a statutory cap on election expenses for political parties, though the limit would apply only to expenditure incurred on 'bought propaganda advertising of all kinds'.

Self-Regulation: Donations to the Labour Party

The Home Affairs Committee effectively recommended that the solution to the problems of political funding was self-regulation. To this end, it proposed that the parties should each adopt a code of practice, though it was left unclear who would draft this code, whether it would apply to all parties, and who would supervise its application. It was recommended, however, that the code would make clear that money does not buy influence or honours, illegally obtained money would not be acceptable, substantial anonymous donations would be refused, and that donations from foreign governments and rulers would be refused. Although they were accepted by the Conservative Party, these rather limited proposals seemed to fall short of what was required. They were nevertheless supplemented by a proposal that party accounts should be made publicly available to those who request them, and that the accounts should be independently audited. The code of practice would provide that party accounts should itemise benefits in kind, income over which the party has control (such as sales and fund-raising events), and expenditure. But there would be no sanction if a party refused to comply with the code, was late with the publication of the accounts,[27] or provided an incomplete picture of its finances.

The Labour Party's response to these proposals was to adopt its own guidelines which were 'intended to provide a workable voluntary framework pending

---

[27] As happened with the Conservative Party in 1998 when accounts for the year ending 31 March 1998 were not published until the end of November in controversial circumstances.

the enactment of appropriate legislation'.[28] They were also designed to demonstrate the party's commitment to accountability, transparency and probity in public life, which it proclaimed applied to the financial affairs of political parties. This was a clear attack on the then government which, encircled by allegations of 'sleaze', had appointed the Committee on Standards in Public Life, but without authorising the Committee to investigate the affairs of the political parties. The two main undertakings in the Labour Party's guidelines were the annual disclosure of all donations in excess of £5,000, and a ban on foreign donations. (In the previous year the Labour Party is said to have declined a gift of £5m alleged to have been offered by a Bangladeshi arms dealer,[29] thereby making an early contribution to ending the arms race between the parties.) While no doubt a demonstration of the Labour Party's commitment to probity in public life, in coinciding with the discomfort and vulnerability of the Conservative Party on funding issues, there was also an element of political opportunism about its new guidelines. By taking these steps, the Labour Party was making clear that the way in which political parties behaved was a partisan political issue. It was also a dangerous initiative for Labour: it was taking the moral high ground on ethical principles to which it would have to live up to at a time when its own fund-raising activities were metamorphosing and large donors were being targeted.

The Limits of Self-Regulation

Although this was an important initiative by the Labour Party, it was not without its limitations. The Party undertook only to disclose the names of donors in its annual report, but not the amounts of the donations. So apart from the fact that a donation made in January 1997 would not be made public until September 1998, there was no way of knowing how much was given by any donor. There was, however, a significant rise in the number of donors and sponsors reported, many of whom were distinguished and prominent names in their respective fields, which included the cinema, literature, music, business, and the law, as well as others. In 1996 17 donors were named, this rising to 55 in 1997 and 97 in 1998. The number of sponsors also rose from seven to 11 and then to 38. Another feature of the guidelines is that although widely defined, not all receipts were to be treated as donations and therefore subject to disclosure. So although a donation included donations in cash or in kind, sponsorship, and fund-raising events, it did not include advertising, sales, exhibitions and conferences, unless an element of political giving was involved in what were otherwise said to be 'services provided on an arm's length basis'. It may well be that these items should not be treated as donations. But it was left to the Labour Party to decide whether

---

[28] Labour Party, *Donations to the Labour Party* (nd).
[29] *Sunday Telegraph Magazine*, 17 May 1998. The same arms dealer is said to have offered his jet to Bob Dole to help him fight his unsuccessful campaign for the US presidency.

any income was a donation or sponsorship (and therefore declarable) or a commercial activity (and therefore not declarable).

It is also the case that the self-denial of foreign donations was not likely be a major problem for Labour, given that as a party it did not receive as many such donations as the Conservatives were believed to receive. But it would be a mistake to assume that there were no Labour supporters overseas, with Labour International being a particularly active body. In 1998, the Labour Party is thought to have had 1,500 members in forty different countries, with the best-organised groups being in Brussels, New York, Washington DC, Boston, Paris and Rome. Overseas members have voting rights in internal party elections and have a right to be represented at Conference following an amendment to the Labour Party rules in 1997. They could also donate to the party, provided they fell within the generous definition of who did not count as a foreign donor. Thus donations would be accepted from foreign nationals resident in the United Kingdom, or from British citizens resident overseas who were entitled to vote in United Kingdom general elections. The latter category would include people who at that time had been out of the country for up to 20 years, since reduced to 15. Under the terms of these rules, the Labour Party did not receive any foreign donations, though it would clearly have been possible for the Party to have accepted under the rules high-value and other donations from foreign nationals living in the United Kingdom and from British nationals living overseas.

Questions for the Labour Party

Whatever their limitations, the Labour Party's guidelines were in advance of the practices of the other parties by some way, and they set an example that others were eventually forced to follow. But it was not until after the 1997 general election that the Conservative Party under the leadership of William Hague announced that they too would publish the names of those who donated more than £5,000 annually, and that they too would no longer accept foreign donations. The Liberal Democrats followed suit at the same time, and the SNP held out for only a little longer. They maintained a policy of secrecy, apparently on the ground that it was necessary to protect prominent businessmen from discrimination in the award of government contracts.[30] They were also strongly committed to keeping open the possibility of funding the party by Scots living overseas, whether they could vote in this country or not. If it was possible for the Labour Party to raise money in London to fight elections to the Scottish Parliament, why should the SNP not be free to raise money in Lisbon or Los Angeles to do the same? There is no convincing response to this. Yet although the Labour Party was thus seen to be taking the moral high ground, with all the imperfections in the

[30] *Sunday Times*, 31 May 1998.

detail, they had also fashioned a rod for their own back in an era where they too relied heavily on large private donations.

Blind Trusts

The Labour Party's initiatives were reinforced by the commitment in the 1997 election manifesto to oblige parties to declare the source of all donations above a minimum figure, and to ban foreign donations. But the Labour Party was by no means above criticism, and a number of complaints began to be made about the party's fund-raising activities. The first of these related to the funding of the office of the Leader of the Opposition. An account of this was given in evidence (written and oral) to the Neill Committee by the Labour Party and its representatives.[31] There it was claimed that the practice of making money available to finance the Leader of the Opposition via so-called blind trusts had been in operation for many years. It was said that both John Smith and Hugh Gaitskell each used the device to raise money for their private offices. In the case of Tony Blair, the Labour Leader's Office Fund was established in 1995, the rules being drawn up by two top QCs who 'advised that the donors to the fund should not be revealed' to Mr Blair. This was to avoid 'any suggestion that the making of donations might be intended or might be motivated by any ulterior purpose'. A board of three peers was appointed to administer the trust and to ensure that only appropriate donations were accepted. These arrangements for what was referred by the Conservative press as Labour's 'slush fund' were approved by the Parliamentary Commissioner for Standards as not being in conflict with the Code of Conduct for Members of Parliament introduced after the First Report of the Committee on Standards in Public Life.[32]

Mr Blair was not alone in raising money in this way: the press reported that four other blind trusts had operated to support members of the Labour Shadow Cabinet before 1997.[33] But although there was no evidence to question the integrity or propriety of any of these arrangements, not everyone believed that blind trusts could be truly blind. The point was well made by Henry Drucker, an erstwhile advisor to the Labour Party on fund-raising.[34] According to Dr Drucker,

---

[31] See Cm 4057-I, 1998, paras 4.71 and 9.22.

[32] *Daily Telegraph*, 13 December 1996.

[33] See *The Times*, 28 November 1997, where it is reported that some members of the Shadow Cabinet had established their own funds, while others drew on the Labour Front Bench Research Fund. Not all Shadow Cabinet members drew on the fund for support. See also Cm 4057-1, 1998, paras 4.71 and 9.23.

[34] Oxford Philanthropic, *Creating a Victory Fund for New Labour* (May 1996). The Labour Party prepared a convincing rejection of some of the proposals in this document: The Labour Party, *Reasons for Rejecting the Report from Oxford Philanthropic* (December 1998).

> I know few donors and no very large donors, who are willing to give substantial sums unless they know that the [recipient] appreciates what they have done. It does not happen.[35]

This proved to be very embarrassing for Labour, which stood accused of double-standards.[36] Committed to the principle of transparency of political donations, the Party refused to name the donors to the blind trusts, and indeed was unable to do so. Yet because not everyone believed that the trusts were really blind, it gave rise to the suspicion that those who had given to the party when it was in opposition could benefit from their secret donations, now that it was in government. For his part, however, the Prime Minister expressly repudiated these allegations. When confronted in the House of Commons, Mr Blair said that '[D]r Drucker left the services of the Labour Party. Since then, he has launched a series of attacks on the Labour Party to which I do not attach any credibility'.[37]

Large Donations

Blind trusts were only part of the problem for New Labour. Another feature of Labour Party funding at this time was the fact that it was receiving some very large donations. Although the Party refused to publish details of the amount of donations received, some leaked out. In 1997 it was reported in the press that the Party was now receiving donations of £1m, at least three of which were in the public domain by the end of the year: those from Matthew Harding, David Sainsbury and Bernie Ecclestone, on the last of which more later. Apart from the Ecclestone affair (though perhaps partly because of it), the press were beginning to ask questions about donations and to relate them to government policy decisions, sometimes reaching conclusions that were very unpleasant yet difficult to refute. As is well known, it is sometimes impossible to prove a negative. A symptom of the kind of battering that was to beset New Labour was the story on the front page of the *Sunday Times* on 16 November 1997 about David Sainsbury's £1m donation. This was all the more timely for the fact that it was published on the same day that the Prime Minister was to appear on the BBC's *On the Record* programme, to be interviewed by the journalist John Humphreys about the £1m donation from Bernie Ecclestone. The purpose of the interview was to apologise for the way in which the circumstances surrounding that latter donation had been mishandled, and to provide reassurance that no impropriety had taken place.[38]

According to the *Sunday Times*, the Labour Party 'received substantial donations of several million pounds from business tycoons, some linked to companies

---

[35] Fifth Report of the Committee on Standards in Public Life, The Funding of Political Parties, vol 2, Cm 4057–II, para 1683.
[36] *Daily Telegraph*, 13 December 1996.
[37] HC Debs, 29 April 1998, col 327.
[38] *Sunday Times*, 16 November 1997, *The Guardian*, 17 November 1997.

which stood to make huge profits from ministerial approval of controversial planning decisions'. These included million-pound-donor Sainsbury whose company 'has been given government approval to build a huge and controversial out-of-town supermarket near Richmond-upon-Thames, Surrey'. The scheme allegedly had been endorsed by the planning minister shortly after the election when the environment department's planning inspectorate said it had no objection. This in itself is an indication that there was little substance in a story that would have been newsworthy only if the minister had overruled the inspectors who had advised against the development. It was prudently made clear that there was 'no suggestion of impropriety by any of the property developers and donors involved' in the story. But it was claimed nevertheless that the 'spate of multi-million-pound planning proposals puts the government is a politically embarrassing position', the implication being that there appeared to be a conflict of interest where donors to party funds were also benefiting from government decisions. Sainsbury was said to have two other superstore sites which needed official approval, and attention was drawn to the fact that another of the large superstore chains was a reported Labour Party sponsor. Along with Sainsbury Homebase, this particular company was said to be

> the biggest player in the out-of-town development business. It has 23 warehouses but plans to triple the number to 70 over the next few years. As with Homebase and Sainsbury supermarkets, some of these will require planning approval by . . . ministers.

The Ecclestone Affair

If matters such as the foregoing were sources of nagging irritation for the Labour Party, the Ecclestone donation was a potential disaster, which has dogged the Blair administration from its earliest days. It was not just that a large donation was made to the Labour Party that gave rise to so much difficulty. Also important was the way in which the affair was mishandled, fuelling the appearance of 'sleaze' and the sense that all was not quite right. The story dominated the news for a three-week period in November 1997, and started with a disclosure on 5 November that the government was proposing to push the European Commission to exempt Formula One from a proposed directive banning tobacco advertising. Although this is reported to have provoked fury from within the Commission, it was claimed that a ban would 'simply force the sport into eastern Europe and Asia, from which tobacco sponsored programmes would still be beamed into Europe'.[39] Accused of 'bowing to intense lobbying from Formula One', and supported by only one other EU Member State, the government

---

[39] *The Guardian*, 5 November 1997.

'remained committed to a ban on tobacco advertising but said it should be done in a sensible and pragmatic way'.[40]

A Large Donation

But more serious revelations were about to be made. On 16 October, Tony Blair met Mr Bernie Ecclestone, the head of Formula One; Max Mosley, the president of the Fédération Internationale de l'Automobile; and David Ward, a lobbyist who had previously been an adviser to John Smith. There is presumably nothing untoward about meetings at 10 Downing Street between the Prime Minister and leading business people. But what caught the imagination of the press in this case was that Max Mosley was not only 'a prominent Labour supporter', but that as such he had given 'thousands of pounds to Party funds' as a member of Labour's Thousand Club.[41] The press were also intrigued by the fact that the lawyer husband of Health Minister Tessa Jowell had been a non-executive director of a Formula One company, Benetton. This led to angry responses from both Mrs Jowell and her husband, the former claiming that suggestions of impropriety in his dealings were deeply offensive,[42] and the latter claiming that he had been subjected to unjustified intrusion into his business affairs to create embarrassment for his wife.[43] The Department of Health explained that both the Secretary of State (then Frank Dobson) and the Cabinet Secretary were 'fully satisfied that no conflict of interest arises for [Mrs Jowell or her husband] and that they have fully observed the Prime Minister's guidance to ministers on conduct and procedures'.[44]

Worse was to follow when it was revealed that Mr Ecclestone had himself made a substantial donation to the Labour Party before the election. But although the Prime Minister was aware of the donation, Downing Street insisted it had no bearing on the decision, that 'no request was made regarding policy', and that the crucial argument was the warning that the loss of sponsorship could lead to a loss of jobs. A statement by Mr Ecclestone confirmed that he had met Mr Blair in 1996 and had been impressed, that he had made a donation in January 1997, and that he 'never sought any favour from New Labour or any member of the Government, nor has any been given'.[45] Questions were then asked about the size of the donation, which the Labour Party initially refused to reveal. It was not until Mr Ecclestone himself had revealed that it was £1m that the party itself formally acknowledged the full amount. But by this time – in an attempt to defuse what was now a 'sleaze row' – the Labour Party had consulted the new Chairman of the Committee on Standards in Public Life (Sir Patrick

---

[40] *The Guardian*, 6 November 1997.
[41] *The Observer*, 9 November 1997; *Scotland on Sunday*, 9 November 1997.
[42] *Scotland on Sunday*, 9 November 1997.
[43] *The Observer*, 9 November 1997.
[44] *Scotland on Sunday*, 9 November 1997.
[45] A minute of the meeting was subsequently published. See *The Guardian*, 17 November 1997.

Neill QC). Although the terms of reference of the Committee had not yet been extended to include party funding (this was not done until 12 November), Sir Patrick advised the party to return the money. Sir Patrick made no criticism of the party for originally accepting the donation, but he concluded that 'in light of the way in which Government policy has developed, Ministers could well conclude that, in the special circumstances of this case, their freedom of action would be, and would be seen to be, enhanced, if the donation were to be returned'.[46] Sir Patrick's confidence in his judgment was said to have increased when he subsequently discovered that the donation was a sum of £1m: 'Every pound makes me feel I am more correct'.[47]

Impact of the Donation

Although Sir Patrick is reported as having accepted government assurances that the donation did not influence the decision on tobacco sponsorship, it was also claimed that 'establishing that fact was not his job'.[48] But whatever the effect of the donation, it is clear that it caused lasting damage to the Labour Party and the Labour government. Moreover, while it was only the start of a large number of other allegations about New Labour 'sleaze', it is clear that the Ecclestone affair affected the way in which these subsequent stories were reported and the prominence they received. Although it did not bring down the government in the way that the first Labour government was brought down by the *Workers' Weekly* case in 1924, the Ecclestone affair surprisingly demonstrated the same ineptness and inexperience of the ways of government by the Blair administration.[49] It also attracted strong criticism from the government's traditional supporters, including the following pointed remarks in a *Guardian* editorial:

> We have seen the unedifying spectacle of Labour squirming to avoid telling the people it affects to serve the truth about its own sources of funding. It has taken them five days to admit that the party was given £1 million by the Formula One boss Bernie Ecclestone. At first they refused to comment at all. This moved to a refusal to confirm or deny receiving any money. This shifted to an admission that it was 'more than £5,000'. Finally Mr Ecclestone himself came clean and admitted it was a cool £1 million.[50]

But although questions of style and spinning were important, the more damaging allegations, which were reported internationally,[51] were that big money gets big favours. According to *The Guardian*, 'Mr Ecclestone's million

---

[46] Letter from Sir Patrick Neill QC to Lord Sawyer, 10 November 1997. See Appendix 1 where this letter and the letter to which it responds are printed in full.

[47] *The Guardian*, 13 November 1997.

[48] *Ibid.*

[49] This story is told in K D Ewing and C A Gearty, *The Struggle for Civil Liberties* (1999), ch 3.

[50] *The Guardian*, 12 November 1997

[51] For example, *Washington Post*, 12 November 1997.

clearly bought him an audience with Mr Blair', whose decision was said to look 'uncannily like Cash for U-turns'.[52]

Yet that was not the end of it. Fresh controversy was provoked when it was revealed that on 7 November the Labour Party had consulted Sir Patrick not about whether it should retain the £1m donation, but whether it should accept another donation from Mr Ecclestone, said to have been offered 'since the election'. The letter to Sir Patrick from the then General Secretary of the party included the following passage:

> The position which we have adopted thus far has been to refuse this further donation, but we wish to be advised whether this is a position which we need to maintain. This approach distinguished between a pre-election donation, which, of course, was not a factor in the Government's decision, which was taken in the national interest as the Government judged it, and the receipt of post-election donations where an appearance of a conflict of interest might be thought to arise.[53]

The fact that Sir Patrick advised the return of a donation about which he had not been asked is perhaps an adequate answer to those who complained that he had allowed himself to be used by the government.[54] Nevertheless, he wisely announced that he was getting 'out of the business of giving any more specific advice',[55] having given his advice without consulting the members of his Committee, even though he was 'sure that they would concur'. But while the reputation of the Committee on Standards in Public Life was enhanced rather than diminished by this sorry saga, there were final twists in the tail. Having agreed to give back the money to Mr Ecclestone (which the press reported he did not want and which Labour proposed to give to a cancer charity), the Labour Party (thought to be about £4.5m in debt at the time) had to replace it. That problem was resolved by the announcement later in November that a donation of £1m was to be made by Robert Earl, the owner of the restaurant chain Planet Hollywood, said in one newspaper report to live in Florida 'in superstar style'.[56] It is assumed that this British-born businessman was not a foreign donor for the purposes of the Labour Party's guidelines.

The Neill Committee

One effect of the Ecclestone affair was to hasten the inquiry into the funding of political parties by the Committee on Standards in Public Life. It is true that the Labour Party election manifesto had included a commitment to clean up party

---

[52] *The Guardian*, 12 November 1997. See Appendix 1, where this is refuted.
[53] As reported in *The Guardian*, 14 November 1997.
[54] In his letter of 10 November, Sir Patrick also advised the Labour Party that they were right not to accept the second donation, which Mr Ecclestone claimed had not been offered. See Appendix 1.
[55] *The Guardian*, 13 November 1997.
[56] *The Guardian*, 24 November 1997; *The Observer*, 23 November 1997.

funding, and that the Queen's Speech on 4 May 1997 had included a commitment to 'restore confidence in the integrity of the nation's political system by upholding the highest standards of honesty and propriety in public life'. But hardly could the Prime Minister have imagined that the need to 'consider how the funding of political parties should be regulated and reformed' should arise with such urgency and in response to a controversy that had engulfed the Labour Party, rather than what was now Her Majesty's Loyal Opposition. The terms of reference of the Committee on Standards in Public Life were extended on 12 November 1997 to enable the Committee to review the issues relating to the funding of political parties, and to recommend changes to the arrangements then in force.[57] The Committee undertook an extensive consultation exercise, with written submissions by political parties and others being followed by public hearings at which the Committee took oral evidence from many of those who had submitted written evidence.[58] The views of the parties were – as might be expected – all over the place, as each party sought to maximise its own advantage from funding reform.

Regulating Income

So what was the Neill Committee to do? Should it cap donations as the Liberal Democrats proposed? Should it cap spending as Labour proposed? Should it recommend State funding which both Labour and the Conservatives opposed? The Committee's starting point was transparency and the reporting of large donations, which was about as far as most of the press wanted it to go.[59] Although recognising the strength of the arguments in favour of privacy, and that the right to privacy should not be invaded unless there is a compelling case for doing so, the Committee also recognised that there was a public interest in knowing 'when a donation is made to a political party which is significant enough to prompt questions or to raise suspicion about its purpose'.[60] It was

---

[57] Although he established the Committee in 1995, John Major refused to allow it to examine the question of party funding. See HC Debs, 22 May 1996, col 95. The Conservatives also opposed a Labour private member's bill which would have required disclosure of donations and a ban on foreign funding. See HC Debs, 31 January 1996, cols 1003–10.

[58] For an account of the Committee generally, see J Fisher, 'Regulating Politics: The Committee on Standards in Public Life', in J Fisher, D Denver and J Benyon (eds), *Central Debates in British Politics* (2003), ch 23. For its work relating to this particular inquiry into the funding of political parties, see L Klein, 'On the Brink of Reform: Political Party Funding in Britain' (1999) 31 *Case W Res J Int'l L* 1. For an account of the report, see N Ghaleigh [1999] PL 43.

[59] See *The Times*, 14 April 1998 (sceptical of contribution limits and spending limits and against State funding); *The Scotsman*, 4 June 1998 (advocating disclosure and a ban on foreign donations, but no other limits on source or size, so that 'voters would be able to decide for themselves if it were morally right for a party before an election to accept funds from a particular source. In that way, and it is the realistic way, the electorate and not parliamentary legislators would be the final arbiters on donations'). The Committee, however, went much further in the direction of regulation, and the press was generally favourable, having to catch up with the Committee. See below, pp 19–20.

[60] Cm 4057–I, 1998, para 2.28.

proposed that parties should be required to disclose on a quarterly basis donations of £5,000 nationally and £1,000 locally. A donation for this purpose would
be widely defined to include sponsorship and donations in kind. In terms of the
source and size of donations, it was recommended that there should be a ban on
foreign donations, the SNP being the only party seriously opposed to this,[61] with
'SNP supporters overseas [contributing] regularly to the party'.[62] A foreign donor
would be someone not on the electoral register in the United Kingdom, or a legal
person such as a company which is not incorporated or based in the United
Kingdom.[63]

But although there should be a restriction on who may give, it was specifically
recommended that there should be no limit on the size of donations from a
particular donor, surprising perhaps in view of the fact that it was a massive
donation which was the immediate cause of the inquiry. Nevertheless, it was
thought that 'individuals should have the freedom to contribute to political
parties, and the parties should be free to compete for donations'. That was said to
be 'part of a healthy democracy'.[64] However, the Committee did not appear to be
unmindful of the problems caused by large donations, drawing attention to its
proposed spending limits which would lessen the need for large donations, opti-
mistic perhaps given that the limit was set at around £20m for the large parties.
The Committee also drew attention to its plans for disclosure which would
'remove illegitimate pressure, whether apparent or real', and its proposals for tax
relief for small political donations which would encourage the parties to broaden
the base of their support.[65] But although recommending tax relief for small
donations, the Committee set its face against public funding, though it did
recommend greater State support for the Opposition parties in Parliament
(including specifically the Leader of the Opposition), as well as a small sum of
£2m to be made available to qualifying parties for policy development purposes.

Regulating Expenditure

As already indicated, the Neill Committee by a majority recommended the introduction of controls on national party election spending to complement those

---

[61]   See SNP, *The Price of Democracy: Submission to the Committee on Standards in Public Life* (1998),
pp 11–12. The case was also made in oral evidence.

[62]   *The Times*, 16 February 1998 The party's most prominent overseas donor was said to be the actor
Sean Connery who the SNP acknowledged gave them £4,800 each month. See *The Scotsman*, 4 June
1998. But there were earlier press reports of the party opening a string of fund-raising offices in the
United States where there are an estimated 20 million people of Scottish descent: *The Independent*, 21
September 1994. But 'harnessing the wealth of the Caledonian diaspora' was not very successful. See
The Scotsman, 17 February 1998 – only £1,000 raised from people who were not British nationals. It
seems that those of Scottish descent inherited financial prudence in greater measure than national
identity. Sean Connery was of course born in Edinburgh.

[63]   Cm 4057–I, 1998, paras 5.20–5.27.

[64]   *Ibid*, para 6.7.

[65]   *Ibid*.

already in force for candidates.[66] Spending limits would not seriously impinge on the right of free speech unless they were set too low, and it was thought possible to set limits at a level that was low enough to be effective without also violating human rights. However, not all the members of the Committee were as persuaded as some of the witnesses about the equality or level-playing-field argument in favour of spending limits. It was conceded that the Conservative Party and its allies had out-spent the Labour Party and its allies at every election since 1955, often by very wide margins. While the Committee declared itself agnostic about whether high spending brings electoral success, it accepted that 'common sense suggests that one major party's ability to spend substantially more than the other may well have made a difference to the outcome' in five post-war elections where the results were very close.[67] But although it could not be proved that high spending buys elections, the Committee seemed persuaded of the need for spending limits to contain the acceleration in spending by the parties, referring particularly to the costs of the 1997 election. The Committee was concerned that these accelerating costs gave rise to a need 'to raise even larger funds to pay for the spending'.

According to the Committee, this need to raise even greater sums would remain if there was no limit on spending, and it was 'at least probable' that 'limits on campaign spending are necessary to prevent undue concentration on fund raising'.[68] But it was not only political parties that would be constrained in this way. So far as 'third party' spending was concerned, the Committee was disarmingly frank: 'any individual or organisation that incurs election expenses should be subject to an expenditure limit'.[69] The Committee was aware that there would be problems in defining an election expense for this purpose but was inclined to take a wide view that this ought not to be confined to propaganda overtly promoting or opposing a political party. In the view of the Committee, however, it was 'simply naïve to imagine that organisations that send out explicitly political messages in the midst of election campaigns, or shortly in advance of them, are engaged innocently in generalised, non-partisan promotional activity'.[70] Also for consideration was the amount of the limit, a matter to be treated with care in view of obligations under the European Convention on Human Rights. But although the Convention suggested the need for a limit which was not too restrictive, the Committee rejected as too generous the Labour Party's suggestion that a third party should be allowed to spend 10 per cent the maximum permitted by the political parties, and proposed £1m instead.

Conclusion

The Neill Committee's recommendations were warmly received by the press

---

[66] The sole dissenter was John McGregor, a former Conservative Cabinet minister.
[67] Cm 4057–I, 1998, para 10.28.
[68] *Ibid*, para 10.29.
[69] *Ibid*, para 10.76.
[70] *Ibid*, para 10.79.

which variously praised it as an 'excellent job',[71] and a 'bedrock for the next century'.[72] The recommendations were also accepted by the government,[73] which is not surprising given that they were broadly consistent with the proposals in the Labour Party's written evidence.[74] There were two exceptions. The first was the Neill Committee's recommendation that there should be income tax relief for small donations to political parties, a proposal which the Labour Party strongly opposed in oral evidence. This was rejected ostensibly because it would be a cost to the Treasury (albeit a small one), that would be better spent on other projects to improve public services. For this the government was criticised by members of the Committee. The second was the Neill Committee's recommendation that there should be no spending limits in referendum campaigns. The Labour Party had proposed that there should be such limits, just as there should be limits on election expenses. But although the Committee accepted that the case in principle for imposing spending limits in referendum campaigns is 'a strong one', it would nevertheless be 'futile and possibly also wrong to attempt to impose such limits in connection with referendums'.[75] Not everyone was convinced, with *The Times* finding it 'curious' that there should be spending limits for elections but not for referendums.[76] With these exceptions, the Neill proposals formed the basis of the PPERA, which (i) created the Electoral Commission, a new regulatory authority for political parties, and (ii) subjected the latter to a highly complex and very detailed regulatory framework.

But despite the warmth with which the press received the Neill settlement, subsequent events make clear that the creation of a new regulatory framework for party funding and a new regulator for political parties has not resolved the problems the settlement was designed to address. Paradoxically, the problems appear to be as great as ever, and there is a sense that the PPERA is simply a step on the way to further reform rather than an end in itself. The Labour Party has been unable to remove the stain of 'sleaze', with one newspaper identifying various forms of 'sleaze': cash for coronets; cash for access; cash for jobs; and cash for policy.[77] Having attacked the Conservatives over the years for rewarding political donors with political honours,[78] the Labour government was being accused

---

[71] *The Independent*, 14 October 1998.

[72] *The Times*, 14 October 1998.

[73] See HC Debs, 9 November 1998, col 58 where the Home Secretary (Jack Straw) announced that the government would 'act quickly to implement its main findings'.

[74] There was, however, concern in some quarters that the spending limit of £20m was not really a reduction, given that it would apply only to spending incurred in the twelve months before the election, with the result that it would not really relieve the pressure for large donations. There was also some alarm about the amount of support for the Opposition parties proposed, on the ground that it was bizarre that the best funded and what had then been the least open party should benefit in this way.

[75] Cm 4057–I, 1998, paras 12.4–5.

[76] *The Times*, 14 October 1998.

[77] *Scotland on Sunday*, 7 January 2001.

[78] See, however, the approach adopted by the then Political Honours Scrutiny Committee (since abolished) to nominees, where the making of a political donation was said to be a 'bonus point rather than a minus'. See Cm 4057-II, 1998, para 3124.

of the same, as it moved to address the problem of Labour under-representation in the House of Lords. This was part of an even bigger problem of alleged cronyism and the use of political patronage by the New Labour government.[79] The Labour Party has always denied any impropriety, but allegations of honours for those who had donated was not the whole of it. There were also allegations that the government was using its power of patronage to punish those who had donated to other parties. This is despite the fact that the estwhile Conservative Party Treasurer and major donor, Michael Ashcroft, was ennobled by a Labour government. [80] Just as embarrassing for the Labour Party, however, are the innuendos that donors had enjoyed certain commercial benefits in return, whether in the form of government contracts or lobbying of foreign governments on their behalf.

These latter innuendos surfaced in 2001 and 2002 in relation to a number of specific donations. They were followed on cue in 2006 by a fresh eruption in the wake of the general election in 2005 when it was revealed that the two main parties had funded their campaigns with loans from wealthy individuals to the tune of £35m, the Labour Party receiving £14m and the Conservatives £21m. At the same time, it was also revealed that four Labour Party lenders had been nominated for a peerage, and concerns were raised that the parties may have undermined the spirit of the Neill settlement, by funding their campaigns with commercial loans which they claimed did not need to be disclosed, as they fell outside the definition of a donation. This was part of the background that led to SNP backbencher Angus MacNeil calling in the police; and to the subsequent arrest of four people. This was also part of the background that led the Prime Minister in March 2006 to appoint Sir Hayden Phillips to conduct yet another review of party funding, with terms of reference which required him to examine whether State funding should be enhanced in return for a cap on donations. The pages which follow provide an opportunity to assess what the next step in the process of reform should be, and the issues of principle that should underpin any additional regulation in this field. The Phillips review is thus the fourth official review of party funding since 1976, and the fifth if the parallel inquiry by the House of Commons Constitutional Affairs Committee is included. It is likely to be last only until the next one, following another funding controversy – whether real or contrived – that will inevitably result, no matter how generously the parties are funded, and no matter how tightly they are regulated.

---

[79] See D Osler, *Labour Party plc* (2002).

[80] There was nevertheless enough concern about the 'shabby' treatment of Sean Connery, for the SNP to complain in their evidence to Neill that 'There has been widespread discontent in Scotland at the revelation that a knighthood for Sean Connery, approved by the outgoing Secretary of State, was disallowed by the present Government on the grounds of his support for the SNP. This is the absolute obverse of the question posed by the Committee about donations being perceived to buy influence' (SNP, above). The outgoing government to which the SNP referred was the government of Mr Major, and the present government to which it referred was the Labour government of Mr Blair. Mr Connery eventually received his knighthood: the best that can be said then is that his donation delayed rather than prevented it.

2

Regulatory Objectives

The funding of political parties is a problem in all parts of the world.[1] It is a problem in developed countries and in developing countries. It is a problem in established democracies and in emerging democracies.[2] And it is a problem that varies from country to country. But the causes are the same. In the competition for political office, there is an insatiable appetite for victory in systems where the winner takes all, and where some are prepared to adopt fair means or unfair means to capture the levers of power. And from those who exercise political power, there are those who seek a share of the spoils, and who are prepared to adopt fair means or unfair means to secure private benefits, or personal advantage or favour. For these and other reasons, funding scandals have woven tangled webs of deceit and corruption, which have ruined careers and reputations, of even the mightiest members of the political classes, in even the most advanced and sophisticated democracies. But whatever the cause of the party funding problem wherever it may arise, there is a need to deal with it, a need that few countries can claim to have addressed satisfactorily.[3] As we have seen, the funding controversy of 2005–2006 in the United Kingdom led to fresh investigations into how party funding should be reformed in this country.[4] But before we can agree what needs to be done, we need first to identify the objectives of any new funding regime.

The Prevention of Corruption and Conflicts of Interest

Perhaps the first objective of a regime for the regulation of party funding is to prevent corruption in the political process.[5] Corruption is a strong word, not to be used lightly. It is a word that spans a wide range of conduct and the conduct of

---

[1] Transparency International, *Global Corruption Report* (2001).

[2] For a good global review, see IDEA, *Funding of Political Parties and Election Campaigns* (2003).

[3] For a review of different national solutions, see K D Ewing and S Issacharoff, *Party Funding and Campaign Financing in International Perspective* (2006).

[4] See p 21 above.

[5] See *Buckley v Valeo*, 424 US 1 (1976).

a wide range of people, with different shades of meaning. Indeed, it is a word with no agreed definition or understanding, with each attempt at a definition found to be as inconclusive as the last.[6] At one extreme, however, is bribery.[7] Although bribery on any systematic scale is now unknown, whether by way of donations to political parties or otherwise, Britain has not been immune from other extreme forms of political corruption, with the most notorious example being the selling of political honours by Lloyd George in the early years of the twentieth century.[8] This was particularly pernicious in view of the fact that those who were honoured by a peerage became members of the legislature as a result, as did their heirs until most of them were removed by the House of Lords Act 1999. But corruption is not confined to the direct purchase of personal and political benefits, and includes what one American commentator has described as 'favouritism':

> even entirely legal contributions from wealthy interests are a source of concern. The worry is favoritism. Groups that give funds to elected officials expect help in the legislative process. They may also expect special treatment on individual problems in dealing with the bureaucracy or in seeking contracts and concessions. If the interests of such groups or individuals conflict with those of the general public, this undermines democratic values.[9]

Here the concern is not with something unlawful or within the legal definition of corruption. Rather, the concern is that donations create the risk of (i) providing donors with opportunites to influence decisions or to promote their personal interests, or (ii) enhancing the possibility of benefits or advantages being conferred on donors.[10]

---

[6] See O Kurer, 'Corruption: An Alternative Approach to its Definition and Assessment' (2005) 53 *Political Studies* 222. See also K D Ewing and N S Ghaleigh, 'Donations to Political Parties in the United Kingdom' (2006) 6 *Election Law Journal* (forthcoming). Kurer writes of 'a set of contradictory descriptions of the phenomenon of corruption, all of which have major disadvantages' (p 226). He advances the case for an alternative which emphasises (i) the conduct of the holders of public office, (ii) the violation of objective principles (such as treating like cases alike), and (iii) the need for private advantage (p 227).

[7] The starting point of bribery suggests that in defining corruption it is useful to distinguish between policy decisions and discretionary decisions which are made for the benefit of an individual or company. These latter include tax breaks, the award of political honours, the award of a government contract or licence, government approval to buy a business, or the release of a convict from prison. All of these decisions may have the appearance of having been made in the exercise of legal authority, but they may in fact have been made in return for a payment in the form of a bribe or donation to the funds of a governing party, or otherwise. In systems where corruption is a problem, it is decisions of this latter kind that are most likely to be susceptible to corrupt influences, though the possibility of policy decisions being bought ought not to be overlooked. There are policy decisions of universal application which may disproportionately benefit a particular company or donor.

[8] See G MacMillan, *Honours for Sale: The Strange Case of Maundy Gregory* (1954).

[9] S Rose-Ackerman, *Corruption and Government* (1999), p 133.

[10] Thus, a donation to a political party may not give rise directly to a *quid pro quo*, and it may indeed not have been made for that reason. But the risk in systems where corruption is a problem is that the donation may nevertheless make the party peculiarly responsive to the interests of the donor, who may enjoy access to ministers as a result of the donation. Even if the donation does not directly

In the past, it was thought that the nature of the British political system was such that corruption of any kind by donations to political parties was difficult to perfect.[11] Political parties were much more ideologically driven than they are today; they had more settled and predicable sources of funding; and there were limited needs for money in an era not yet touched by the commercial marketing of the parties and their leaders. There may also have been a shared acceptance of higher ethical standards. But even then there were areas of concern. Although there is no evidence of peerages and knighthoods being bought or sold in the post-Lloyd George era, the questions about political honours did not end with Lloyd George and re-emerge in more recent times. There has long been a worry about the coincidence of honours being granted to the executives of companies that made political donations to the Conservative Party. There is also a sense that the award of government contracts must also have been an area of vulnerability, and indeed until 1957 government contractors were barred from membership of the House of Commons.[12] It is true that this problem was minimised by the fact that public services were delivered by government directly, and not by the private sector on its behalf, and by the fact that there has been for some time a rigorous auditing of central government expenditure.[13] Nevertheless, it was the private sector that built the hospitals, prisons and offices on behalf of central government departments, and the private sector that made the arms and equipment used by the armed forces. The opportunities for corruption were real, yet they did not appear publicly to have touched the parties, for reasons about which we can now only speculate.

In recent years, however, we have seen a change in the British political culture, with expanding opportunities for corruption of various shades of meaning. Ideological divisions between the parties are much less pronounced than in the past, the role of the State has changed, and the funding needs and opportunities of the parties have expanded. All the parties are now competing with each other for private donations and all are cultivating a much closer relationship with the business community, at a time when membership of political parties is in decline. Indeed, such is the close proximity that suspicions are raised that large donors are now in a position to influence party policy. These suspicions appear to have been fuelled by the manner of press reporting of one especially high profile £1m donation to the Labour Party, even though it is 'now pretty well accepted' that the

secure policy changes or other benefits for the donor in these systems, such access in itself may help to put the donor in an unrivalled position when a decision is taken. Such potential access is to be questioned, if for no reason other than that the donor is securing a privilege which is not available to other citizens.

[11] It still is, and it is not suggested that there has been any corruption of any kind by way of donations to political parties in recent times. However, the prevention of corruption remains an important regulatory objective in this area in this as in other countries, with the changing role of the State calling for more rather than less vigilance, as explained in the text.

[12] For similar restrictions in Australia, see Commonwealth of Australia Constitution 1900, s 44(iv) and (v).

[13] On which see E L Normanton, *The Accountability and Audit of Government* (1966).

donation was not made to influence policy.[14] But it is in the changing role of the State that the risk of influence is most pronounced, when taking into account the close links between the party of government and the business community. The issue here is that the State is cast more and more in the role of contractor or licenser of public services which have been 'privatised' or 'liberalised', to use current euphemisms for 'transferred' to the private sector. The State, increasingly, no longer provides public services, but authorises others to do so, and in the process wields a great discretionary power that can confer great benefits on anointed heads. These are the areas where the risk of corruption is greatest, and where safeguards need to exist to prevent the operation or appearance of undue influence on decisions that ought to be taken in the public interest, and not the commercial interest of someone who has made a political donation.

Although the prevention of corruption is one of the key objectives in regulating the funding of political parties, it is important to emphasise that the problems in the United Kingdom are thought by many to be insignificant compared to other countries.[15] But although this is a claim which could become rather hollow with over-use, it is also important to emphasise that corruption will not be prevented by regulating political parties alone.[16] The regulation of party funding is only part of what must be an approach that addresses other relationships between business and other interests on the one hand, and public officials and elected politicians on the other.[17] (One issue which has grown in recent years – for example – is the role of lobbyists who may seek access to politicians and non elected officials.) In each case, there is a need for a regulatory framework that deals with the relationship of the public official and commercial organisations as well as individual businessmen and women.[18] Yet although the regulation of party funding is not enough on its own to deal with the threat of corruption, it is nevertheless an essential part of an overall strategy. It is true that the payment of money to a political party is different from the payment of

[14] *The Times*, 15 April 2002 (*T2*).

[15] For an account of the motives of donors in the United States, see D Lowenstein, 'On Campaign Finance Reform: The Root of All Evil is Deeply Rooted' (1989) 18 *Hofstra Law Review* 301, where it is suggested that donors give in order to seek and secure influence.

[16] Indeed, as part of an anti-corruption or anti-conflict of interest package, the regulation of political parties may only be a very small part of the whole. Any political system faced with corruption and introducing such an overall package would wish to address potential problems presented by the personnel of government, in the form of the executive and legislative branches, as well as those who advise them and implement their policies. Such a package would have to address not only the personnel of national government, but also the personnel of regional and local government as well (where relevant and appropriate). But is important not to under-estimate the need to address political parties as part of any such package. Apart from reasons given in the text, the political party provides a channel to the government and in systems where corruption is a problem, the danger could arise of donations being made to a governing party with a view to influencing the policies or decisions of the government, and with a view to government responding to the donor's interests.

[17] For colourful accounts of business and politics in the United Kingdom and the USA respectively, see D Osler, *Labour Party plc* (2002), and G Palast, *The Best Democracy Money Can Buy* (2002).

[18] In Britain, that framework is composed of a series of dated criminal statutes and a variety of codes of conduct that apply to MPs, ministers and civil servants.

money directly to an individual, and that the conferring of a benefit on a company because it donated to a political party is different from the conferring of a benefit on a company in the unlikely event that it gave money to a minister. But although the public official in the case of a donation to a political party can say that he or she did not benefit directly and personally, the challenge to democracy is the same.

Equality of Opportunity and Fair Competition for Political Office

The second objective of a party funding regime is based on the principle of political equality which lies at the heart of liberal democracy. In practice, this principle is little more than a fiction, undermined by the great disparities of wealth and fortune that exist between individuals in a liberal version of democracy. Those with greater economic resources have correspondingly greater political influence, and they are able to exercise their considerable economic power in the political arena in a number of ways. Nevertheless, we cling to the idea of equality in the political arena as one of the fundamental principles of democracy, and indeed in this sense it is all-pervasive. We operate a system of universal suffrage whereby everyone is entitled to vote regardless of their means, so much so that steps have been taken to enable and encourage the poorest among us to register to vote. Under the Representation of the People Act 2000, the homeless are now permitted to register, even though they are not resident in a particular constituency, provided that they can show some connection with it.[19] Everyone, regardless of their means, has only one vote (except in the Scottish Parliament and Welsh Assembly where everyone has two votes), and everyone's vote notionally is of equal value.[20] It is true that the value of some votes is greater than others because parliamentary constituencies are not all the same size. But any differences here are due to a system of distribution of the constituencies that takes into account geographical factors as well as the number of electors.[21] The distribution of the constituencies is not based on a formula that places fewer voters in constituencies populated by rich people in order to enhance their relative voice.

It is not only in the choice of a representative in government that the principle of equality applies. We also take steps to ensure that we all have a fair opportunity to stand for political office, reflecting the principle that no one should be denied the opportunity to stand for elected office or accept the responsibility of election because of a lack of means. Candidates have an opportunity to ensure that their message is communicated to the electorate, with free postage for literature and

---

[19] 2000 Act, s 6, amending Representation of the People Act 1983.
[20] On the elimination of plural voting, see D E Butler, *The Electoral System in Britain* (2nd ed, 1963).
[21] See *R v Boundary Commission, ex p Foot* [1983] QB 600.

the free use of public buildings for meetings.[22] These measures apply regardless of the means available to the candidate, the likely support for the candidate, or the representative nature of the party he or she represents.[23] From early times, moreover, steps have been taken to ensure that individuals have an opportunity to become an elected representative on equal terms with other candidates, and that no one should be able by reason of great personal wealth to have an unfair or disproportionate opportunity to secure election. Legislation introduced in 1883 makes electoral bribery and corruption an offence, thereby denying the wealthy the opportunity literally to buy election, with corrupt and illegal practices being widely defined to include treating electors, paying electors to display election material, and at one time the use of cars to convey voters to the polls.[24] These attempts to control the unfair advantage of the wealthy candidate are reinforced by other controls, such as spending limits, which were also introduced in 1883. By limiting the amount of money that all the candidates can spend in an election, the law thereby prevents the campaign from becoming a one-sided affair, and prevents the campaign from being saturated by the views of the candidate who has raised the most money.[25]

These principles apply with equal force to the political parties as they apply to candidates. Here we have a recognition that in the context of electoral politics, the principle of political equality means fair rivalry in the election campaign, and fair electoral competition. It clearly cannot mean genuine equality, even if this could be quantified in electoral terms. Some parties will enjoy an advantage because they have better policies, better candidates or a better campaign. But what equality means here is that no party should have an unfair advantage because it has greater financial resources than its rivals. It also means that no elector should have an unfair advantage because he or she has vast wealth that he or she is prepared to use to influence and perhaps determine the outcome of an election.[26] Nor does the principle of equality in this context mean that all parties must have exactly the same resources to spend at an election or the same opportunity to reach the electorate. Some parties are very small, have little popular

[22] See ch 8 below.

[23] But it is to be pointed out that in order to prevent frivolous candidates, it is necessary for candidates to pay an election deposit of £500 which is retuned only if the candidate in question secures 5 per cent of the vote.

[24] For an account of the Corrupt and Illegal Practices Act 1883, and the background to it, see C O'Leary, *The Elimination of Corrupt Practices in British Elections 1868–1911* (1962).

[25] See ch 7 below.

[26] This reminds us that when we consider equality in the context of the political party, the question arises about whose interests are being promoted by equality. It is not only the equality of the party that is relevant, but also the equality of the elector. The point was made forcefully by the Supreme Court of India in the following terms: 'It is obvious that pre-election donations would be likely to operate as post-election promises resulting ultimately in the casualty of the interest of the common man, not so much ostensibly in the legislative process as in the implementation of laws and administrative or policy decisions. The small man's chance is the essence of Indian democracy and that would be stultified if large contributions from rich and affluent individuals or groups are not divorced from the electoral process': *Kanwer Lal v Amarnath* AIR 1975 SC 308, per Bhagwati J at p 315; K C Sunny, 'Election Laws', in S K Verma (ed), *Fifty Years of the Supreme Court of India* (2000), ch 5.

support and traditionally attract few votes. Only one of two parties have a realistic chance of forming the government, and in modern times only two of our national parties have been in government. So when we promote the cause of equality in the sense of fair rivalry or fair electoral competition, there must also be a recognition of a principle of proportionality. Treating all parties in the same way and giving all parties access to the same benefits is not necessarily the same as treating them all fairly.

The principle of equality of electoral opportunity is not unrelated to the regulatory goal of preventing corruption in electoral politics, just as the regulatory goal of preventing corruption is not unrelated to the regulatory goal of promoting equality. As we have seen, the law of corrupt and illegal practices is one way of reducing the electoral power of wealthy candidates, even though this may be a secondary goal. Conversely one effect of equalising measures in the interests of fair rivalry or fair electoral competition may be to reduce the 'arms race' between the main parties whereby each is locked in an endless battle for more and more money to fuel bigger and more expensive campaigns. The need for money leads to temptation and to errors of judgement, and to the possibility that money is taken from sources that are thought to be ethically unacceptable. An example might be the decision of the two main parties in 2005 to raise funds by loans rather than donations, thereby side-stepping transparency obligations imposed by law.[27] If the effect of steps taken in the interests of fair rivalry or fair electoral competition is to reduce the need of the parties to spend money or to restrict the purposes for which it might be spent, this in turn may diminish the risk that the parties will solicit or receive money from improper sources, or from sources that will compromise them or their elected officials. But much will depend on the nature and content of the equalising measures introduced. Equality at a level that is unattainable is not likely to have much of an impact, either in promoting fair rivalry or in reducing the risk of corruption.[28]

A Need to Ensure that Political Parties are Adequately Funded

A third objective of a party funding regime is to ensure that political parties are adequately funded, in the sense that they have enough funds to enable them to carry out their functions. Political parties perform a number of crucial constitutional roles in liberal democracies,[29] and have been said judicially to be 'essential

---

[27] See ch 6 below.

[28] Thus, spending limits introduced by the PPERA were arguably too high to meet regulatory objectives. See Ch 7 below.

[29] Although curiously their role is not always acknowledged in the constitutional law of some jurisdictions which have written constitutions. The absence of any reference to political parties is particularly noticeable in the United States and in other common law constitutions, on which see S Issacharoff, 'Introduction: The Structure of Democratic Politics' (2000) 100 *Columbia Law Review* 593.

to the proper functioning of democracy'.[30] They provide a channel for political participation, they provide for the collective representation of citizen's views, and they provide the personnel of government and opposition.[31] They also provide a vehicle for the narrow personal ambitions of individuals who see politics as a career, success in which brings great rewards for some. Those among us who do not like political parties nevertheless find it difficult to live without them. We vote for them (though significantly fewer of us now do so), we ask their elected representatives to help us when we have a problem with national or local government, and we expect the parties to govern in our interests. This all costs money, which has to be raised from either private or public sources, or from a mixture of both. The State's interest in the funds of the political parties and the State's interest in ensuring that there is an adequacy of funding arise from the nature of the functions which the parties perform. Although in form private bodies governed by private law,[32] political parties perform a number of public functions. As such they are a bridge that connects the private with the public spheres, and in particular they are the organised form that ensures that the voice of the people is heard in government.

It is thus because of the functions which the parties perform that the State's interest is engaged. This is a matter to which we return in chapter 8, where it is argued that not only does the State have an interest in ensuring that the parties are adequately funded, but that it has a responsibility to do so. In the meantime, an early recognition of the State's interest in ensuring that the parties are able to fulfil their public role of representing people in government can be seen in the early years of the twentieth century following the decision of the House of Lords in the *Osborne* judgment.[33] It was held in that case in 1909 that trade unions could not lawfully raise a political or parliamentary levy of their members to affiliate to the Labour Party and pay the salaries of their sponsored MPs. That was a decision that not only damaged the cause of trade union parliamentary representation and the cause of the development of the Labour Party. More importantly, it undermined the ability of British citizens without private means to stand for election to Parliament, and would have deprived British electors of the right to be represented in Parliament by the person of their choice. The immediate response was the introduction in 1911 of salaries for MPs to perform a role which had previously fallen to the parties and their supporters, but which the Labour Party would in the future be unable to perform.[34] As it happened, the *Osborne* judgment was partially reversed by the Trade Union Act 1913 so that trade unions could again lawfully collect a political levy which could be used for

---

[30] *United Communist Party of Turkey v Turkey* (1998) 26 EHRR 121. See A R Mowbray, 'The Role of the European Court of Human Rights in the Promotion of Democracy' [1999] PL 703.

[31] See also P Webb, *The Modern British Party System* (2000), ch 9.

[32] On which see ch 4 below, where the rather primitive legal status of political parties is discussed.

[33] *Amalgamated Society of Railway Servants v Osborne* [1910] AC 87.

[34] See W B Gwyn, *The Costs of Democracy* (1962), pp 206–226.

purposes of parliamentary representation.[35] The salary – set initially at £400 per annum – survived, and has since been greatly expanded to include other costs incurred by MPs.[36]

But in contending that the State has an interest in ensuring that the parties are adequately funded is to beg the question of what adequacy means for this purpose. Adequacy in relation to what? This is by no means a simple or trite question, because there is no settled view of what political parties are for, how much money they need, and how that need could best be met. On one view, political parties are simply electoral machines for the purpose of winning elections. On another view, it is the function of political parties to 'dominate the State and "colonize" important segments of its institutions and society, like public administration (at all levels), public enterprises, education, the media, etc.'[37] In Britain, the system of party government is closer to the former view, whereas in Germany the system of *parteienstaat* is closer to the latter. But despite this uncertainty, what we can say is that in all liberal democracies political parties have a number of core needs: the recruitment and training of candidates, the contesting and conduct of elections, and even in the case of the government party, the holding of government to account. What distinguishes these needs from other activities of the parties is that they relate to the interface between the public and the party, in connection with which it may be said that there is a public interest engaged in addition to the narrow sectarian interests of party members. But in suggesting that the State has an interest in ensuring that these core needs are met, we still have a problem of determining the extent of the need that the parties have in relation to each of these items. How much money do the parties need to recruit and train candidates, to run an effective campaign, or to oppose and hold government to account?

Apart from identifying need, there is a separate question of how that need can best be met. Here the interest of the State can be addressed in a number of ways. It can encourage and promote the private funding of the parties, or it can supply the funds that the parties must have to meet these needs. But in determining choice of regulatory strategy, it is important not to overlook its implications for the other regulatory objectives identified in this chapter. Steps to promote the private funding of the parties may lead to conflict with the need to prevent corruption and to promote political equality in terms of fair rivalry and fair electoral competition. But steps to promote a greater role for the State in meeting the needs of the political parties may undermine attempts to ensure high levels of citizen participation in the funding and activities of political parties, an objective

[35] Trade Union Act 1913, amended by the Trade Union Act 1984; now Trade Union and Labour Relations (Consolidation) Act 1992, ss 71–96.

[36] See P Strickland, *Members' Office Costs – The New System* (House of Commons Library, 2001). Additional benefits include an annual staffing allowance, an allowance for IT equipment, an incidental expenses provision for office running costs, an additional costs allowance to maintain a home in London, a mileage allowance, and free stationery, telephone and postage.

[37] H-J Puhle, 'Still the Age of Catch-allism? Volksparteien and Partieienstaat in Crisis and Re-equilibration', in R Gunther et al, *Political Parties: Old Concepts and New Challenges* (2002), p 70.

that is considered below. Another option, then, is a synthesis of private funding and State support, whereby the State provides some support to help parties meet core needs. The parties are thereby relieved of the obligation to finance these activities but must raise money privately for other purposes (or if they want to spend more on core activities than the State provides where it is permissible to do so). This support may be provided in cash or in kind, with the provision of free mail and the free use of public buildings at election time for parliamentary candidates being good examples of support in kind.[38] Another example would be the provision of free broadcasting time for the parties during a general election campaign,[39] reflecting the fact that the 'days of soap-box oratory are over, so are the days of political pamphleteering'.[40]

Promoting Citizen Participation in the Funding of Political Parties

The most obvious way by which parties can be adequately funded is by the contributions of their members and supporters. Indeed, it may be said to be a fourth regulatory objective of a party funding regime that citizens should be encouraged and not discouraged to take responsibility for the funding of political parties and to take part in the activities of political parties.[41] But why? Although political parties may be an important and indispensable institution of liberal democracy, it does not follow that they should be popularly funded, or that they should have an active membership. It is perfectly possible to contemplate the existence of 'leadership' parties of the kind we see in France, where there are parties in name only, which are funded by the State and have few, if any, members.[42] It is possible also to contemplate the élite parties of eighteenth- and nineteenth-century Britain, in which political parties were loose 'organisations' that existed for the purpose of securing the election of like-minded individuals who would support or oppose a government.[43] Parties of this kind could develop policies (the policies of the leadership), present candidates for election (candidates loyal to and chosen by the leadership), and provide the basis for the recruitment of the government and opposition. The costs of discharging these

[38] See ch 8 below.

[39] See ch 8 below.

[40] *Rambachan v TTT*, 17 July 1985 (Trinidad and Tobago High Court, Unreported), Deyalsingh J, referred to by A Fiadjoe, *Caribbean Public Law* (2nd ed, 1998), p 142.

[41] In identifying this objective, it is important to acknowledge the different ways by which individuals may make a contribution to political parties. They may do so directly through a membership fee or small contribution; or they may do so indirectly through an intermediate organisation which is a donor or contributor to the funds of a political party.

[42] For a brief account of this problem, see Y-M Doublet, 'Party Funding in France', in K D Ewing (ed), *The Funding of Political Parties: Europe and Beyond* (1999), ch 5.

[43] See M Duverger, *Political Parties* (1959), ch 1.

responsibilities could be met either by sympathetic donors or by the State. Moreover, the State could just as well meet the last of the three preceding regulatory objectives identified above if faced with parties of this kind, as it could in relation to parties of grass-roots members, which are associated with twentieth-century government and universal suffrage.

So why do parties need members, and why should the State be concerned with whether they have members or not? Much of the work by political scientists on this question is on the private benefit to the parties themselves of party activists,[44] rather than the public benefit of such activism to the community at large.[45] But one reason why members are important from the latter perspective is that they are necessary to give legitimacy and stability to the process of government. As already pointed out, political parties are the key institution which links the private sphere with the public sphere, that is to say links the people with their government. This reflects Kelsen's claim that in a parliamentary democracy, 'the political party is an essential vehicle for the formation of the public will'.[46] Yet there are many – not without cause – who see liberal democracy as an illusion, as a process in which economic power governs through political institutions.[47] Citizens are not engaged in a process of self-government, but in a process of self-delusion in which they themselves are governed by others. If liberal democracy is to have legitimacy (and ultimately stability), it can only be because people are active participants in the process of representative government, which is seen to work. The most direct and practical way by which citizens can engage with this process is through membership of and participation in political parties. These organisations provide citizens potentially with the opportunity to take part in the development of public policy through all its phases, and to secure its implementation in a campaign for public office. It is the great responsibility of the political parties themselves to ensure that they effectively discharge their constitutional duties in a way that enables citizens meaningfully to enjoy the opportunities of this kind that representative democracy is supposed to provide.

The State has a clear role to play in helping the parties to discharge these responsibilities, though it cannot be fully responsible for the irresponsibility of the parties themselves. The State's role is twofold. In the first place, it must refrain from any form of regulation that will have a negative impact by discouraging

---

[44] Parties need members if they are to recruit candidates for the multitude of offices that must now be contested in local, devolved, national and European government. They need members to work for the party at election and other times, members who will form a volunteer army and whose activities will serve to reduce the cost of politics. And they need members to pay the bills and to fund the activities of the party, and to reduce the risk of corruption by making the parties less dependent on large donors.

[45] See D Denver and G Hands, 'Constituency Campaigning' (1992) 45 *Parliamentary Affairs* 451, and P Whiteley and P Seyd, 'The Labour Vote and Local Activism' (1992) 45 *Parliamentary Affairs* 582.

[46] H Kelsen, *General Theory of Law and State* (1949), p 294.

[47] For a compelling and still relevant account, see R Miliband, *Capitalist Democracy in Britain* (1972). Also, H J Laski, *Parliamentary Government in England* (1938).

party political activity by citizens or discouraging the parties themselves from seeking new members, supporters or activists. It ought also to refrain from reinforcing what some have seen as the oligarchic tendencies at work in the political parties,[48] which appear to be at least as pronounced today as they have ever been.[49] On the other hand, the State may take steps that will have a positive impact by encouraging (it cannot require) party political activity by citizens.[50] This commitment may take different forms, from membership, small donations to party funds, participation in the affairs of a party, standing for public office, and providing professional assistance to a party. One kind of potentially negative intervention is large-scale public funding of the parties on the model to be found in several European democracies. In some of these countries (such as Spain) where the needs of the parties are largely met by the State, the parties have very few members. Conversely, one kind of intervention which may have a positive impact is to be found in Germany where the State funding for the parties is tied to electoral success and levels of membership, creating incentives for the parties to increase voter turnout and party membership.[51] Intervention of a positive kind can also require the parties to follow certain democratic procedures prescribed by the State,[52] just as the State prescribes procedures for the government of other organisations, such as trade unions.[53]

The State's interest in promoting citizen participation in the funding and activities of political parties may thus be said to relate to both the political legitimacy and stability of parliamentary democracy on the one hand, and the constitutional functions of the parties on the other. But an additional reason why there is a public interest in promoting high levels of active membership in and support for political parties relates to the other regulatory objectives which have

---

[48] This is a phenomenon of party government associated with the work of R Michels, *Political Parties* (1915), and applied in the British context by R McKenzie, *British Political Parties* (1955). One of the great concerns about the operation of political parties is that they become controlled not by the membership but the bureaucracy or leadership of the party, or both. The rules of the party may say that party policy is determined by the membership in a representative forum, and that candidates for public office are selected by the members of the party. But the reality may be very different. If it is thought that membership participation is desirable, care needs to be taken to ensure that regulation or intervention does not relieve the parties of the need to seek new members, or make it unnecessary to retain these members by engaging them in the affairs of the party.

[49] J Fisher, 'Political Parties: Organisational Change and Intra-Party Democracy', in J Fisher, D Denver and J Benyon (eds), *Central Debates in British Politics* (2003), p 137, at p 154.

[50] This is clearly a matter which has a particular urgency in Britain, at a time when party membership is in freefall. Both of the major parties have seen membership levels fall dramatically since 1990, with the Conservatives now thought to have a membership of around 300,000, and the Labour Party much less. See p 7 (n 25) above.

[51] See S Scarrow, 'Party Decline in the Parties' State? The Changing Environment of German Politics', in P Webb et al (eds), *Political Parties in Advanced Industrial Democracies* (2002), ch 4.

[52] That is to say that there may be a third role for the State here: if membership participation is desirable, the regulation of political parties should be designed to promote and encourage membership participation in the affairs of the parties. This is a matter to which we return in ch 10.

[53] See Trade Union and Labour Relations (Consolidation) Act 1992, ss 46–70. This is a matter to which we return in ch 10.

already been identified. A large number of members or supporters making small donations would provide a secure income base for the parties, which would relieve them of the need to seek large donations from wealthy individuals or corporations. It would thus contribute to the objective of preventing corruption in the political process, and would do so without the need for State funding of the parties. It is much better from the point of view of preventing corruption that 100,000 people each pay £10 than one individual donates £1m, even though the latter may be easier to collect and may be much less trouble to manage. Yet it is not only the objective of preventing corruption that would be served by a high level of membership. So too – as already indicated – would the objective of ensuring that the parties are properly funded. The more money the parties are able to raise from their own members and supporters, the less pressure there will be on the State to provide for the core needs of the parties. The State may thus have a direct financial interest in stimulating party membership and the making of small donations by as many individuals as possible.

Respect for the Nature and Diversity of Party Structure

Although there are thus a number of objectives of party funding regulation, there are also a number of factors that constrain the way in which these objectives are met in any particular jurisdiction. Thus, while the foregoing objectives may be universal in their ambition, their application in any particular situation must always have regard to the peculiar circumstances of each specific country. There is no common regulatory system that can be applied to every country, regardless of the stage of political development of the country in question, the nature and structure of its political parties, and the form of its constitutional arrangements. One constraint is the nature of the party structure in a particular jurisdiction, the need to respect which may be said to be a fifth regulatory objective. It is at this point that our fourth and fifth regulatory objectives overlap, in the sense that party structure may be based on the need for political representation of hitherto excluded or disadvantaged groups. As part of the objective of promoting participation, it is necessary simultaneously to respect those institutional structures that facilitate participation or make such participation possible.[54] It is thus important to recall that – perhaps for different reasons – political parties are different and may be different in different countries. Political scientists have identified various types of political party, not all of which take the form of mass organisations of thousands of individual

---

[54] To this end regulatory strategy must avoid measures which will intentionally or otherwise undermine the 'plurality of political parties representing the different shades of opinion to be found in a country's population': *United Communist Party of Turkey v Turkey, supra* n 30.

members. One classification of political parties is that by Duverger who drew a distinction between 'élite' or 'cadre', and 'mass' parties.[55]

Duverger also observed the existence of what he referred to as 'intermediate' parties, of which the Labour Party was the best and most successful, but by no means the only example.[56] As an 'intermediate' party, the Labour Party was said to be also an 'indirect' party, in the sense that it includes – as members – bodies which are themselves organisations of individuals. Apart from individuals who join the Labour Party, membership includes both trade unions and socialist societies such as the Fabian Society, the Society of Labour Lawyers and the Christian Socialist Movement.[57] A full list of these affiliated members is shown in Boxes 2.1 and 2.2. The individual members of these latter organisations are involved in the Labour Party: 'but only in an indirect manner. They do no belong to the party itself; they belong to an organisation that is a collective member of the party – which is not the same thing as individual membership.'[58] The Labour Party historically may be said to have been a mixed rather than an exclusively indirect party, that is to say that it had qualities of a mass party with a large (and now rapidly declining) individual membership, and an indirect party with a large number of indirect members. The point is acknowledged by Duverger who writes of the Labour Party having been a purely indirect party but transformed into a

---

BOX 2.1
Trade Unions Affiliated to the Labour Party 2006

AMICUS	Musicians' Union
ASLEF	NACODS
BECTU	NUM
BFAWU	TGWU
CATU	TSSA
COMMUNITY	UCATT
CWU	UNISON
GMB	USDAW
Loom Overlookers	

Source: Labour Party.

---

[55] M Duverger, *Party Politics and Pressure Groups* (1972), ch 1. For the development of this classification and the emergence of others, see P Mair, *Party System Change* (1997), ch 5; S B Wolinetz, 'Beyond the Catch-All Party: Approaches to the Study of Parties and Party Organisation in Contemporary Democracies', in Gunther et al, *supra* n 37, ch 6.

[56] Duverger, *supra* n 55, p 17.

[57] See Appendix 3.

[58] Duverger, *supra* n 55, p 17.

BOX 2.2
Political Parties and Socialist Societies Affiliated to the Labour Party 2006

Co-operative Party	Christian Socialist Movement
Fabian Society	Jewish Labour Movement
Labour Campaign for Lesbian & Gay Rights	Society of Labour Lawyers
Labour Disabled Members' Group	Labour Housing Group
Labour Irish Society	Labour Students
National Union of Labour and Socialist Clubs	Scientists for Labour
Socialist Education Association	Socialist Health Association
Socialist Environmental Research Association	

Source: Labour Party.

---

mixed party when in 1918 individual members were admitted alongside the affiliates.[59] The need to respect the diversity of party structure is a need that arises because there is no ideal party type, or at least no party type which is so superior that it deserves being specially recognised by the State.

The need to respect the diversity of party structure arises also because of the functions that different organisational forms serve. In the case of the British Labour Party, the party was formed in order to facilitate the political representation of working-class and trade union interests, and to ensure that working people were represented in Parliament.[60] The continuing trade union link can be defended on the ground that it allows for the formal representation of working people in the political system,[61] and for providing an institutional forum for their voices to be heard. But the link not only provides representation and voice, it is also a way of balancing political influence. Individual wage-earners acting alone are powerless in a system in which one individual can write a cheque for £5m,[62] and in which newspaper proprietors and transnational corporations have great political authority. Collective representation through affiliated membership in a small way helps to create a still imperfect balance in the political process, and helps to ensure that a particular constituency is heard more loudly and its views taken more seriously. But in addition to representation, voice and influence, the trade union link helps to guarantee the presence of working people in representative institutions. As has been pointed out by the SAP in Sweden, close links with the trade union movement helps to ensure that wage-earners are present in

---

[59] Duverger, *supra* n 43, p 7. For an account of these constitutional changes, see G D H Cole, *A History of the Labour Party from 1914* (1948), p 44.

[60] For a good account, see H Pelling, *Origins of the Labour Party* (2nd ed, 1965).

[61] On the importance of party form and representation, see L Minkin, *The Contentious Alliance* (1992), ch 21.

[62] See ch 5 below.

political institutions.[63] Apart from voter apathy and declining party membership, the other concern about the political process in modern liberal democracies is the unrepresentative nature of governing institutions.[64]

It is true that this form of party structure appears now to be under constant challenge. It has been abandoned by the social democratic parties in Sweden (in 1990) and Norway (in 1997), both of which – influenced by liberal ideological values – moved to individual membership only, both suffering dramatic falls in membership as a result.[65] But these were in any event the weakest examples of the model, with affiliation taking place at local rather than national level. It is also under siege in Canada as a result of changes to federal election law that now tightly caps donations to political parties.[66] Yet despite these retreats, we should not write off this particular form of party organisation, though it becomes more difficult to sustain as trade union membership and influence are rolled back throughout the world. Nevertheless, apart from the British Labour Party, we find examples of this model in Australia (Australian Labor Party), Ireland (Irish Labour Party) and New Zealand (New Zealand Labour Party). Of these latter three parties, the best known is the Australian Labor Party, which is the oldest and largest party in Australia. It too allows for individual and affiliated membership through its State branches, and for trade union representation at conferences of both the State and Federal parties. An internal party review conducted in the aftermath of the party's 2001 general election defeat reaffirmed the union–party link, while proposing that union delegations to party conferences should be reduced from 60 per cent to 50 per cent (as now operates in Britain). But it was recommended that the party otherwise seeks new union affiliations and develops closer working relationships with the unions.[67]

The Protection of Human Rights

The sixth and final regulatory objective is to ensure that any regulation is consistent with human rights standards. These too operate as a potential restraint on regulators, though in a different way from the restraint caused by the need to respect the diversity of party structure. The latter is a constraint of an institutional or political nature, whereas the need to respect human rights is a constraint of a constitutional or legal nature. These two constraints do, nevertheless, overlap, and are at points mutually reinforcing.[68] A regulatory measure that

---

[63] See K D Ewing, *Trade Unions, the Labour Party and Political Funding* (2002), p 20.

[64] Although the occupational spread and social class of the members of political institutions is very narrow, it remains wider in the Labour Party than in others: see J Fisher, *British Political Parties* (1996), chs 3–5.

[65] Ewing, *supra* n 63, p 17,

[66] See ch 9 below.

[67] Australian Labor Party, *National Committee of Review* (2002).

[68] See for a vivid example, *California Democratic Party v Jones*, 147 L Ed 2d 502 (2000).

imposed a uniform structure on the political parties and failed to respect the different origins and diverse structures of the parties would stand condemned for violating the right to freedom of association. This is a right that does not mean simply the freedom of the individual to be in association with others to share common interests and to promote common objectives. It also means the freedom of the association to determine who its members will be and to determine its own rules and constitution free from State interference. These are not simply formal rights unrelated to issues of political substance. The European Court of Human Rights has emphasised the importance of 'the plurality of political parties representing the different shades of opinion to be found within a country's population'.[69] Political scientists in turn have drawn attention to the importance of party membership and structures to party ideology and impact, the point being particularly well made by Epstein in relation to the Labour Party:

> It is hard to see how there could have been an important British Labour Party without massive trade union support. There could perhaps have been a middle class party, like the Liberals (or the American Democrats) receiving union money and votes. And this may still occur in the future. But if there was to be a sizeable socialist working class party, as has in fact been the British case, then the unions were clearly necessary. No socialist party anywhere else has ever been as successful as the British without union support.[70]

It is nevertheless surprising that human rights should be presented as a source of potential regulatory restraint. The First Protocol to the European Convention on Human Rights provides by Article 3 that States are under a duty 'to hold free elections at reasonable intervals by secret ballot under conditions which will ensure the free expression of the opinion of the people in the choice of the legislature'. Given this obligation, how is it that human rights standards are not unequivocally the friend rather than the foe of regulation? One possible explanation is that human rights standards are designed above all to protect individual liberty and corporate freedom. Both the regulation of political parties and the regulation of elections are designed in part to prevent the risk of undue influence (i) on parties and governments on the one hand, and (ii) in determining electoral outcomes on the other. In promoting these objectives, regulation will inevitably undermine the liberty of individuals and the freedom of corporations to do what they want, or to spend what they want. In some countries these liberty-based concerns are greater than in others, and it is in the United States in particular that major difficulties have arisen. Here the Supreme Court struck down unequivocally any attempt to limit the amount of spending which candidates and others were permitted to spend in an election. In the memorable words of the Court:

---

[69] *United Communist Party of Turkey v Turkey, supra* n 30, p 148.
[70] L Epstein, *Political Parties in Western Democracies* (1968), p 147.

the concept that government may restrict the speech of some elements of our society in order to enhance the relative voice of others is wholly foreign to the First Amendment, which was designed to secure the widest possible dissemination of information from diverse and antagonistic sources and to assure unfettered interchange of ideas for the bringing about of political and social changes desired by the people.[71]

The promotion of electoral equality is thus just not a permissible constitutional objective. This is what it means to say that fundamental rights are a potential regulatory restraint.[72]

But although similar problems have been encountered with equalising measures in Australia and Canada,[73] the nature of the problem is not the same in every country. There are few jurisdictions so uncompromising as the American. Partly this is because of the major drafting differences in the different constitutional texts protecting human rights or fundamental rights. The European Convention on Human Rights (enforceable in the British courts following the Human Rights Act 1998) is very different in structure from the US Bill of Rights (as is the Canadian Charter of Rights and Freedoms). As a result, the Convention can accommodate a wider range of restraints on some human rights than could be contemplated in the United States.[74] The European Convention on Human Rights can also accommodate a greater ideological plurality than can the US Bill of Rights. Although the Convention is still tilted heavily in the direction of individual liberty, it is a liberty that in many cases allows restraints to be imposed where these are said to be 'necessary in a democratic society'. For this purpose, democracy is sufficiently open-ended to allow for a wide range of complementary principles to emerge. So although there is a right to freedom of expression in Article 10 of the ECHR, there is no question of the right to free expression being absolute, as some judges and scholars claim for the First Amendment in the United States. On the contrary, the right to freedom of expression is the most heavily qualified of all Convention rights, with Article 10(2) providing that the right may be qualified on one of a number of different grounds.

But this is not to deny that problems do arise with these more modern human rights instruments. The problems may be of a qualitatively different kind, but there may be problems nevertheless in determining the boundaries of regulation, and in striking a balance between the protection of human rights and the

---

[71] *Buckley v Valeo, supra* n 5, at pp 48–9.

[72] On the implications of this for restricting the boundaries of debate about permissible options for reform, see S Issacharoff and P S Karlen, 'The Hydraulics of Campaign Finance Reform' (1999) 77 *Texas Law Review* 1705.

[73] For Australia, see *Australian Capital Television v Commonwealth of Australia* (1992) 66 AJLR 695.

[74] The Canadian Charter can also accommodate a wider range of ideological interests: see *Libman v Quebec* (1997) 151 DLR (4th) 385, and *Harper v Canada (AG)* [2004] SCC 33. For comment, see C Feasby, '*Libman v Quebec (AG)* and the Adminstration of the Process of Democracy under the Charter: The Emerging Egalitarian Model' (1999) 44 *McGill LJ* 5; C Feasby, 'Issue Advocacy and Third Parties in the United Kingdom and Canada' (2003) 48 *McGill LJ* 11; A Geddis, 'Liberté, Egalité, Argent: Third Party Election Spending and the Charter' (2004) 42 *Alta Law Review* 429; and J Hiebert, 'Elections, Democracy and Free Speech: More at Stake Than an Unfettered Right to Advertise', in Ewing and Issacharoff, *supra* n 3, ch 13.

promotion of other regulatory objectives.[75] These problems have already arisen for the United Kingdom with the European Court of Human Rights holding that the Representation of the People Act 1983, section 75 violated Article 10.[76] This provision – first enacted in 1918 – was designed to complement the spending limits imposed by law on parliamentary candidates.[77] These could easily be undermined if so-called third parties (interest groups, corporations, trade unions) were free to spend without restraint promoting or opposing a particular candidate. In order to avoid this risk, section 75 provided that third parties could only incur election expenses of £5. If they wanted to spend more, they would need the permission of one of the candidates, and if the permission was given the expenditure incurred by the third party would count towards the spending limit of the candidate in question. This was held to be in breach of Article 10, not because spending limits were prohibited, but because the £5 limit was too low. The Court did not, however, indicate what an acceptable limit would be, and the legislation was changed to allow third parties to spend up to £500 each in every constituency.[78] But anyone prosecuted for exceeding this limit will almost certainly claim immediately that it violates their right to freedom of expression as guaranteed by the Convention.[79]

Conclusion

The aim of this chapter has been to consider the objectives of any regime for the funding of political parties, and the obstacles that may have to be overcome or taken into account in devising and developing a new regulatory strategy. Here it is proposed that there are six principal objectives of any such strategy, and that a successful strategy will involve a synthesis of them all. Two of these objectives are objectives of principle, which are drawn from the fundamental values of liberal democracy. On the one hand, there is a need to ensure that political parties are not exposed to the risk of corruption and that public power is not used secretly for private purposes or personal gain. On the other hand, there is a need to ensure that those who compete for political office have a fair chance of doing so, and that they are not overwhelmed by the greater financial resources of their rivals. Two of the other objectives relate to the role of political parties in the political process. On the one hand, there is a need to ensure that the parties are adequately financed in the sense that they have enough money to meet their core

---

[75] A matter of growing concern is the political advertising ban, a very important equalizing measure which imposes serious restraints on media freedom. See ch 7 below.

[76] *Bowman v United Kingdom* (1998) 26 EHRR 1.

[77] See K Ewing, *The Funding of Political Parties in Britain* (1987), ch 4.

[78] PPERA, s 131. See ch 7 below.

[79] So although restrictions in the interests of electoral equality may be imposed in the European democracies, there is uncertainty about the permissible content of any such regulation, which will inevitably lead to regulatory and prosecutorial restraint.

needs and to perform the functions which are expected of them. On the other hand, there is a need also to ensure that the parties are supported by as many people as possible, willing to support them with small contributions and membership fees.

But although these different considerations help to drive the development of policy, two other objectives operate as possible restraints. The first is the nature and structure of the political parties in a particular jurisdiction. As we have seen, political parties in different countries sometimes take different forms, so that it is not possible to have a system of regulation that applies equally to all parties in all countries. Regulation must reflect political reality, constitutional principle (in the shape here of freedom of association) and organisational choice. Not unrelated to this, though also raising a range of different issues, is the need to respect human rights in the development of policy for the regulation of political parties. In some countries the regulation of political parties has given rise to problems on the altar of constitutional law and fundamental rights. These problems have been most marked in the United States, though there is now an expanding body of important jurisprudence developing in other countries as well, notably in Canada.[80] And although constitutional protection for freedom of expression has been a particular cause for concern, there are also other constitutional rights that operate as a potential restraint on the development of policy in this field, as in other fields.

---

[80] For a consideration of both, see Ewing and Issacharoff, *supra* n 3, chs 9–13.

3

Regulatory Methods

Introduction

Having considered the different objectives which should inspire policy in relation to party funding, it is necessary now to consider how these objectives can best be developed and implemented. Different countries have adopted different methods or combinations of methods for these purposes, though as we shall see there are effectively only four ways by which these objectives can be promoted.[1] In the absence of consensus about the most appropriate method for a particular jurisdiction, partisan considerations may come into play, with each party seeking the regulatory regime most favourable to its interests.[2] Where such partisan interests can be contained, there will be other factors that determine choice of regulatory method. These include the constitutional arrangements in a particular country, the nature of the regulatory problem, which may present differently in different jurisdictions, and the form and structure of the political parties to be regulated. There will also be powerful ideological forces at work, with party funding regulation being built in all countries on an ideological fault line pulling simultaneously in the different directions of liberty and equality. Regulators thus have a choice of regulatory methods; this chapter assesses these different regulatory methods with reference to the different regulatory objectives considered in the previous chapter.

Transparency and Disclosure

The first and the oldest method of regulation of party funding is transparency and disclosure. The case for transparency is compelling and has been frequently

---

[1] See K D Ewing and S Issacharoff, *Party Funding and Campaign Financing in International Perspective* (2006).

[2] A good example of legislation being used for partisan reasons to inflict damage on the funding of a major political party is the Trade Disputes and Trade Unions Act 1927, which was passed partly to undermine trade union funding of the Labour Party. For details, see K D Ewing, *Trade Unions, the Labour Party and the Law* (1983), ch 3. A similar motivation was behind the mandatory political fund balloting provisions of the Trade Union Act 1984. See K D Ewing, 'Trade Union Political Funds: The 1913 Act Revised' (1984) 13 *ILJ* 227.

made.[3] In terms of regulatory objectives, transparency is an indispensable (though by no means sufficient) tool in the fight against corruption, to the extent that it may discourage donations being given for corrupt reasons, and to the extent that it allows donations and policy favours to be traced and identified. And to the extent that it may have a tendency towards donor restraint, it is conceivable that transparency may also help to meet the objective of fair electoral competition by closing income gaps that might otherwise exist between the parties. But it cannot be said that transparency will meet the funding needs of the parties. Indeed the reverse is the case, in the sense that a requirement that the parties should disclose the names of donors and the amount of their donation may operate to discourage some people from giving a donation, or to reduce the amount that they might otherwise have donated. Nor is it clear that transparency will encourage more people to play a bigger role in the funding of the parties, though it is conceivable that some people may be encouraged by the fact that the parties are not in the pockets of wealthy backers.

Similarly, it is unlikely that the need to respect the diversity of party structure will be affected one way or another by transparency and disclosure, unless transparency would reveal a structure which causes embarrassment and is not otherwise known. But this is as improbable as it would be an unconvincing reason for regulatory inaction. A more difficult issue, however, relates to human rights, in connection with which it might be argued that disclosure is a violation of the individual's right to privacy, to the extent that it involves disclosure not only of the income and expenditure of the parties, but also of their donors and the size of their donations. This is an argument that was raised by the Conservative Party in 1998 in opposing the introduction of mandatory disclosure legislation, then being considered by the Committee on Standards in Public Life.[4] But although the issue has been raised in a number of courts in different parts of the world, there is no court that has been prepared to say that the mandatory disclosure of political donations is a breach of fundamental rights. This is because the courts have taken the view that the individual's right to privacy must yield to a greater interest, namely the right of the public to be informed about the identity and extent of private funding of the political parties.[5]

This is not to say that human rights considerations have no bearing on the substance of transparency and disclosure legislation. Although in principle the courts have accepted that transparency does not violate fundamental or constitutional rights, there may nevertheless be exceptions. One issue relates to political parties on the fringes of the political process whose members and supporters are liable to reprisals by third parties, including employers, landlords and

---

[3] See S Issacharoff and P Karlen, 'The Hydraulics of Campaign Finance Reform' (1999) 77 *Texas Law Review* 1707.

[4] Committee on Standards in Public Life, *The Conservative Party's Evidence*, Cm 4057–I, 1998, App V: 'there is a perfectly honourable case to be made for anonymity' (p 239).

[5] See *Buckley v Valeo*, 424 US 1 (1976).

neighbours, to say nothing of the police and other agents of the State.[6] In these cases, where small donations to fringe parties may be of greater news value than larger donations to mainstream parties, there may be a chilling effect in the sense that people are discouraged from giving reportable amounts. On this point, the courts in the United States have accepted that there may be circumstances where the individual's right to privacy and freedom of association will take priority over the public's right to know.[7] Apart from thus possibly restricting who may be required to disclose, human rights concerns may also require limits being imposed on what must be disclosed. So although the law may require that the names and addresses of donors be reported to a public body such as an Electoral Commission, privacy concerns may require only the name of the donor to be publicly disclosed.[8]

It is thus clear that transparency means that the political parties should be required to publish annual audited accounts at the end of every financial year, and that they should be required to publish the names of donors and the size of donations. But although the general principle might thus be obvious, there are a number of issues of a practical nature to be considered in the implementation of a transparency and disclosure strategy. How should a donation be defined? Should it be simply a cash payment, which can at least be objectively identified and quantified? Or should it include support in kind, or loans at less than the commercial rate, or the costs of employees who are seconded to work for a party? Having defined a donation, which donations should be disclosed? All donations? Or only those above a certain amount? If the latter, what should that amount be? Having defined what should be disclosed, there is then the question of the intervals at which disclosure should take place. Should it be annually, at the same time as the party accounts are published? Or should it be more frequently, and if so, what should the intervals be? Should special rules be introduced for disclosure during election campaigns so that voters know before rather than after an election who has supported a party or candidate? There is also the question of the different levels of party organisation and party representatives. Should a disclosure regime apply only to the donations to the national party, or include all levels of party organisation?

Contribution Controls

The second regulatory strategy is to control who may give to political parties and

---

[6] This is a problem not only for the disclosure of donations, but also for laws requiring party registration where (as in Australia and Canada) the registration regime requires parties to identify a minimum number of members as a pre-condition of registration.

[7] *Brown v Socialist Workers '74 Campaign Committee*, 74 L Ed 250 (1983).

[8] See, for example, Political Parties, Elections and Referendums Act 2000 (PPERA), Sch 6, para 2(2) (donation report to include donor's name and address) and s 69(4) (donation register not to include donor's address).

how much they may give. The first example of contribution controls in modern democracies is provided by the United States, which in 1907 banned political donations by corporations, a similar measure being adopted in Canada the following year.[9] This was the era of the *Osborne* judgment in Britain when the courts rather than the legislature decided that trade union political contributions were unlawful, though there were no comparable restraints in this country on corporate donations.[10] The latter in any event were ineffective where they operated in Canada and the United States,[11] and the ban on trade union political activity was partially lifted in Britain in 1913.[12] Contribution controls of different kinds now operate in a number of jurisdictions, though few are so pure as Quebec where only electors may make a contribution to a political party.[13] But controls will typically take one of two forms, or both. The first is a ban on donations from certain sources, such as foreign governments, corporations as mentioned, or trade unions; while the second is a limit on how much a permitted donor may give in any one year.[14] In terms of regulatory objectives, contribution controls of either kind might be seen directly to address concerns about political donations being given for corrupt reasons. A ban on donations from prescribed sources will help to ensure that the parties are no longer responsive to these interests, while a cap on contributions will ensure that no party will be held to ransom by the withholding of the donation in future years. Nor is the offer of a capped donation likely to turn the heads of elected officials, assuming that the cap is set at a modest level.

The impact of contribution controls on electoral equality is much more equivocal. On the one hand, it might be argued that they will have a positive effect, in the sense that they will reduce the influence of prohibited sources and large donors on a particular candidate or party and in the election itself. In the process, contribution caps will thus create an equality between electors.[15] Equally important, contribution caps may also create an equality between candidates and parties, by restraining the fund-raising advantage of candidates and parties that have access to large numbers of wealthy supporters, and the ability to collect vast sources of money from these supporters. Such a candidate or party is then well placed to dominate the campaign, and to drown out its less well-funded (but

---

[9] See K D Ewing, 'Legal Control of Party Political Finance', in I Loveland (ed), *A Special Relationship? American Influences on Public Law in the UK* (1995), ch 10.

[10] *Amalgamated Society of Railway Servants v Osborne* [1910] AC 87.

[11] In the United States the ban was outflanked by the emergence of political action committees funded by employees and shareholders, a device upheld by the Supreme Court, and in Canada the ban was outflanked by weak enforcement regimes. See Ewing, in Loveland, *supra* n 9.

[12] Trade Union Act 1913.

[13] See L Massicotte, 'Financing Parties at the Grass-Roots Level: The Quebec Experience', in Ewing and Issacharoff, *supra* n 1, ch 8.

[14] For a review of contribution controls, see IDEA, *Funding of Political Parties and Election Campaigns* (2003), pp 193–97.

[15] The large donor may help to define the issues a party promotes, and may help to give greater prominence to these issues. If his or her favoured party is successful he or she may have a disproportionate political influence afterwards, in terms of access to officials, influence in the development of policy, and preference in terms of government benefits.

perhaps no less well-supported) rivals.[16] But although the equalising tendencies of contribution caps between electors is clear,[17] the equalising tendencies between parties is much more equivocal. Thus, it is possible that a ban on large donations may create unequal competition between the parties at an election and that large donations are necessary paradoxically to enhance equality between the parties. A good example of this is provided by the 2001 general election in Britain, before which the Conservative Party received two donations of £5m.[18] Although these were unprecedented in their size, they nevertheless played an important part in ensuring that each of the main parties had roughly similar amounts to spend on their campaigns. An equally good example is provided in Box 3.1 in relation to Conservative proposals to cap trade union donations to the Labour Party.[19] This in a sense compounds the paradox, as it reveals that – depending on the political circumstances – a contribution cap can create electoral disadvantages for parties of the centre-left just as it can cause disadvantages for parties of the centre-right.

In terms of other regulatory objectives, the impact of contribution controls on ensuring adequacy of funding is likely only to be negative. A ban on funding from prescribed sources and a restriction on how much may be accepted from permitted sources is likely to lead only to a reduction on the funds available to the parties. However, contribution controls are not likely in themselves to give rise to fundamental rights objections. A challenge to a ban on foreign donations is unlikely to get very far, and no court has held that a ban on corporate contributions violates constitutionally protected rights. By the same token, a limit on the amount that a donor may contribute has been upheld by the US Supreme Court which concluded that such a restriction did not violate protected rights to freedom of expression.[20] But there reaches a point at which contribution controls become entangled with considerations of party structure, a situation that gives rise to difficult freedom of association concerns. This is because a limit imposed by the State on the amount an individual or organisation may donate to a political party will not just regulate the money which flows to the parties. It could also potentially affect the structure and organisation of those parties which are composed of individual and collective members. In these so-called 'indirect' parties,[21] collective members affiliate on a basis related to the membership of their own organisation, so that in Duverger's terms there will be more indirect members of the party from a union which has a million members than one

---

[16] On donations and political equality, see n 15 above. See also J Hopkin, 'The Problem with Party Finance' (1994) 10 *Party Politics* 627, and J Rowbottam, 'Political Donations and the Democratic Process: Rationales for Reform' [2002] PL 758.

[17] Though this may depend on the level at which these caps are set, with the equalising benefits of a cap of £50,000 being marginal.

[18] *Daily Telegraph*, 5 August 2001.

[19] See also ch 9 below in relation to the impact of contribution caps in Canada.

[20] *Buckley v Valeo, supra* n 5.

[21] See pp 35–38 above.

BOX 3.1
Contribution Limits and Party Funding Inequality

Although contribution limits in some cases may help to promote equality between parties, in other cases they will have the opposite effect. This can be illustrated by the Conservative Party proposals in 2006 that there should be a cap on contributions of £50,000 per donor which should apply equally to individuals, companies and trade unions.[1] Although superficially attractive, this would have the effect of benefiting the Conservative Party, perhaps because in general it continues to enjoy the support of wealthier members of the community than does the Labour Party. As we shall see in later chapters, the Conservative Party received three times as many personal donations as the Labour Party and twice as many company donations. The size of the average personal donation to the Conservative Party was almost double the size of the average personal donation to the Labour Party. Between 2001 and 2005, the Labour Party received 726 individual donations of up to £75,000, amounting to a total of £4.3m. In the same period, the Conservative Party had 2,149 individual donations, amounting to a total of £14.4m.[2] (It does not follow that there were 726 and 2,149 donors respectively, as some of these donations may have been made by the same people, with many donors making multiple donations.) Under Political Parties, Elections and Referendums Act 2000 (PPERA), a donation for this purpose means a donation in excess of £5,000,[3] so the fact that the Conservatives had twice as many donors at this level is not an indication that they had more supporters. It is at best an indication that even when they were at the nadir of their electoral fortunes, they had twice as many donors with money to spare. To impose a contribution cap in these circumstances that applied to trade unions would mean that the Conservatives would have a significant funding advantage because there are only seventeen trade unions affiliated to the Labour Party which currently supply about two-thirds of the Labour Party's donation income.[4] However, to introduce a contribution cap that excluded trade unions would potentially give the Labour Party a funding advantage. The traditional role of trade union funding in an unequal society has been to allow parties of the centre-left to compete on fair terms with parties of the centre-right, which have traditionally enjoyed support from corporations and rich individuals.

---

[1] A Tyrie, *Clean Politics* (2006).
[2] K D Ewing, *The Funding of Political Parties – The Trade Union Case for Reform* (2006), p 15.
[3] PPERA, s 62(4).
[4] See pp 124–125 below, and K D Ewing and N S Ghaleigh, *The Funding of Political Parties*, Submission to Constitutional Affairs Committee, 10 April 2006.

which has a thousand members.[22] But the effect of a contribution cap would be that each union would be permitted to contribute the same amount, regardless of the difference in the size of their memberships.[23]

A contribution cap that applied indiscriminately in this way would thus undermine the organisational base of indirect parties. The State would be saying, in effect, that this form of party organisation is no longer to be permitted. Apart from raising questions about freedom of association, such a position would undermine another regulatory objective, which is to promote citizen participation in the funding of political parties. One of the most significant ways by which individuals currently take part in funding political parties in Britain is by the annual affiliation fee that trade unions pay to the Labour Party, on behalf of those of the political levy-paying members they choose to affiliate. In this way, the Labour Party is sustained by the contributions of some 2.5 million trade unionists. Although many people would prefer trade unionists to be fully paid-up individual members of the Labour Party, it is not really for the State to dictate the manner in which citizens associate with political parties. It is much better that trade unionists should associate indirectly from a distance and with a long spoon than not at all. It would, of course, be possible in principle to have a system of contribution controls that was able to distinguish between large personal donations, company donations and trade union affiliation fees. In 2006, the Power Commission proposed a contribution cap of £10,000 for individuals and that organizations should be capped at £100 per member.[24] This is a well-intentioned – if unprecedented – proposal. But in a system such as the British where only one party relies on membership organizations for financial support, the other parties may be unwilling to accept such an arrangement.[25]

Spending Controls

The third regulatory strategy moves from the regulation of the supply side to the regulation of the demand side. Here the aim is to regulate by controlling the spending which the parties may lawfully incur, principally, though not exclusively, through the medium of spending limits, particularly at election time. This

---

[22] M Duverger, *Party Politics and Pressure Groups* (1972), ch 1.

[23] For an account of the problems likely to arise, see K D Ewing, *Trade Unions, the Labour Party and Political Funding* (2002).

[24] Power Commission, *Power to the People* (2006), p 211 (Recommendation 19).

[25] Although the problem of the indirect party is perhaps the thorniest problem that has to be confronted with a system of contribution controls, there are also others. To whom would a contribution cap apply, and what would be the amount of any proposed cap? Practice varies greatly in those countries where there are caps. Many of the questions which were raised in the context of reporting and disclosure apply here too. Thus what is a contribution? It clearly includes donations of cash. But what about donations in kind?

strategy may entail banning certain kinds of expenditure,[26] or the amount that may be spent by electoral actors, or both. In terms of regulatory objectives, this is a strategy that plays to the concerns about political corruption. Spending limits in theory reduce the need for money by capping the 'arms race' between the parties, reducing if not eliminating the temptation on the part of the parties to seek or accept funding from tainted sources, or with strings.[27] Spending limits also play strongly to the second regulatory objective in the sense that they promote financial equality between the principal parties and their candidates. It is not a genuine equality to the extent that not all parties or candidates will be able to raise enough money to spend at or near the limit that the law imposes. But it is equality in the sense that the main parties or candidates are likely to be competing on the same terms financially, and fair because it means that those with greater resources do not enjoy a competitive advantage for that reason alone. Spending limits also help to promote the objective of ensuring that the parties have adequate funding. One consequence of a limit on the amount of money which can be spent on election activities is that more money will be available for other activities in which the parties are engaged, whether it be servicing members, training candidates and officials, or attending to internal democratic procedures.

But not all regulatory objectives are met by spending limits. It is possibly the case that spending limits could discourage the party or candidates from seeking support or contributions from electors. Once the budget needs are met, there is no point in seeking donations that cannot be spent. In this sense, spending controls may be particularly unfair where a candidate or party enjoys high levels of support, which the spending limits prevent from being displayed in the campaign. But there is another way in which spending limits may have a chilling effect on citizen participation not just in the affairs of political parties, but in this case in the conduct of elections. In order to be successful as a strategy, spending limits must apply not only to candidates and parties, but also to others who might want to engage in the campaign and influence the outcome of the election. These so-called third parties include trade unions, interest groups promoting a host of causes (from opposition to abortion to protection of the countryside), and companies notably in the form of newspapers. Unless the spending limits are extended to these bodies, the limits on the candidates and parties can easily be undermined and indeed eclipsed by third parties which could campaign for or against individual candidates or specific parties with impunity. If this is to be avoided, people will be either prohibited from engaging in certain kinds of electoral activity, or constrained in terms of the volume and intensity of their engagement.

[26] The classic example is television advertising. The advertising ban in Britain is very unusual, though no less justifiable for that – see *R v Radio Authority, ex p Bull* [1997] 2 All ER 561.

[27] For an argument that spending limits perform an anti-corruption function, see J-C Tham and D Grove, 'Public Funding and Expenditure Regulation of Australian Political Parties: Some Reflections' (2004) 32 *Federal Law Review* 397.

This brings us to a second concern with spending limits. One of the main problems with this particular strategy is that more than any other form of regulation it is seen to threaten constitutionally entrenched rights. In the landmark decision of the US Supreme Court in *Buckley v Valeo*[28] limits on the electoral spending of candidates and others were struck down as violating the constitutional right to freedom of expression in the First Amendment to the US Constitution, thereby permitting 'economic inequalities to be translated into political inequalities'.[29] Problems of a less dramatic nature have also been encountered in Canada where the lower courts on two separate occasions struck down third-party spending limits as violating the freedom of expression guarantees in the Charter of Rights and Freedoms.[30] The Supreme Court of Canada has now accepted that spending limits are a permissible restraint on freedom of expression in the interests of political equality, though the courts retain the power to determine where the balance between liberty and equality is to be struck in these cases.[31] As we have seen, similar problems have been encountered in the European Court of Human Rights where the Representation of the People Act 1983, section 75 was found to be in breach of Article 10 of the ECHR.[32] Here the court indicated that it was not opposed to spending limits in principle but to the fact that the limit in the British legislation was too low.[33] The legislation provided that an individual or organisation could spend up to only £5 promoting or opposing the election of a candidate. But the Court did not indicate what an acceptable limit might be.

This uncertainty about the amount of permissible limits on third-party spending is only one of a number of problems associated with spending limits as a regulatory strategy.[34] So far as the parties and candidates are concerned, the same question arises. If there are to be spending limits, what should they be? Should they be the same for all parties, regardless of the size of the party, the number of its members and the number of seats it is contesting in the election? Once that question is resolved, there is then the question of what constitutes an election expense of a candidate or a party. Political parties are permanent organisations that do not spring into life for the purposes of an election only to disappear when it is over. Indeed, there is a sense in which we live in an era of

---

[28] 424 US 1 (1976).

[29] C Sunstein, 'Political Equality and Unintended Consequences' (1994) 94 *Columbia Law Review* 1390, at 1413.

[30] *Attorney General v National Citizen's Coalition* (1985) 11 DLR (4th) 481; and *Somerville v Canada (AG)* (1996) 184 Alta R 241.

[31] See the battle between courts and legislature in Canada, as discussed in the articles referred to on p 40, n 75 above.

[32] *Bowman v United Kingdom* (1998) 26 EHRR 1. See pp 40–41 above.

[33] N S Ghaleigh, 'Election Spending and Freedom of Expression' [1998] CLJ 431 – 'the Court accepted that while money may be speech, expenditure limits are not per se an objectionable fetter on freedom of expression' (p 453).

[34] For a comparative review of this issues, see A Geddis, 'Democratic Visions and Third-Party Independent Expenditures: A Comparative View' (2001) 9 *Tulane Journal of International and Comparative Law* 5.

permanent elections: in addition to the Westminster elections, we also have the European elections, the elections to the Scottish Parliament and Welsh Assembly, as well as London and other local government elections. How can we say which expenditure incurred by a party is or is not an election expenditure, particularly when everything that a party does is directed ultimately to electoral success? Does this mean that there should be annual spending limits, not election spending limits?[35] Would the former be practicable, or even desirable?[36] And once that question is resolved, what is the sanction for non-compliance with the law? In the case of a failure to report and disclose contributions, or a violation of contribution limits, it is easy to contemplate the possibility of these failings and violations to be punishable by a fine and perhaps the forfeiture of the contribution. But what would be a dissuasive and proportionate sanction for a candidate who has overspent, or a party that has done the same?[37]

State Aid and Public Funding

So far, we have concentrated on the State's role or potential role as regulator of the political parties. But the State has another role as well, a role that involves supporting rather than regulating the parties.[38] This can take the form of aid in kind for the parties by the State,[39] or the direct subsidy of the parties by the State. State support and subsidies of both kinds are to be found in almost every Western democracy, which is not surprising as they play strongly to a number of the regulatory objectives identified above. So far as the elimination of corruption is concerned, state aid and/or public funding reduce and may eliminate the need of the parties to seek large personal or corporate donations if their needs have already been met by the State. This indeed is one of the principal reasons for introducing State funding: to release the parties from the thrall of the large donors.[40] Similarly with regard to electoral equality and fair electoral competition. Here the provision of core needs by the State ensures that the parties are able to communicate with electors, and reduces the income differences that might otherwise exist between them. This would be even more the case where the

---

[35] The only known example of a jurisdiction with an annual spending limit is the small Canadian province of New Brunswick. An annual limit, introduced in 1978, applies to registered parties, registered district associations of the registered parties and registered candidates. There are also election spending limits in New Brunswick.

[36] To introduce annual spending limits is to reflect a one-dimensional view of political parties as electoral machines. Is this appropriate? Or is it just realistic?

[37] See *Pierre-Bloch v France* (1998) 26 EHRR 202.

[38] For a good account of the role of the State in meeting (slightly different) regulatory objectives, see A Geddis, 'Towards a System of Taxpayer Funding for New Zealand Elections?' (2002) 10 *Otago Law Rev* 181.

[39] For a discussion of various forms of aid, see pp 176–185 below (broadcasting, mailshots, use of public buildings for meetings).

[40] But for an argument that it may not be effective, see Tham and Grove, *supra* n 27.

support is targeted specifically on electoral activity, which may be regarded as the most basic core need of political parties. In the United States, public funding of the election campaigns of candidates has been seen by some as an answer to both of these regulatory concerns,[41] being strengthened in those few States where it has been adopted by an obligation on the part of candidates who accept public funding to forego the use of private funds for campaigning beyond that which the public funding allocation allows.[42]

So far as the other funding needs of the parties are concerned, State aid or public funding helps here too: depending on the nature of the support provided and the level of support provided, the core needs of the parties will be met, as may much else besides. But this in turn brings us to one of the main drawbacks with State support and public funding (apart from an unwillingness on the part of the taxpayer to pay for the parties),[43] which is that neither State support nor public funding obviously ensure that citizens will be encouraged to support the parties financially or that the parties will be encouraged to promote member participation. The danger of a regime in which the political parties are an annual charge on the Consolidated Fund is that they will become another arm of government: that is to say, public bodies, publicly funded, with no incentive to recruit members beyond those required for electoral candidature and political reproduction. Not only would there be no need to recruit members, but there might be a positive disincentive on the part of an incumbent leadership to do so. For a party with guaranteed funding, members would be an irritation. The risk is then that public funding (particularly on a large scale) would reinforce the oligarchic tendencies within the parties identified by Michels so many years ago.[44] Those who controlled the money provided by the State would control the party machine, such as it would be: there would be no leadership accountability and no internal party democracy.

So far as other regulatory objectives are concerned, it is not clear that State aid or public funding would necessarily conflict with the need to respect diverse forms of party structure or undermine party organisation. The most that could be said is that it would make intermediate parties less dependent on their collective members, but it is not likely to make the parties independent of these members. Intermediate or indirect parties flourished in countries (such as Sweden and Norway) and continue to operate, if not flourish, in countries (such as Australia) where there is either State aid or public funding, or both. The human rights issue is more sensitive in the sense that State aid and public funding inevitably require taxpayers to support financially political parties they strongly

---

[41] See R Briffault, 'Public Funding and Democratic Elections' (1999) 148 *U Pa L Rev* 563. But for a sceptical approach, see B Smith, 'Some Problems with Taxpayer Funded Political Campaigns' (1999) 148 *U Pa L Rev* 591.

[42] This system is used in Maine and Arizona.

[43] On public resistance to State funding, see Electoral Commission, *The Funding of Political Parties* (2004), para 2.9.

[44] R Michels, *Political Parties* (1915).

oppose and in some cases despise.[45] The spectre often raised is of the taxpayer who may end up supporting either fascist parties or parties linked to terrorist organisations, or both. In these situations the taxpayer might complain that his or her right to freedom of conscience is being violated by being forced to sustain such parties. It might also be argued that people's right to freedom of association is being undermined in the sense that the individual is being forced by the government's use of income and other tax to associate with organisations to which these people object. Unlike the trade unionist who pays the political levy of his or her union,[46] the taxpayer is not normally consulted about whether he or she wants public money to be used in this way, nor does he or she have a right to claim exemption from the obligation to contribute to any such programme.[47]

It is thus clear that State support or public funding are no less free of difficulty in terms of regulatory objectives than are any of regulatory options already considered. Apart from the problems identified so far, there are also others. The first is one of political priority. How can the use of public funds be justified at a time of growing pressures on public services and at a time of growing disillusionment with electoral politics generally and political parties in particular? Why should taxpayers be expected to fund organisations that in many countries have lost popular support, at a time when 'political space is becoming multi-dimensional'?[48] Parties are losing members and electors are staying away from the polls, with national elections (to say nothing of European and local government elections in Britain in particular) in many countries in the late twentieth century having the lowest levels of participation for decades. But quite apart from such basic considerations of principle, there are difficult practical questions to confront, these relating to (i) what form of aid the State should provide, (ii) how much aid it should provide, (iii) to whom the aid should be provided, and (iv) for what purposes aid should be provided. These questions require us to have a clear view of how much money the parties need, which in turn may require us to have a clear view of their functions, though – as we have seen – neither matter is settled. Having addressed these questions, others appear. Thus, can the taxpayer be expected to fund the parties without getting anything in return, in terms of the greater accountability of the parties – not only for their finances but also for the manner in which they are organised?

[45] This is an issue that arose in Canada and was raised in legal proceedings. See K D Ewing, *Money, Politics and Law* (1992), ch 4.

[46] See ch 4 below.

[47] Taxpayers have no right to withhold part of their taxes as a protest against the use of public money for purposes which they oppose: *Cheney v Conn* [1968] 1 All ER 779.

[48] A Panebianco, *Political Parties: Organisation and Power* (1988), p 271. Some of the possible consequences are captured by Katz and Mair who write about parties which 'by privileging the party in public office, the parties have risked being seen as privileging themselves, and, whether directly or indirectly, to have been using state resources in order to strengthen their own position in terms of subsidies, staffing, patronage and status': R S Katz and P Mair, 'The Ascendancy of the Party in Public Office: Party Organizational Changes in Twentieth-Century Democracies', in R Gunther et al, *Political Parties: Old Concepts and New Challenges* (2002), ch 5, at p 134.

Self-Regulation or State Regulation?

There is thus a choice of regulatory method, and a choice to be made between regulation and support. But if regulation is thought necessary or appropriate, there is a separate question about whether it can be secured by the actors themselves or whether regulation by the State is necessary. There are many forms of self-regulation or extra-legal regulation in the area of party funding, in Britain and elsewhere.[49] The evidence suggests that there are two reasons why it may take place. The first is that the parties themselves may take the initiative, perhaps because of an ethical commitment to particular principles,[50] perhaps because of an obligation to members, or perhaps because of public pressure. Self-regulation in fact made a significant contribution as a strategy in the British context. The Labour Party has published its accounts annually since 1900, even though it was not under any obligation to do so, and even though neither of the other two main parties did so until much more recently. This appears to have been done as part of the obligations of transparency and accountability the party owed to its members. More recent self-regulatory initiatives of the party, however, bear the smell of political opportunism to some extent. At the time when the Conservative Party was tainted by the stain of 'sleaze' in the 1990s, the Labour Party announced not only that it would ban foreign donations, but also that it would identify the names of those who contributed more than £5,000 annually.[51] But unlike the Conservative Party at the time, the Labour Party was not in receipt of substantial foreign donations,[52] while the commitment to name donors was not matched by a commitment to publish the amount of their donations.

Self-regulation may also occur in response to external pressures. One possibility is that the parties or donors agree to accept some restraints in the shadow of the State, following recommendations of public bodies, or for fear that otherwise they will be faced with legislation. A good example of the latter is the agreement between the government and the TUC in 1984 whereby the trade unions undertook to inform members of their right not to pay the political levy, the substantial part of which was used to pay Labour Party affiliation fees. The then Conservative government was in the process of implementing the Trade Union Act 1984 which required trade unions to ballot their members every ten years for authority to continue to promote political objects.[53] The government was also proposing to introduce legislation whereby trade union members would

---

[49] The best-known example of extra-legal regulation is in Argentina where politicians participate in what are called 'transparency agreements' supervised by an NGO called Poder Ciudadano. For a brief account, see Transparency International, *Global Corruption Report* (2001), p 192.

[50] See the example of the Irish Labour Party which returned a cheque of £50,000 from a multi-millionaire businessman 'with a covering letter outlining the need to end the links between big business and politics': *Irish Independent*, 23 January 2000.

[51] See pp 7–10 above.

[52] Following its election defeat in 1997 the Conservatives also undertook not to accept foreign funding.

[53] See K D Ewing, 'Trade Union Political Funds: The 1913 Act Revised' (note 2 above).

contract in to the political levy rather than contract out, as was then and is now the case. It was feared that this could lead to a loss of revenue for the Labour Party as some trade unionists who pay the political levy under the present rules would not take the trouble to contract in if the procedures were changed. Faced with the threat of further legislation of this kind, the trade unions agreed to government demands that they take steps more actively to inform and remind members of their right to contract out. Under the terms of this most unusual agreement, the unions also accepted the need to provide members with a right of access to political fund accounts along with an information sheet about the political fund.[54]

A more recent and very different example of self-regulation is the agreement between the five main parties in Scotland before the elections for the first Scottish Parliament in 1999.[55] At that time the Neill Committee report had been published, but not implemented by the government. The five parties agreed, on January 14th 1999, however,

1   That there should be a £1.5 million limit on all expenditure from each party at national level applicable from today until May 6th;

2   that all parties will declare donations at national and local level from January 14th in line with the Neill recommendations;

3   that no party will accept foreign donations except in circumstances outlined in the Neill report;

4   that all parties will support the establishment of an independent panel to define, audit and adjudicate these arrangements which will have appropriate administrative and secretarial support and which will report at the end of the period covered by this voluntary agreement;

5   that the parties unanimously request Professor Anthony King to chair such a panel;

6   that an urgent request for a decision on funding be made by the Scottish Labour Party on behalf of the Group to the Minister of State for Devolution . . . and that a decision be made to allow the voluntary agreement to take effect without delay as quickly as possible.[56]

A Scottish Election Commission of three members (with Professor King as the Chair) was duly established with a grant of £20,000 from the government.[57] Legislation was subsequently introduced to impose the £1.5m limit on national

---

[54] For an account, see K D Ewing (1984) 13 *ILJ* 125. The text of the agreement is reproduced in K Ewing, *The Funding of Political Parties in Britain* (1987), pp 201–02.

[55] The parties to the agreement were the Scottish Green Party, the Scottish Conservative and Unionist Party, the Scottish Liberal Democrat Party, the Scottish Labour Party, and the Scottish National Party.

[56] For background to the meeting, see *The Herald*, 14 January 1999.

[57] *The Herald*, 28 January 1999. The other two members were Dr Joan Stringer (Principal of Queen Margaret University College, Edinburgh), and Anthony Taylor (formerly Director of Finance with Fife Regional Council).

party election spending,[58] but the Commission gave guidance of the type of items which should be included, though it was said to be 'impractical to devise a detailed schedule'.[59] The Commission still retained primary responsibility for reporting and disclosure and for ensuring that the ban on foreign funding was complied with, and to this effect gave guidance on what should be reported and when. But as the Commission pointed out, it was

> . . . a voluntary body; it neither has nor seeks powers of compulsion. Nevertheless, the Commission, acting on behalf of the main political parties, is concerned that the Neill report recommendations, as interpreted by the Commission, should be complied with. If it receives complaints from any of the political parties or from members of the general public suggesting that the recommendations are not being complied with, or if it has reasons of its own to believe that they are not being complied with, it will investigate the matter to the best of its ability and, if it thinks fit, issue a statement of its views. Any such statement or statements will be issued as rapidly as possible. They may be issued at any time, including during the election campaign itself.[60]

But although it has an important role to play in regulating the affairs of political parties, self-regulation is unlikely to be enough on its own.[61] In the first place, it may not be universal in the manner of its application: what one party has agreed to be bound by will not necessarily be matched by the others. Thus while by the 1980s all three main parties in Britain published their accounts despite the absence of any legal obligation to do so, the amount of information that each party provided varied, as indeed did the frequency, consistency and timing of the publication of these accounts. A second concern is that even where the parties agree to be bound by the same rules and procedures, the way in which these rules and procedures are applied will be determined by the parties themselves, and not by any external or public body. The temptation may be to announce a grand gesture of principle, but to take a narrow approach to what it means in practice. So a party may announce that it will ban foreign donations, but take a very narrow view of what is a foreign donation for this purpose; or announce that it will limit its election expenses but take a very narrow view of what counts as an expense for this purpose. And the third problem is perhaps more obvious still. What happens if the party fails to comply with its self-regulatory constraints? Who is there to monitor the situation, and what are the sanctions for breach of the rules voluntarily adopted? All of which is to suggest that while self-regulation may have a role (perhaps as a precursor to and as a companion of State regulation), it will require an element of supervision if its benefits are to be fully realised.

---

[58] SI 1999 No 787, reg 42. Note the formula used for this purpose: 'No sum shall be paid and no expenses shall be incurred by a registered political party at a general election for return of members to the Scottish Parliament whether before, during or after such an election, on account of or in respect of the conduct or management of the election, in excess of £1,500,000'. It was an offence to exceed the limit.

[59] Scottish Election Commission, *Memorandum of Guidance to the Political Parties in Scotland* (1999), p 6.

[60] *Ibid*, p 8.

[61] See also pp 9–10 above (Home Affairs Committee Report, 1993).

Supervision and Enforcement

The drawbacks of self-regulation thus point not only to State regulation of party funding, but also to State supervision and enforcement of any regulation as an alternative. To this end, the experience of legislation in Britain since 1883 and the experiences of other countries suggest that an essential precondition of successful regulation is the existence of a separate body dedicated to the enforcement of such legislation. This is not to say that there will be no enforcement whatsoever, or that the law will not be obeyed, in the absence of a regulatory body. In the absence of such a body, a supervisory role would inevitably be assumed by the rival political parties, while investigations by the press and by others would also take on a greater significance in ensuring compliance. It should not be overlooked that the absence at the time of a separate supervisory body did not prevent the prosecution, albeit unsuccessful, of Fiona Jones for alleged election expenses irregularities after she won Newark for the Labour Party at the general election in 1997.[62] But it remains the case, nevertheless, that if the law is to be applied consistently, there is no substitute for enforcement by a specialised agency established for the purpose of supervising the legislation, and dedicated to ensuring that it is enforced. For although we can point to prosecutions under the Representation of the People Act 1983, some commentators nevertheless have been surprised by the small number of cases, with the *Jones* case being the first prosecution in Britain in relation to election expenses at a parliamentary election since 1924. This has led to suspicion that there existed an unwritten understanding between the parties not to examine too closely the election returns of their rivals for fear of a rebound.

But it is not enough that there should be a separate body for this purpose. The body in question must be independent of the parties, it must have a large enough budget to enable it to perform its functions, and it must have adequate powers. Many countries have responded to the need for a specialised agency by establishing an Election Commission (Australia), an Electoral Commission (United Kingdom) or a Federal Electoral Commission (United States). In Canada the task is vested in one person, the Chief Electoral Officer. The difference between these bodies is that the Commonwealth agencies are non-partisan while the FEC is bi-partisan. What this means is that the former have no representatives of the political parties on the agency in question, whereas the membership of the latter is confined to the two main parties who enjoy equal representation. One of the advantages of a bi-partisan Commission is that it will be composed of experts in the field, people who have fought elections and who know how political parties work. But the disadvantage exposed by the US experience is that it leads to inaction, either because there is institutional paralysis or institutional reluctance to enforce the law. The US experience suggests that cosy deals are struck between the parties not to enforce the law for reasons of political opportunism or

---

[62] See ch 7 below.

advantage rather than the public interest. In other words, there is a danger that a bi-partisan Commission will serve the interests of the regulated rather than the regulations, and become nothing more than an institutionalised form of ineffective self-regulation.[63]

Although the case for a bi-partisan agency was rejected by the Neill Committee,[64] the creation of a genuinely independent body in parliamentary democracies is a genuinely difficult exercise.[65] Appointments at this level are made by the Crown, which in practice means the Prime Minister, whether in the United Kingdom, Australia or Canada, or any other parliamentary democracy in the Westminster tradition. There is clearly a danger that appointment by a head of government alone to a body such as this will lead to the politicisation of the agency. It is therefore necessary to secure the independence of any such body that it is appointed in a way which meets the approval of all the parties and that all have a role to play in the appointment process.[66] Equally important is the security of tenure of those appointed, who like judges should be protected from attempts to remove them by government for the honest and good faith discharge of their duties. Similar problems arise with the budget of any such body, which in the Westminster system of government will be determined by Parliament. This typically means that the budget will be determined by the government, which in most parliamentary systems has a tight grip on the legislature. Yet in order to be effective, any such body must have responsibility to determine how much it needs to police the democratic process, and not be left to make do with what the government decides to give it. Nor can it be placed in the position of having its budget cut because it has offended the governing party by the vigour with which it has discharged its duties and the failure to treat the governing party more favourably than any other party.

So far as the powers of regulatory bodies are concerned, there are two factors pushing in the direction of restraint that have to be overcome. The first is that the powers will be contained in primary legislation sponsored by government, and that no governing party is likely to welcome any more intrusion by the State than it can possibly avoid. Yet to be effective, a supervisory body will need powers of access to records, files and documents held by the parties. It will also need powers of investigation, including where necessary the right of access to the premises of the parties and the power to remove evidence. Powers of this nature lead us to the second factor tending towards restraint, especially if they are to be exercised without any independent judicial supervision. These are the human rights concerns we encountered at various points in this chapter. Powers of entry, search

---

[63] For a pithy account of the problems associated with the Federal Election Commission, see L Klein, 'Sanctions for Violation of Campaign Finance Laws in the USA', in K D Ewing and N S Ghaleigh (eds), *The Challenge of Party Political Funding: Comparative Perspectives* (2001), ch 3.

[64] Cm 4057–I, 1998, para 11.8.

[65] But compare the relatively upbeat account in C A Hughes, 'The Independence of Commissions', in G Orr, B Mercurio and G Williams, *Realising Democracy* (2003), ch 16.

[66] Similar problems arise in relation to the audit of government spending. See A W Bradley and K D Ewing, *Constitutional and Administrative Law* (14th ed, 2006), ch 17.

BOX 3.2
The Electoral Commission

An independent Electoral Commission (currently with five members) was established by the Political Parties, Elections and Referendums Act 2000 (PPERA), with the legislation dealing with three matters essential to its integrity: the manner of its appointment, its financial independence from government, and its powers. So far as the first is concerned, the Prime Minister must consult the leaders of the main parliamentary parties, and all appointments must be approved by the House of Commons, as well as by the Speaker.[1] In order further to eliminate the risk of abuse, it is a qualification for appointment that the individual in question has not been an officer, employee or contributor of more than £5,000 to a political party within the previous ten years.[2] So far as the financial independence of the Commission is concerned, this is secured by virtue of the fact that the budget is determined not by the Treasury but by a Speaker's Committee established under the Act, the Committee making recommendations to the House of Commons for approval.[3] The Committee is a committee of nine (including the Speaker), of whom one is the chairman of the Home Affairs Committee of the House of Commons, two are Ministers of the Crown, and the other five are MPs who are selected by the Speaker but must not be ministers.[4] Turning finally to the powers of the Commission, these are formidable. Charged with a general duty to monitor compliance with the Act, the Commission has wide powers to demand the production of material for inspection as well as extensive powers of entry, search and seizure, all without the need for a warrant.[5] These are powers which are not available to the police in a murder investigation, and it goes without saying that only the most robustly independent body stands between these powers and their abuse.[6]

[1] PPERA, s 1.

[2] *Ibid*, s 3(4). But unlike the Chief Electoral Officer for Canada, who is appointed until the age of 65 and has the same status by statute as a federal court judge, Electoral Commissioners in Britain are appointed for renewable fixed terms of up to ten years. The members of the Electoral Commission do, however, enjoy the same security of tenure as High Court judges during their period of office in the sense that they can be removed only for misconduct or incapacity and only after an Address by the House of Commons.

[3] PPERA, Sch 1, para 14.

[4] *Ibid*, s 2.

[5] *Ibid*, s 146.

[6] Under the Police and Criminal Evidence Act 1984 a search warrant issued by a magistrate is normally required before the police may enter and search private property, and a search warrant will only be granted where there is reasonable grounds to believe that there is evidence on the premises of an indictable offence which the police are investigating. Where the material is excluded or special procedure material, an application must normally bemade to a judge for an order that the material in question be surrendered to the police. It is possible to argue that some of the material held by political parties about donors would fall within this category. This is not to say that the Electoral Commission should not have such wide powers.

and seizure of the offices of political parties are far-reaching powers to take in a democracy, and there ought to be a great reluctance about arming the State in this way for obvious reasons.[67] Such powers are also likely to confront difficulties under human rights instruments. In order to avoid these difficulties, care would have to be taken that such powers do not disproportionately trespass upon the right of private property, the right of privacy (which a political party enjoys along with other organisations and individuals), and the right to a fair trial, to say nothing of the right to freedom of association. Otherwise there is the question of the power of any such agency to impose penalties for violation of the legislation. At this point consideration needs to be given to the relationship between the supervisory body and the agency or agencies responsible for the prosecution of criminal offences.

Conclusion

This chapter has been concerned with the different regulatory strategies that may be pursued to promote the different regulatory objectives identified in chapter 2. These strategies take various forms, but include principally the following: transparency of the finances of the political parties (including not only income and expenditure, but also the identity of the principal donors and the amounts of large donations); the control of donations, sometimes in the form of a prohibition of donations from impermissible sources, and sometimes in the form of a cap on the size of donations from permissible sources; the control of expenditures, most usually in the form of a cap on election expenses or parts thereof, applying not only to political parties but also to candidates and third parties; and the provision by the State of facilities, resources or funds to the parties, perhaps to help them meet core objectives and to do so without the need to solicit or accept donations from questionable or improper sources. These strategies may be pursued in different ways, but principally by self-regulation or by legislation. Although there is a role for the former, it is likely to be mainly as a complement to legislation, which in itself may not be enough. There may, however, be circumstances where some form of supervised self-regulation is the only option available. The other issue identified in this chapter as part of a successful regulatory strategy is the need for effective supervision of the legislation by an independent agency. This requires an independent regulatory authority with adequate powers, which the authority is prepared to use in a non-partisan way.

These methods all point to the need for some form of regulation and to some form of State intervention. It is important to emphasise, however, that these different methods provide the possibility of different forms of State intervention. Indeed, in some circles a distinction is drawn between models based on

---

[67] But see PPERA, s 146. See Box 3.2.

disclosure and state funding (which are seen not to be regulatory), and systems based on contribution and spending controls (which are seen to be regulatory). But the distinction seems to be groundless. All forms of intervention have regulatory aims in the sense that they are designed directly or indirectly to mould conduct; and all forms of intervention will require some kind of regulatory supervisory or enforcement machinery to ensure that legal obligations (such as reporting and disclosure) are met. It should also be emphasised that although there are different forms of intervention or regulation, it does not follow that any particular regulatory method is more efficient then the others, or indeed that any method of regulation is efficient.[68] But assuming a commitment to regulation, there is no reason why any national strategy must involve a choice of only one method, and why it could not involve a synthesis of all regulatory methods.[69] All depends on the nature of the party funding or campaign financing problem in the jurisdiction under review. But once the process of regulation begins, the experience of every country suggests that there is an irresistible dynamic in the direction of more and more regulation – as the recent experience of Australia, Canada and the United States makes very clear.[70]

---

[68] In the United States, there is an emerging wringing of hands about the utility of regulation. Some of this is related to a concern about the impact of regulation on political freedom (L BeVier, 'Campaign Finance Reform: Specious Arguments, Intractable Dilemmas' (1994) 94 *Columbia Law Review* 1258); some to a scepticism about regulation in meeting policy objectives such as those identified above (B Smith, 'Faulty Assumptions and Undemocratic Consequences of Campaign Finance Reform' (1996) 105 *Yale L J* 1049); and some to concerns about the ability of reform to make things better (C Sunstein, 'Political Equality and Unintended Consequences' (1994) 94 *Columbia Law Review* 1390).

[69] See ch 9 below for the experience of Canada.

[70] See Ewing and Issacharoff, *supra* n 1.

4

Party Autonomy and Public Accountability

Introduction

Political parties enjoy no special or distinctive legal status. Despite the importance and the public nature of the functions they perform, they remain unincorporated associations governed by private law. There is thus an unequivocal rejection in British constitutional law of Kelsen's notion that it would be acceptable to make political parties into organs of the State, in view of the decisive role they play in the election of legislative and executive organs.[1] The relationship between political parties and the State continues to be dominated by a series of liberal principles that emphasise the independence of parties within the State. So although they may perform public functions, political parties are not yet public bodies, and not yet subject to public law.[2] In recent years, however, there has been a growing recognition in legislation of the significance of political parties, which are now subject to a greater degree of regulation than in the past. In particular, there is now in place a system for the registration of political parties, with the conditions of registration having been strengthened considerably by the Political Parties, Elections and Referendums Act 2000 (PPERA). So although unincorporated associations governed by private law, political parties are now publicly accountable for the way in which they conduct some of their internal affairs. This chapter charts the evolution of political parties from autonomous bodies governed by common law in the interests of their members, to bodies that are now accountable by legislation to the public, and in the process seeks to identify a number of underlying principles that define the legal position of political parties in the British constitution.

[1] H Kelsen, *General Theory of Law and State* (1949), p 295.
[2] Compare P Joseph, *Constitutional and Administrative Law in New Zealand* (2001), p 1030 where it is suggested that the greater role ascribed to political parties by New Zealand electoral law following the introduction of the mixed member proportional (MMP) system has transformed political parties into public organisations, exercising public statutory functions. This in turn may lead to their being subject to legal scrutiny under the New Zealand Bill of Rights Act 1990.

Diversity of Party Structure

The first brush between the courts and political parties was not a happy one. *Amalgamated Society of Railway Servants v Osborne*[3] was concerned essentially with whether trade unions could in association with socialist societies form a political party called the Labour Party.[4] The case was decided at a time when there was no State support for political parties and no remuneration of MPs by the State. In the speech of Lord Shaw of Dunfermline, the case also contains one of the most detailed examinations of the constitution and rules of the Labour Party by any court before or since. Although concerned with whether working people could secure parliamentary representation, this dimension was largely lost in a fog of legality: the political question was translated into the legal question whether it was within the powers of a trade union registered under the Trade Union Acts 1871-76 to impose a compulsory levy of their members for political purposes. In answering in the negative, Lord Macnaghten said:

> It can hardly be contended that a political organisation is not a thing very different from a combination for trade purposes. There is nothing in any of the Trade Union Acts from which it can be reasonably inferred that trade unions, as defined by Parliament, were ever meant to have the power of collecting and administering funds for political purposes.[5]

In this way the case was presented simply as a matter about the powers of the trade union: there was no recognition that the decision had profound implications for the survival of a political party, or for the freedom of individuals and groups to form political parties to secure better parliamentary representation.

The Struggle for Diversity

This is not to say that these matters were completely ignored. Two members of the court examined the rules and constitution of the Labour Party. Holding that the raising of money for political purposes was not beyond the powers of a trade union, they nevertheless held that it was unlawful to raise money for a party organised in the way that the Labour Party was organised. Lord James of Hereford was troubled by the requirement in the rules of the union that all parliamentary candidates supported by the union must sign and accept the conditions of the Labour Party and be subject to its whip. Objection was taken to this on the ground that

> the member undertakes to forgo his judgment, and to vote in Parliament in accordance with the opinions of some person or persons acting on behalf of the Labour Party. And such vote would have to be given in respect of all matters, including those of a most

---

[3] [1910] AC 87.

[4] For full details, see S and B Webb, *A History of Trade Unionism* (1920), ch 11, and K D Ewing, *Trade Unions, the Labour Party and the Law: A Study of the Trade Union Act 1913* (1982), ch 2.

[5] [1910] AC 87, at p 97.

general character, such as confidence in a Ministry or the policy of a Budget – matters unconnected, directly at least, with the interests of labour. Therefore I am of opinion that the application of money to the maintenance of a member whose action is so regulated is not within the powers of a trade union.[6]

This is a theme developed at greater length by Lord Shaw of Dunfermline. He drew attention to the fact that the Labour Party was a federation of trade unions, trades councils, socialist societies and local labour associations, their object being to organise and maintain a parliamentary party with its own whips and policy, the policy being formulated and controlled by the annual conference of delegates. Lord Shaw continued in a manner which revealed a certain degree of concern for this particular model of party organisation:

> How this works in practice is not stated, but it appears to be possible that the annual conference, which constitutes the ultimate governing body, may be composed according to money contributions by trade councils and local labour associations in such a way as to swamp larger component organisations, including the Amalgamated Society of Railway Servants, whose representation is confined to one voting card per 1,000 members. The case, therefore, is not simply that of contributions for payment of members of Parliament to be selected and supported by the appellant society itself, but one in which, while the duty of support is laid on the society, the securing of the election of the member and the parliamentary policy which he is bound to pursue is controlled by another body, a federation of societies, to whom the appellant society has consented to delegate these important functions, in which federation the opinions of the appellant society may be merged or submerged, as the case may be.[7]

The *Osborne* judgment had three immediate consequences: it led to a number of judgments against other unions, gradually turning off the tap of union funds to the Labour Party;[8] it led in 1911 to the introduction of parliamentary salaries so that working people could be elected to Parliament; and it led to a campaign for legislation partially to reverse the decision. In this campaign, the trade unions were supported by the Lord Chancellor (who did not sit in *Osborne*). In a memorandum to Cabinet colleagues, Lord Loreburn pointed out that it was 'incontestable that until 1909 the doctrine laid down in the *Osborne* case had never been asserted by any court of law'.[9] In supporting a reversal of the decision, Lord Loreburn dismissed the foregoing line of argument presented by Lords Shaw of Dunfermline and James of Hereford, as well as another line of argument in which the Lords expressed concern about the individual trade unionist being required unwillingly to pay a political or parliamentary levy as a condition of membership of a trade union. According to Lord Loreburn:

> The truth is that when men agree to be bound by majorities they encounter a risk of having to do something they dislike or to quit the association. Real freedom consists in leaving bodies of men free to combine for objects which are in themselves proper, and

---

[6] *Ibid*, p 99.
[7] *Ibid*, pp 109–110.
[8] See Ewing, *supra* n 4, chs 2 and 3.
[9] TNA, CAB 37/103/44.

leaving each man free to judge for himself whether, having regard to these objects, he chooses to accept the combination and make the sacrifice which combination involves, if sacrifice there be.[10]

The legislation to reverse *Osborne* was nevertheless controversial, and it took two attempts before the Trade Union Act 1913 reached the statute book, and before the right of trade unions to affiliate to the Labour Party was fully restored. In this way, however, the diversity of party structure was now recognised by Parliament.

The Principle of Consent

By the Trade Union Act 1913, the Labour Party thus secured the right to exist, largely in the form in which it had been born. But under the same Act that right came at a price. In the first place, a union had to conduct a secret ballot of its members to determine whether they wanted their union to adopt political objects. If a majority agreed, the union had then to adopt political fund rules by which political objects would be financed from a separate political fund to which all members of the union had a right not to contribute. In other words, members had (and still have) the right to 'contract out' of paying the levy. This right was to be contained expressly in the political fund rules, as were the accompanying requirements that payment of the political levy was not to be made a condition of membership of the trade union, and that anyone who claimed exemption from paying the levy was not to suffer any disability (such as loss of benefits or expulsion) for doing so. Anyone complaining of a breach of the political fund rules could complain to the Chief Registrar of Friendly Societies, who would determine whether there had been a breach of the rules and the steps within his powers to be taken to remedy it. This is a jurisdiction which is now exercised by the Certification Officer for Trade Unions and Employers' Associations, from whom an appeal lies to the Employment Appeal Tribunal (EAT), though neither is kept busy by the flow of complaints.

The costs of diversity were nevertheless increased in 1984, by the strengthening of one of the principles of the 1913 settlement. That settlement is based on the principle of consent – both collective and individual; collective in the sense that majority support in a ballot was needed to establish a political fund, and individual in the sense that members could choose not to comply with the decision. But although trade unions were required to hold a ballot to adopt political objects and establish a political fund, there was no obligation to ballot the members at any time thereafter to determine whether they continued to support the union's engagement in the political process. That is to say, there was no continuing need for collective consent, and no need for trade union members regularly to affirm their consent to political objects on a periodic basis. That was changed in 1984 – by a measure designed by the Thatcher government to weaken

---

[10] *Ibid.*

the Labour Party – with trade unions now required to ballot their members every ten years for authority to maintain political objects and incur political expenditure.[11] But although a majority of the members of the union may vote in favour of retaining political objects, the individual members of the union are not bound by this collective result, in the sense that they may still exercise their right not to pay the political levy. The principle of individual consent is thus unaffected.

The Principle of Party Autonomy

The *Osborne* case and its aftermath are concerned with the question of who may establish a political party, and who may be members of a political party, and on what terms. Once the party is established, we encounter a third principle that complements the principles of diversity and consent which we have now identified: so far as the internal affairs of the parties are concerned, the governing principle of British law appears strongly to be autonomy of party organisation. There is little direct regulation of the internal affairs of the parties by legislation, though the parties are not exempt from the ordinary law. As a general rule, it is for the parties themselves to determine who is eligible for membership, how they are structured and organised, how they develop policy and select candidates, how their leader is to be chosen or elected, and how and in what circumstances members may be disciplined or expelled.[12] Although there is some legislation dealing with these matters, the role of the courts is mainly to ensure that the party operates in accordance with its own rules, and to enforce these rules where there is a breach. But not only is there autonomy in the sense of an absence of State intervention, there is autonomy also in the sense that the courts have expressed reluctance about being drawn into rule-book disputes, preferring the parties themselves to resolve internal conflicts. In *Lewis v Heffer*,[13] it was pointed out that

> The courts exist (one hopes) as a last resort for the members of a party or organisation who feel that the only way they can assert their rights inter se is to ask the court to define what those rights are. They do not exist simply to give the kiss of life to some faction which is otherwise not viable.[14]

In the same case, it was thought necessary for another member of the court to point out that no organisation can survive a steady shower of writs, and no organisation can possibly be made to work by a series of injunctions.[15]

---

[11] See K D Ewing, 'Trade Union Political Funds: The Trade Union Act 1913 Revised' (1984) 13 *ILJ* 125. See now Trade Union and Labour Relations (Consolidation) Act 1992, Ch VI.

[12] Powers of expulsion are often extremely wide. see Labour Party Rules, rule 2A8 – No member of the party shall engage in a sustained course of conduct which in the opinion of the [National Constitutional Committee] is prejudicial, or in any way which in the opinion of the NCC is grossly detrimental to the party.

[13] [1978] 1 WLR 1061.

[14] *Ibid*, at p 1079 (Geoffrey Lane LJ).

[15] *Ibid*, p 1077 (Ormrod LJ).

Internal Organisation and Management

Lewis v Heffer[16] is a good example of the principle of autonomy in operation. In that case, there was a bitter dispute between two factions in the Newham North-East Constituency Labour Party (CLP), each said to be striving for mastery of the general meeting of the local party. After many court cases, the Labour Party National Executive Committee (NEC) suspended the officers and committees of the local party, pending a full inquiry into the dispute within the CLP, and entrusted the conduct of its affairs to the party's national agent. Julian Lewis – the leader of one of the factions – brought legal proceedings challenging the suspension. He claimed that the NEC had no power under either the national party or the CLP rules to take such a step, and that even if did have such powers, their exercise in this case was unlawful and in breach of the rules of natural justice. At a time when the Court of Appeal was flexing its muscles against public authorities and trade unions, on this occasion it showed remarkable forbearance to the autonomy of the party, despite having recognised the importance of the matter before it. According to Lord Denning:

> Whichever faction gets the mastery of the local general meeting selects the parliamentary candidate for the constituency. It selects of course a man of its own way of thinking. It is a safe Labour seat. So the faction which wins will have a representative in Parliament. He will there propagate its ideas. And, if there are other members of Parliament of like mind, he will, with them, be able to put their objectives into operation. This local struggle may have its counterpart in other constituencies. So the outcome may influence the standing of the Labour Party in Parliament, and thus affect the policies of Parliament itself. Hence its importance.[17]

On the question of the rules authorising the suspension, the court acknowledged that there was nothing expressly set out to authorise the action being challenged. But here the court deferred to the law of the party, with Lord Denning holding that

> The NEC have exercised disciplinary powers over the local Labour Parties or their members. When there have been dissensions within a local party, the NEC have held enquiries and reorganised them. They have expelled members and suspended them. All these measures have been reported to the annual party conference and no exception has been taken to them, or no serious exception as far as I can see. In a body like this, rules are constantly being added to, or supplemented by, practice and usage; and, once accepted, become as effective as if actually written.[18]

In a similar vein, Ormrod LJ thought that it must require an extraordinarily strong and clear case to justify the court in holding a well-established practice like the power of suspension to be unconstitutional or ultra vires, more particularly where the organisation concerned is a voluntary, unincorporated and

---

[16] [1978] 1 WLR 1061.
[17] *Ibid*, pp 1064–65.
[18] *Ibid*, p 1072.

essentially informal body.[19] Such deference was all the more remarkable for the fact that the faction that benefited from the decision was the Left,[20] trying to unseat the incumbent moderate MP, Reg Prentice (who later defected to the Conservatives). But given that the power to suspend existed, what about the claim that it had been improperly exercised because there had been a breach of natural justice? The latter are the procedural rules of the common law that require a hearing to be given to someone who is facing a disciplinary penalty or some other prejudice.[21] On this point, it was held that the rules of natural justice did not apply (though they would apply in the case of a *disciplinary* suspension or expulsion, as discussed below). According to Geoffrey Lane LJ:

> It seems to me that this suspension was an administrative action which by its very nature had to be taken immediately. It was impossible for the NEC at that stage, and I emphasise those words at that stage, to hear both sides. In most types of investigation there is in the early stages a point at which action of some sort must be taken and must be taken firmly in order to set the wheels of investigation in motion. Natural justice will seldom if ever at that stage demand that the investigator should act judicially in the sense of having to hear both sides. No one's livelihood or reputation at that stage is in danger. But the further the proceedings go and the nearer they get to the imposition of a penal sanction or to damaging someone's reputation or to inflicting financial loss on someone, the more necessary it becomes to act judicially, and the greater the importance of observing the maxim, audi alteram partem. It seems to me in the present case . . . natural justice does not demand that anyone should be invited to provide an explanation or excuse before that suspension was imposed.[22]

The Selection of Candidates

Apart from matters of internal party organisation and management, the principle of autonomy is reflected also in matters such as the selection of delegates to party conferences and the selection of candidates to contest elections on behalf of a party.[23] A good example of the latter is *Mortimer v The Labour Party*,[24] which was concerned with the rules adopted by the Labour Party to select a candidate for the London mayoral election in 2000.[25] Under the rules adopted by the NEC, the

---

[19] *Ibid*, p 1076.
[20] Although it is clear that at least one member of the court took against the plaintiff: *Ibid*, at p 1079 (Geoffrey Lane LJ).
[21] For a detailed account of the rules of natural justice, see H W R Wade and C Forsyth, *Administrative Law* (9th ed, 2004), chs 12–14.
[22] *Lewis v Heffer, supra* n 15, pp 1078–79.
[23] See *Hudson v GMB* [1990] IRLR 67, below p 75.
[24] Case No HC 1999 OY944.
[25] Candidate selection has given rise to a number of complaints to the courts by people who have failed to secure their party's nomination, though these generally have failed. Another case is that involving Denis Canavan, a Labour MP who the Labour Party refused to select to contest his Westminster constituency for the Scottish Parliament. This gave rise to legal proceedings that were unsuccessful. See *The Herald*, 12 August 1998. But problems are not confined to the Labour Party. See *Weir v Hermon* [2001] NIJB 260, and *Donaldson v Empey* [2004] NIJB 1.

candidate was to be chosen by an electoral college of three parts: one third to consist of the affiliated trade unions and socialist societies in Greater London, one third to consist of MPs and MEPs, and one third to consist of paid-up party members in Greater London. The NEC decided that only those individuals who were fully paid-up members on 24 September 1999 would be eligible to vote and that only those affiliated organisations which had paid their affiliation fees up to the end of 1998 would be able to participate. Under the rules of the party, affiliation fees were to be paid in full by the end of the year to which they related, but the Manufacturing, Science and Finance union (MSF) operated a practice whereby it paid its affiliation fees in arrears. On this occasion, the union did not pay its 1998 London affiliation fees until August 1999, though this was before the NEC rules for the selection of the London mayoral candidate were developed.

The effect of the selection rules was to disqualify MSF from taking part. This led six members of the union (but not the union itself) to bring legal proceedings, seeking a declaration that the union was an affiliated organisation, and that the claimants were therefore entitled to participate in the selection of the Labour Party's candidate for London mayor. But the claim failed. The starting point for Jonathan Parker J was that

> no individual or organisation had any right to participate in the selection process under the Labour Party Rules. It was entirely a matter for the National Executive Committee to decide what form the selection process should take and who should be eligible to participate in it. Thus the court is not here concerned with the construction of a contract or a statute, but rather with the procedure which the National Executive Committee in its discretion decided to approve.[26]

It is not clear on what principles that discretion must be exercised. But in this case the court found that the so-called freeze date of 31 December 1998 for affiliated organisations was neither arbitrary nor capricious, and that the MSF London Region enjoyed no special position in relation to the selection process by reason of its practice of late payment of affiliation fees and the Labour Party's acceptance of these late payments. Unlike in *Lewis v Heffer*, the practice was found not to have crystallised into a legal form. In any event, the court also found that the claimants had no standing to bring the case in the first place. The dispute was one between the Party and the union. It was not between the Party and the members of the union, who were said not to have any contractual right in relation to the selection process.

Autonomy of Party Organisation: The Role of Legislation

Subject to the rules of natural justice, political parties are thus exposed to little legal scrutiny by the courts, which are concerned principally to ensure that they

[26] Case No HC 1999 OY444, pp 7–8.

act in accordance with their own rules, but in the process performing this role from some distance. It is thus a case of autonomy under the rules, and autonomy in the application of the rules, though we should not underestimate the power of the courts to intervene in internal party affairs, should they wish to.[27] Apart from rule-book disputes, however, the courts may be asked to intervene to enforce a statute of general application against a party, such as the Sex Discrimination Act 1975, the Race Relations Act 1976 or the Disability Discrimination Act 1995. There can be little objection to the principle of autonomy under the law, as we will discuss in the following section. Nor can there be any objection to the principle that political parties should be subject to the ordinary law relating to discrimination: no party should be permitted to discriminate on the grounds of sex, race or disability. But equally, the application of the ordinary statute law can have important implications for party autonomy within the uniquely political sphere that the parties occupy, and the attempts which the parties may make to broaden the base of representative political institutions. In these cases, it may be necessary for Parliament to intervene to restore the autonomy of the party.

All-Women Shortlists: A Threat to Autonomy

One of the most contentious issues of this kind in recent times relates to the practice of all-women shortlists, whereby parliamentary candidates in some constituencies were chosen from shortlists consisting only of women. This practice was adopted by the Labour Party in the 1990s in an attempt to increase female representation in Parliament, and was challenged in *Jepson v Labour Party*[28] on the ground that it violated the Sex Discrimination Act 1975, which by section 13 applies to an authority or body which can confer an authorisation or qualification which is needed for or facilitates engagement in a particular profession or trade. The latter provision was found by an industrial tribunal to apply to MPs, and the tribunal thought that it was immaterial so far as section 13 was concerned that

> a person seeking to be considered for approval as an official candidate for a major political party has further hurdles to overcome before he or she can achieve a position as a Member of Parliament. He has to be actually selected as the candidate in competition with others and then gain the approval of the electorate at an election. However, in that sense he is in no different position from a person denied approval by a body under s 13, who does not as yet have any particular work to do and who would need selection by others before obtaining such work.

It was rather bad luck for the Labour Party to be caught by the Sex Discrimination Act 1975 in this way. Section 33 of the same Act had expressly disapplied

---

[27] Nor should it overlooked that there are a number of collateral restraints in labour law which have implications for the organic relationship between trade unions and the Labour Party. See *Birch v NUR* [1950] Ch 602, *Leigh v NUR* [1970] Ch 326.

[28] [1996] IRLR 116.

aspects of the Act so far as they might affect the constitution, organisation and administration of political parties. This was designed to protect arrangements for the representation of women within the government of political parties (such as the provisions in the Labour Party Constitution reserving a fixed number of seats on the NEC for women). But section 33 did not apply to exclude the operation of section 13 so far as the latter applied to political parties.

Although an important challenge to the autonomy of political parties over candidate selection, Parliament has since intervened to reverse the *Jepson* ruling, which was never appealed to a higher court. The Sex Discrimination (Election Candidates) Act 2002 applies to arrangements made by registered political parties for the selection of a party's candidates in what is referred to as a relevant election. The arrangements in question apply only to those adopted for the purpose of reducing inequality in the numbers of men and women elected as candidates of the party. The relevant elections to which the Act applies are parliamentary elections, elections to the European Parliament, elections to the Scottish Parliament and the Welsh Assembly, and local government elections. In these cases, it is expressly provided by the 2002 Act that none of the provisions in Parts 2–4 of the 1975 Act are to apply. This has the effect of (i) giving the political parties an immunity from the general law, and (ii) restoring autonomy (for prescribed objectives) in terms of candidate selection (at least so far as gender is concerned). Similar provision is made to amend the Sex Discrimination (Northern Ireland) Order 1976, and the Act unusually contains a sunset clause whereby it is to expire at the end of 2015 (though the expiry date may be extended by order of the Secretary of State).

Party Autonomy and the Race Relations Act

As it happens, the Sex Discrimination (Election Candidates) Act 2002 may have been unnecessary. The issue of discrimination in the selection of candidates resurfaced in the courts, but this time under the Race Relations Act 1976. Like the Sex Discrimination Act 1975, this also makes unlawful certain forms of discrimination by a body or authority which can confer an authorisation or qualification, which is needed for or facilitates engagement in a particular profession.[29] In *Sawyer v Ahsan*[30] the applicant (a Muslim of Pakistani origin) was a member of the Labour Party and a member of the Birmingham City Council. After having successfully contested two elections as a Labour Party candidate, he was not adopted as a Labour Party candidate in 1998, and claimed that he had been the victim of racial discrimination, losing the selection to a less-experienced white male. Just as the industrial tribunal had held in the *Jepson* case that the Sex Discrimination Act 1975 applied to candidate selection, so the EAT in *Ahsan* held

---

[29] Race Relations Act 1976, s 12.
[30] [1999] IRLR 609.

the same in relation to the Race Relations Act 1976. According to the appeal tribunal, the endorsement of a candidate by the Labour Party was to be regarded as an authorisation of a kind that was needed for engagement in the particular occupation of Labour councillor.[31] *Ahsan* is thus consistent with *Jepson*: both the Sex Discrimination Act 1975 and the Race Relations Act 1976 apply to the selection of parliamentary and local authority candidates.

But that has been changed in relation to the former by the legislation of 2002, though not in the case of the latter. This means that it is still unlawful to discriminate against someone on racial grounds. It also means that it is not permissible to give preference to racial minority candidates for nomination or selection. That conclusion, however, has now been thrown into doubt by the Court of Appeal in *Triesman v Ali*,[32] another case involving Labour Party selection procedures. In this case, the applicants were suspended from office following a disciplinary investigation into alleged breaches of party rules, with the result that neither could be nominated for selection as local authority candidates. They claimed that they had been discriminated against because of their race, on the ground that white candidates had not been similarly treated. But although the applicants succeeded in both the employment tribunal and the EAT, the Labour Party successfully appealed to the Court of Appeal which reversed *Ahsan*, and by implication *Jepson* as well. The view of the appeal court was that s 12 of the 1976 Act was not intended to apply to the selection of local authority candidates, thereby directly repudiating the rhetoric of counsel in the *Ahsan* case that Parliament could not have intended that so potentially harmful a class of discrimination should be left without a remedy. In the view of the Court of Appeal:

> even if being a Labour councillor is being engaged in a profession for the purposes of section 12, we cannot see that the Labour Party in selecting a candidate or accepting a nomination for such candidacy is conferring an authorisation or qualification such as is within the contemplation of the section. It is not the type of qualifying body to which the section is intended to apply, its activities being for its own political purposes.[33]

Autonomy and Legality

Although there is thus a strong commitment to Party autonomy, this does not mean that there is no legacy of regulation of the affairs of political parties.[34] Nor

---

[31] It is true that it was only the electorate that could provide the ultimate authorisation, but in the view of the appeal tribunal the Race Relations Act did not require the authorisation to be sufficient in itself, but only that it should be needed.

[32] [2002] IRLR 489.

[33] *Ibid*, p 495.

[34] But until recently the regulation has been light and collateral. For example, the Trade Union Act 1984 provided that membership of a political party could not be made a condition of being a candidate for the union offices which are regulated by the Act. (Now Trade Union and Labour Relations

does it mean that the parties are above the law. The ordinary law will normally apply to the parties as it applies to others, particularly when a political party engages in activities incidental to its political work. Autonomy is thus complemented by legality, in the sense that the parties are bound by the ordinary law, in the same way as others. So while the State recognises the autonomy of political parties, it does not normally provide them with legal immunities. While the former is clearly consistent with constitutional principle, the latter would be a clear violation and would strike at the very heart of the rule of law. This is not to say that the political parties do not enjoy certain privileges conferred by the State, but this is a somewhat different matter that relates to the nature of the activity they are expected to perform. Some of these privileges are discussed later in this chapter and others are considered in chapter 8 below. For example, only political parties have access to television for party political and party election broadcasts, and political parties nominate the great bulk of the members of the House of Lords. To the extent that the Conservative Party enjoyed immunity from corporation tax, this was wholly fortuitous.[35]

Legality and the Common Law

So far as the principle of legality is concerned, political parties are bound by common law and statutory rules. So far as the common law is concerned, a political party will be bound by contracts made on its behalf, it is liable in tort for the negligence of its staff, and it will have responsibilities as the owner or occupier of property. The common law may also impose duties on a political party in its dealings with its members. Chief amongst these are the rules of natural justice which we encountered in *Lewis v Heffer*.[36] In that case, natural justice arguments were raised unsuccessfully by the plaintiff to challenge the suspension of the local party. But the rules of natural justice do, nevertheless, have a record of successful application in the specific context of discipline and expulsion of members,[37] where the courts will protect the member from arbitrary conduct by the party, as the Court of Appeal made clear in the *Lewis* case. Disciplinary powers will have to be exercised strictly in accordance with the powers of the party, and in accordance with the rules of natural justice where the former fall short of the latter. The rules of natural justice are procedural rules which have been developed by the courts to ensure that the individual has a right to a hearing before disciplinary penalties are imposed, and the right to be heard by a body or tribunal which is free from bias. Although most commonly encountered in the field of

(Consolidation) Act 1992, s 47(2).) The Labour Party rules provide that delegates to party conference must be individual members of the party. The effect of the 1984 measure is that a trade union could be led by an individual who thus may not be in a position to represent the union in Labour Party affairs.

[35] *Conservative Central Office v Burrell* [1980] 3 All ER 42; [1982] 2 All ER 1.
[36] [1978] 1 WLR 1061.
[37] *John v Rees* [1970] Ch 345.

public law in relation to the decisions of public authorities, the rules of natural justice apply also to the disciplinary proceedings of trade unions, voluntary associations and political parties.

But whilst there is a record of application of the rules of natural justice to discipline and expulsion cases involving individual members of parties (leading to the tightening up of party disciplinary procedures), the courts remain reluctant to extend the reach of these principles in the context of party government. Here we find legality tempered by autonomy. A good example of this is *Hudson v GMB*[38] where the plaintiff was aggrieved because the union withdrew her nomination to represent the union at the Labour Party's Yorkshire Regional Council. This was done because the union discovered after Hudson had been nominated that she was a supporter of Militant, an organisation proscribed by the Labour Party. Being a delegate to the Labour Party Regional Conference was said to be a privilege of union membership which could not be withdrawn without proceedings in accordance with natural justice. But this argument was rejected by the court on the ground that the appointment of Labour Party delegates was not something which was sufficiently formalised or enduring to attract the rules of natural justice. According to Hoffmann J, if one of the chosen delegates had been told that he or she was not to go because the union's Regional Committee had decided that someone more important should go instead, that might have been thought discourteous but would not have been a ground for legal complaint. In determining whether natural justice applies, it is necessary to have regard to the ad hoc nature of an appointment and whether it involved any particular status in the union's hierarchy.

Legality and Legislation

Political parties will also be bound by a number of statutory obligations of a kind that apply to others. As a landlord, it will be bound by legislation designed to protect tenants; as an employer it will be bound by employment protection legislation, designed to protect workers from unfair dismissal; and as a processor of data it will be bound by the Data Protection Act 1998, designed to protect members and other people about whom the parties may store information (such as donors or voters). A good example of a political party being bound by legislation of general application is *Oakley v The Labour Party*,[39] which concerned the dismissal of the manager of the party's sales and marketing unit. Ms Oakley had been appointed on a fixed-term contract for a year, and the contract was not renewed when it expired. Instead, the department was reorganised, she was offered other work for four months, and permitted to apply for the headship of the new department, an application that was unsuccessful. The new job involved responsibilities similar to those previously performed by Oakley, but with

---

[38] [1990] IRLR 67.
[39] [1988] IRLR 34.

extended scope, and it was said by Watkins LJ in the Court of Appeal that all this was a little ironic given that the new arrangements had been recommended in a report which Oakley had prepared. The claim for unfair dismissal succeeded,[40] with the Court of Appeal holding that the whole affair was a charade, in the sense that the Labour Party had made up its mind to get rid of the appellant, with the restructuring being simply a pretext for that purpose.

Only in exceptional circumstances will such legislation not apply to political parties, so that it is only exceptionally that legality will give way to autonomy. One example is the Data Protection Act 1998, which applies to political parties as to everyone else, with the result that data may be processed with the consent of the data subjects.[41] There is, however, one exception to the application of the Data Protection Act 1998 to the political parties, which hold and process data not only about members but also voters. This is done as part of voter identification programmes, to enable the parties to target known supporters at election time to encourage them to vote. The processing of this information even within the party could violate the data protection principles, and as a result special provision is made in regulations to permit such processing without the consent of the data subjects.[42] Another example is provided by the new regulations prohibiting discrimination on the grounds of sexual orientation on the one hand, and religion or belief on the other. These provide that it is unlawful to discriminate in relation to an appointment to an office or post, with a number of exclusions that include a 'political office'. This is defined in turn to include 'any office of a political party'. A similar exclusion applies to the Race Relations Act 1976, which was extended in 2003 to apply to office-holders, with the same exception. While it is understandable that someone's beliefs may make him or her ineligible for appointment to an office in a political party, permitting discrimination on other grounds takes the principle of autonomy to curious levels.

From Autonomy to Accountability: Registration and Party Identity

Recent legislation (such as the Sex Discrimination (Election Candidates) Act 2002) strongly reinforces the principle of party autonomy as a guiding legal principle of the law relating to political parties. As already pointed out, however, the principle of autonomy has been complemented by the principle of accountability, though this is an accountability of the parties to the public rather than to their members. But even here, we find accountability tempered by the legacy of

---

[40] Compare *Hotson v Wisbech Conservative Club* [1984] IRLR 422.

[41] This is an issue that could give rise to difficulties in the context of internal party elections, in terms of providing access to data for candidates for party elections.

[42] See The Data Protection (Processing of Sensitive Personal Data) Order 2000, SI 2000 No 417, Sch, para 8.

autonomy, notably in the rules relating to the registration of political parties. First introduced by the Registration of Political Parties Act 1998, these are extremely important. But although they bring political parties formally under the supervision of the State, the rules do so in a way that respects the parties as organisations, both in terms of their ideology and doctrine on the one hand, and their structure and government on the other. Registration was introduced to deal with a number of mischiefs, these set out clearly during the Second Reading debates in both the Commons and the Lords. According to the then Home Secretary (Jack Straw):

> The Bill will help to prevent the use of misleading candidates' descriptions on ballot papers at elections, thus helping to protect the identity of political parties and, therefore, the integrity of the political process. In addition, the Bill will allow, for the first time, a registered party's emblem to be printed on the ballot paper as a way of helping to distinguish as clearly as possible between candidates from different parties.[43]

The problem of party identity was caused by the fact that in order to mislead voters and presumably to cause harm to serious candidates, some election candidates described themselves on the ballot paper as Conversatives, or Literal Democrats.[44]

Registration – From Voluntary to Compulsory

The 1998 Act thus provided for a system of registration of political parties. In making this provision, ministers emphasised two points. The first is that registration was voluntary, though parties would have strong incentives to register. This was because only registered parties could protect their names from being used by others on the ballot paper;[45] only registered parties could put forward lists of candidates for the additional member elections to the Scottish Parliament and Welsh Assembly, as well as the regional lists for European Parliament elections; only a registered party could have its emblem printed alongside a candidate's name on a ballot paper; and only registered parties would be eligible (but not entitled) to be offered party political broadcasts.[46] The second point emphasised by ministers related to concerns about party autonomy, it being pointed out by Lord Williams in the House of Lords that

> the way a party is to be organised, how it selects candidates and what its aims and objects are to be, all remain for each party to determine individually in accordance with its own rules or constitution. Any organisation, large or small, will be able to register provided that it intends to contest an election.[47]

---

[43] HC Debs, 4 June 1998, col 515.
[44] See *Sanders v Chichester, The Independent*, 16 November 1994.
[45] 1998 Act, s 13; Sch 2, amending parliamentary election rules.
[46] 1998 Act, s 14.
[47] HL Debs, 8 October 1998, col 659.

The register was maintained initially by the Registrar of Companies, but has since been transferred to the Electoral Commission, following its creation by the PPERA.

The latter Act repealed the 1998 Act, and re-enacted its main provisions with a number of important modifications.[48] It is the replacement registration provisions of the PPERA that we are concerned with here. These provide that parties are to be registered in order to field candidates in an election.[49] In this way, it is said that the PPERA formally converts the voluntary scheme under the 1998 Act into a compulsory one.[50] Other candidates must appear on their nomination papers as independent or without any description other than their name.[51] The legislation requires the parties to register their leader, their nominating officer and their treasurer.[52] For the purposes of the legislation, the treasurer is the person responsible for ensuring that the party complies with the various reporting and disclosure obligations which the Act introduces,[53] and not the person who may hold the position for the purposes of the party's own internal auditing machinery, where the two positions are held by different people. The statutory position may not be held by anyone who has been convicted of an offence under the Act or an election offence in the previous five years.[54] A party may also register a campaigns' officer who is then responsible for ensuring that the party complies with the spending limits in Parts V–VII of the Act (these apply to general elections and to referendums).[55] Where there is no campaigns' officer, this is the responsibility of the party treasurer.

Registration – Protecting Party Identity

The PPERA requires an application for registration to comply with certain formalities, and the payment of a fee. The application must specify the name of the party, its headquarters, and its officers as explained; it must also supply a copy of its constitution (thereby implying that political parties must have a constitution), as well as details of different accounting units of the party.[56] In addition, the party must make a declaration that it intends to contest one or more relevant elections, which is the closest that we come in the legislation to defining a political party.[57] With these formalities completed, the Electoral Commission is bound to grant the application unless it takes exception to the name of the party

---

[48] See O Gay, 'What's in a Name? Political Parties, Lists and Candidates in the United Kingdom' [2001] PL 245.
[49] PPERA, s 22.
[50] O Gay, *supra* n 48, p 250.
[51] PPERA, s 22(1),(3).
[52] *Ibid*, s 24.
[53] See ch 5 below.
[54] PPERA, s 24(8).
[55] *Ibid*, s 29. See ch 7 below.
[56] *Ibid*, s 28(1); Sch 4, Part I.
[57] *Ibid*, s 28(2).

on one of a number of grounds.[58] It may be the same as a party already registered, or sufficiently similar to cause confusion among the electors; it may
comprise more than the six words allowed by law; it may be obscene or offensive;
it may include words the publication of which would be likely to amount to the
commission of an offence; it may include script other than Roman script; or it
may include words or expressions prohibited by ministerial order. Provision was
also made for the possibility that applications may be made by two parties with
the same or similar names (such as The Labour Party and The Real Labour Party).

In these latter cases, the Electoral Commission was directed to determine the
matter by reference to the history of the respective organisations, and to assess
which had the greatest claim to the name proposed.[59] Registration thus protects
the identity of the party, in the sense that no one else who wants to compete in an
election can use its name. It is like registering a trademark. But not only can no
other organisation use a party's name, no candidates can describe themselves as
candidates of the party, or a similarly named non-existing party (such as Literal
Democrats). Moreover, a party can protect by registration other aspects of its
identity, such as emblems (for example, the Labour Party's red rose and the
Conservative Party's oak tree) to be used by the party on ballot papers.[60] Again
the request for registration can be refused, but only on limited grounds. These
are where the proposed emblem is the same as the emblem of another party
or sufficiently close to cause confusion, where it is obscene or offensive, where it
is of such a character that its publication would be likely to amount to the
commission of an offence, or where it includes a word or expression prohibited
by ministerial order.[61] As in the case of a refusal to register a party name, the
Electoral Commission must give reasons for any refusal to register a party
emblem.[62] The accuracy of a party's entry on the register must be confirmed
every year by the treasurer, when he or she submits the party's accounts to the
Commission.[63]

State Supervision: Registration and Financial Accountability

An important additional requirement for registration introduced in 2000 related
to the financial affairs of the parties. It is now provided that a party may not be
registered unless it has adopted a financial scheme which (i) sets out the arrangements for regulating the financial affairs of the party, and (ii) has been approved
by the Electoral Commission.[64] This is a necessary part of the new legislation

---

[58] *Ibid*, s 28(4).
[59] *Ibid*, s 28(7).
[60] *Ibid*, s 29.
[61] *Ibid*, s 29(2).
[62] *Ibid*, ss 28(9), 29(5).
[63] *Ibid*, s 32.
[64] *Ibid*, s 26.

BOX 4.1
Registered Political Parties

In July 2006, there were 340 registered political parties. These included the three major parties (the Conservative Party, the Labour Party and the Liberal Democrats) as well as the Scottish National Party and Plaid Cymru. The register also includes a large number of small parties on the Left (the Communist Party of Britain, the Revolutionary Communist Party (Marxist-Leninist), and the Workers' Revolutionary Party; and several more) and the Right (the British National Party and the National Front). It also contains a number of local parties (such as the Doncaster First Party and the Durham Taxpayers' Alliance) and numerous residents' associations; single-issue parties (such as the Abolish Forth Bridge Tolls Party, the Countryside Alliance and the NHS First Party); and identity parties (such as the Muslim Party and the Christian People's Alliance). It also includes the colourful – the Chaos Party, the Church of the Militant Elvis Party, the Fancy Dress Party, the Official Monster Raving Loony Party and the Rock 'N' Roll Loony Party. The number of registered parties has more than doubled since 2001 (when there were 152 registered parties) and some of the parties previously registered are no longer entered there (such as the ProLife Alliance). Not all parties are registered, the Socialist Workers' Party being a notable omission. One hundred and fifteen registered parties contested the general election in 2005.

---

dealing with the reporting and disclosure of large donations to political parties.[65] If disclosure is to work, there is a need for the parties to have clear and effective financial procedures. The legislation anticipates the possibility of two different kinds of party organisation: those parties that consist of a single organisation with no division of responsibility for the financial affairs of the party; and those parties with a central organisation and one or more separate accounting units of constituent or affiliated organisations, each with some responsibility for its own financial affairs.[66] The three main political parties fall into the latter category, which is designed for organisations with a national office and a number of relatively autonomous constituency parties or associations. In these cases the financial scheme must identify the central organisation and the different accounting units, and give their names.[67] The scheme must also identify the responsibilities of key officers of the party, notably the treasurer and the

---

[65] See ch 5 below.
[66] PPERA, s 26(2).
[67] *Ibid*, s 26(3).

BOX 4. 2
Exemptions from Financial Scheme

An important – and mildly controversial – provision makes clear that not all parts of a political party are to be included in its scheme. The three exempt categories are trade unions; industrial or provident societies and friendly societies; or any other organisations specified in an order made by the Secretary of State on the recommendation of the Electoral Commission.[1] The purpose of this is to avoid the political parties being responsible for the financial affairs of autonomous organisations over which they have no control, and which – at least in the case of trade unions – are already subject to separate statutory regulation of a very detailed nature. This provision is a reflection of the special peculiarities of political parties that are not necessarily organisations of individual members, but organisations that include both individual and organisational members. The exclusion of trade unions nevertheless caused some irritation on the part of the Conservatives, and whether feigned or not it gave rise to discussion in the House of Lords where the opposition tried unsuccessfully to include trade unions in the financial scheme of the Labour Party. But trade unions are separate organisations, in many cases much bigger than the Labour Party, over which the Party has no financial control or responsibility. Trade unions are also subject to detailed statutory regulation of their own which exceeds that which applies to political parties.

[1] PPERA, s 26(8).

---

nominating officer, as well as the responsibilities of the treasurers of the accounting units.

Financial Accountability and the Publication of Party Accounts

Financial accountability goes beyond the obligation to adopt and register a financial scheme. There is also a statutory duty on the treasurer of a registered party to ensure that proper accounting records are kept in respect of the party.[68] The accounts must be kept in such order that it is possible to disclose at any time the financial position of the party; and they must contain entries showing from day to day all sums of money received and spent by the party, as well as a record of its

[68] *Ibid,* s 41.

assets and liabilities.[69] Financial records must be kept for at least six years. In addition to maintaining and retaining accounting records, the treasurer must, moreover, prepare an annual statement of accounts. These must comply as to form and content with regulations made by the Electoral Commission, and they must be approved by the management committee of the party.[70] These too must be retained for at least six years. Where the gross income or total expenditure of the party exceeds £250,000 in any financial year, the accounts must be audited, and the Commission has a discretion to require the accounts of any party falling below the £250,000 threshold to be audited.[71] In the latter case, auditing can be required on the ground only that the Commission deems it desirable, without any further requirement, though presumably the Commission would need to be able to explain why it was desirable in any particular case to require the auditing of the accounts of a party otherwise exempt.

In 2005, no fewer than 247 parties filed financial reports for the year ending 31 December 2004. These were published by the Electoral Commission in July 2005. Some of these accounts were very basic, especially in the case of the very small parties, sometimes handwritten and showing little by way of income or expenditure. But some were more substantial, as might be expected of the main parties. The income and expenditure accounts of the three main parties for 2004 and 2005 are reproduced in Appendix 2.

- The Labour Party accounts show that in 2004, the party had an income of £29.3m and that it spent £32.1m, with deficit for the year of £2.7m. In the previous year, the Labour Party had an income of £26.9m and expenditure of £24.2m. At the end of 2004, the Labour Party had a debt of £11m.
- The Conservative Party accounts show that in 2004, the party had an income of £20m and expenditure of £26.2m, with a deficit of £6.1m for the year. In the previous year, the Conservative Party had an income of £13.6m and expenditure of £16m, with a deficit for the year of £2.4m.
- The Liberal Democrat accounts show that in 2004, the party had an income of £5m and that it spent £4.6m, with a small surplus for the year of £445,703. In the previous year, the Liberal Democrats had an income of £4m and an expenditure a little less, with a surplus for the year of £91,131.

Party accounts for 2005 (a general election year) show a dramatic change: the Conservative Party raised £24m and spent £39m, Labour raised £35m and spent £49m, and the Liberal Democrats raised £8.5m and spent £8.7m. The combined deficit of the parties for the year was thus just under £30m.

---

[69] *Ibid,* s 41(2),(3).
[70] *Ibid,* s 42.
[71] *Ibid,* s 43.

BOX 4. 3
The Duty to Submit Annual Accounts

The accounts of the parties – and the accounting units where required – must be submitted within three months of the end of the financial year to which they relate, or six months in the case of those parties or accounting units whose accounts must be audited.[1] Once the accounts have been filed, the Electoral Commission is then required to make the statement of the accounts available for public inspection as soon as reasonably practicable.[2] It is a criminal offence to fail to deliver the accounts in the manner prescribed in the Commission's regulations, or to fail to deliver them within the time required by the Act.[3] Liability rests with the treasurer of the party at the time the offence was committed, though it is a defence for the person charged with the offence to prove that he or she took all reasonable steps and exercised all due diligence to comply with his or her obligations. These are significant obligations and penalties to impose on the lay officers of voluntary organisations, which did give rise to concern in Parliament that many organisations that act in a bona fide way do not necessarily have the accountancy skills of a major company, and that the government was coming close to being unable to see the wood for the trees. But although concerns of over-regulation are to be taken seriously particularly at a time when party membership is in decline, these obligations are minimum requirements for any body which is operating in the public domain, and they are no greater than the obligations imposed on the branch officials of trade unions. The view of the government was that at the local level, the Electoral Commission would use a light touch.

[1] PPERA, ss 43, 45.
[2] *Ibid*, s 46.
[3] *Ibid*, s 47.

Transparency of Accounting Units

The duty to maintain accounting records and the duty to prepare annual accounts apply also to the accounting units of the parties (the constituency and regional parties and associations), in those parties which have different accounting units.[72] The duty to maintain and retain financial records in the case of accounting units applies to the treasurer of the unit in question and not the national treasurer of the party, as does the duty to prepare an annual statement of

[72] *Ibid*, s 49; Sch 5.

accounts which in the case of an accounting unit must be approved by the management committee of the unit rather than the management committee of the party. Unlike in the case of the national parties, not all accounting units are required to submit their annual accounts to the Commission. This obligation arises only where the gross income or total expenditure of the unit in the year in question exceed £25,000,[73] though the Electoral Commission has a discretion to require the treasurer of any accounting unit of a political party to submit accounts if it so requires. Accounting units are obliged to have their accounts audited only if the gross income or total expenditure exceed £250,000, a threshold which means that the duty will apply to few local parties or associations, though again the Commission has a discretion to require the auditing of the accounts of accounting units which fall below the threshold.[74]

All three main parties have a large number of accounting units registered with the Electoral Commission. The Conservatives had 683 and the Liberal Democrats 516. However, the financial fortunes of these units vary enormously between and within parties, and not all raise or spend enough money to require them to submit annual financial returns.

- In the case of the Conservative Party in 2004, 271 accounting units (mainly Constituency Associations) submitted financial returns, showing that these accounting units raised about £17m, in addition to the £20m raised by the party nationally.
- In the case of the Liberal Democrats in 2004, 54 accounting units (mainly Constituency Associations) submitted financial returns, showing that these accounting units raised about £ 7.9m, in addition to the £5m raised by the party nationally.
- In the case of the Labour Party in 2004, 28 Labour Party accounting units (mainly Constituency Labour Parties) submitted financial returns, showing that these accounting units raised just under £2m, almost half of which was counted for units other than CLPs (such as the Scottish and Welsh Labour parties).

In 2005, 312 Conservative Party accounting units submitted financial returns, compared to 104 and 46 in the case of the Liberal Democrats and the Labour Party respectively. Since these data were compiled in mid 2006, returns have been submitted for both years by other accounting units of each of the three parties. The additional information does nothing to contradict the indication that the Conservative Party has a very significant locally based organisation.

---

[73] *Ibid*, Sch 5, para 6.
[74] *Ibid*, Sch 5, para 4.

BOX 4. 4
Funding Local Parties

Some Conservative Constituency Associations (CAs) are very wealthy and raise considerable sums of money. For example, in 2004 thirty CAs each raised more than £100,000. These included the Cities of London and Westminster (£360,000), Kensington and Chelsea (£285,435), Aylesbury (£265,153), South West Surrey (£200,029), Chichester (£177,655), Wealden (£170,025), Reigate (£169,119), Surrey Heath (£154,400), Folkestone (£153,430) and North Oxfordshire (£139,771). The Conservative Party has more associations with an annual turnover in excess of £100,000 than the Labour Party has Constituency Labour Parties (CLPs) submitting annual returns. The best performing CLPs were Ipswich and Norwich with £76,728 and £75,224 respectively.

Conclusion

As a matter of legal form, political parties remain primitive institutions: unincorporated associations performing overwhelmingly public functions. Nevertheless, political parties are being drawn into the legal spotlight as legal entities, mainly as a result of the PPERA, which provides that as legal entities they may commit offences which relate to their failure to report donations, their acceptance of prohibited donations, and their spending more than the law permits in an election. In many of these cases, the liability will attach to the registered treasurer of the party in question as well as to the party, though it is the former who will bear the principal responsibility. There are, nevertheless, cases where the party will be liable. In these cases, proceedings for an offence are to be brought against the party in its own name and not that of any of its members. Moreover, for the purpose of such proceedings, any rules of court relating to the service of documents shall have effect as if the association were a corporation. It is also provided that a fine imposed under the Act on an unincorporated association (which would include a political party) following its conviction of an offence is to be paid out of the funds of the association.[75] In this very pragmatic – yet very important – way parties may be said to have an identity and a legal personality distinct from their members.

The emergence of political parties as distinct legal entities parallels the evolution of distinct legal principles to govern political parties. The foregoing analysis suggests that the relationship between political parties and the State is governed by a number of discrete principles, sometimes contradictory and sometimes

---

[75] *Ibid*, s 153.

overlapping, but overwhelmingly coherent as a total package, even if not consciously designed as such. The key principles on which the relationship between political parties and the State is based may be said to include the following: (i) tolerance of diverse party structures; (ii) respect for the individual who should not be required to contribute to a party against his or her wishes; (iii) respect for the autonomy of political parties to develop their own policies, rules and procedures; (iv) recognition of the principle of legality, and a need for political parties to act within the law; (v) the absence of legal immunities or privileges for political parties; (vi) protection for the identity of the political parties, in terms of their names and emblems; (vii) tolerance, if not indulgence, in the sense that there are few formalities required to register as a party, which (unlike some countries) are not required to establish even a minimum number of members; and (viii) growing public accountability of the parties, particularly in relation to their financial affairs.

The main question now is to determine how far political parties can remain autonomous organisations, and how far the principle of accountability will develop and extend. The PPERA has given priority to public accountability for the financial affairs of the parties over the autonomy of parties and their members. These rules of public accountability will take priority over the wishes of the members, though the members may be involved in adapting the new legal regime to the circumstances of their own party. In other jurisdictions, however, public accountability does not end with financial management, but extends also to matters of internal government and organisation. These include the regulation of leadership elections in Canada, and candidate selection in Australia. Neither is as far-reaching as the position in Germany where – in a manner that embraces Kelsen – parties are recognized by the constitution, which requires their 'internal organisation' to conform to 'democratic principles', an obligation fleshed out in some detail by the *Law on Political Parties of 1967*.[76] The case for similar regulation in Britain may be irresistible, with the arguments in favour of developing the principle of public accountability to include internal democracy, as well as financial transparency, being considered more fully in chapter 10 below.

---

[76] See p 245 below.

5

Donations to Political Parties: The Regulatory Framework

Introduction

Donations to political parties are now regulated by the Political Parties, Elections and Referendums Act 2000 (PPERA). The Act addresses a number of concerns about political donations that had been raised in the 1990s, particularly the lack of transparency about political funding on the one hand, and the reliance of at least one of the parties on foreign donations on the other. One of the main aims of the PPERA was to shine a bright light of publicity into the financial affairs of political parties. To this end, the parties are subject to far-reaching and detailed reporting requirements which extend to every corner of mainstream party organisation. This is not to say that there are not exceptions and omissions, as we shall see. Nor is it to say that there are not already cracks appearing in the structure of the Act so carefully constructed, as we shall also see. This chapter is thus concerned not only to give an account of the main features of the regulatory framework introduced by the PPERA, but also to present some of the problems that have arisen in its wake. The main story of the new regime is one of extensive and detailed controls which have been found to be very porous, allowing ample opportunity for financial support for parties to be concealed in various perfectly lawful ways which are discussed in the pages below.

Disclosure and Corruption

As we saw in chapters 2 and 3, one of the main purposes of disclosure is the prevention of corruption, and this appears to be one of the main rationales for disclosure to be found in the Neill Committee report.[1] It is true that we are not so vulgar as to use the word corruption in modern parlance, perhaps because of the debilitating effect on public discussion of English libel law. We prefer to say that

---

[1] Fifth Report of the Committee on Standards in Public Life, *The Funding of Political Parties in the United Kingdom*, Cm 4057–I, 1998, paras 4.3–4.6.

it is designed to improve standards in public life, carefully overlooking the fact that these standards need to be improved only because they are corrupt or have been corrupted.[2] In this sense, dealing with corruption and raising standards in public life are synonyms. But what is meant by corruption and impropriety? As we also saw in chapter 2, there is a great deal of uncertainty in the literature about the former of these terms in particular, so that we are thus thrown back on a linguistic or dictionary definition. Here we find an emphasis on corruption as a word that implies a sense of debasement, and one that also implies a scale of conduct, with a thick or general meaning at one end of the scale, and a thin or narrow meaning at the other end. It is also one that applies in different contexts and involves many different potential actors.

Corruption

The adoption of a linguistic or dictionary definition is not without difficulty, as there are many different linguistic and dictionary definitions to choose from. But one that best captures the foregoing features of the term is the *Chambers' Dictionary* which defines 'corrupt' in the following manner: 'to make putrid, to taint, to debase, to spoil, to destroy the purity of, to pervert', as well as 'to bribe'. There is no suggestion in the report of the Neill Committee of any concern about bribery. But there is a clear concern with a thicker concept of corruption that includes donations that have the effect of enhancing the likelihood of a benefit being conferred on an individual, or provide the donor with an opportunity to influence a decision, or promote his or her personal interests. Issues which, in the words of the Neill Committee, might attract the suspicions of the 'cynical' were said to include access to ministers (or shadow ministers) and the purchase of influence over policy. The Committee also identified the possibility of donations being given because of a desire to be considered for an honour, or in order to enhance the donor's selection for some public position or appointment. In some countries, it was said, allegations were made of donations being made in return for defence procurement contracts and the like.[3] Much of the concern with corruption, however, appears to be with appearance more than reality, for the Committee thought that 'the suspicions which are entertained concerning large givers are *commonly* lacking in any justification'.[4]

The qualification was hardly a ringing endorsement that the concern was solely with appearance rather than reality. Nor was the claim that '*nearly all* give generously either because they support the general aims of the party which they

---

[2] By adopting the language of corruption, it is neither claimed nor implied directly or by innuendo that in the British system money by way of political donations is being given by anyone with the intention of receiving favours or that favours are returned for money by way of political donations received.

[3] Cm 4057–I, 1998, paras 4.3–4.4.

[4] *Ibid*, para 4.5. Emphasis added.

finance, or in order to minimise the risk of the opposing party attaining power'.[5] Nevertheless, in the view of the Committee, disclosure was necessary in order to 'allay the suspicion that each large giver is actuated by some improper motive and that the recipient political party has accepted some tacit obligation to one or more of such givers'.[6] However, in developing its proposals for regulatory reform, the Neill Committee appeared expressly to eschew a still thicker conception of corruption. This is one based on the corruption of principle rather than the corruption of institutions or personnel. Such a conception – which goes well beyond the narrow legal definition to include conduct which is perfectly lawful – would see large donations as being inherently corrupting, because of their impact on one of the first principles of democratic self-government. This is the principle of political equality (including the right to equality of influence) reflected in the modern franchise.[7] But although the Neill Committee appeared simultaneously relaxed and uneasy about large donations,[8] it also expressed the view that '[i]f a party becomes over-dependent on a particular source, that is its own affair, provided its dependence is a matter of public knowledge'.[9] This is despite the Committee's starting premise that 'it is undesirable that a political party should be dependent for its financial survival on funds from a few well-endowed individuals, corporations or organisations', citing the 'familiar maxim' that 'he who pays the piper calls the tune'.[10]

Voter Information

While corruption (as defined) is thus part of the reason for disclosure, corruption (as defined) does not provide a full explanation or rationale. The existence of other reasons is suggested in part by the fact that disclosure is applied equally to all political parties. This would be consistent with disclosure being required as a way of exposing the generally corrupting impact of large donations (that is to say where the concept of corruption in its thickest sense is used). But that is not the case in the United Kingdom where the principal corruption rational is the more instrumental corruption of government, where rewards are given for payments received. Yet if that is the reason for disclosure, it is not clear why we require disclosure from political parties that have no chance of ever forming the government, or indeed of ever having a candidate elected to public office. In these cases, it is difficult to see what the corruption argument is, unless it is an argument based on corruption of party. But this would be a very weak form of corruption in the case of parties with no hope of election (and where the party

---

[5] *Ibid.* Emphasis added.
[6] *Ibid*, para 4.6.
[7] See also O Kurer, 'Corruption: An Alternative Approach to its Definition and Assessment' (2005) 53 *Political Studies* 222.
[8] Cm 4057–I, 1998, para 6.7.
[9] *Ibid.*
[10] *Ibid*, para 4.3.

may simply be the *alter ego* of an obsessive individual). Indeed in these cases there is a strong claim that disclosure conflicts with other objectives of a regulatory strategy, in this case respect for human rights and specifically the right to privacy.[11] If there is no serious corruption rationale associated with donations to political parties that have no chance of forming government, the only public interest in requiring disclosure is that electors are entitled to know who is backing the parties that are fielding candidates in an election.

Further evidence that corruption is thus not the only objective of disclosure is provided in part by the timing at which disclosure is required. As we shall consider more fully below, the legislation requires disclosure of donations to take place every three months.[12] There is nothing exceptional about this: timely disclosure would be consistent with an anti-corruption rationale. But disclosure must also take place every week during an election campaign,[13] this being necessary on the ground that the information is urgently needed at an election time, because it 'may have a bearing on the response of other potential donors and it may impact upon voters' intentions'.[14] So here we have an explicit acknowledgement that the purpose of disclosure is the arming of electors and others with information that they may need to make a decision (for whom to vote and to whom to donate). But although important, this is an inadequately considered rationale, and it is one that may be incompletely implemented. Thus, the obligation to disclose donations on a weekly basis during an election campaign applies only to the political parties: there is no corresponding obligation on the candidates, the people against whose name the electors place their crosses. Although there is a duty on the part of candidates to disclose the identity of donors, this applies only in a post-election return,[15] by which time it is too late for the elector whose decision would be influenced by the company the candidates keep. It also denies the local press the opportunity to expose donors and to raise questions about their motives.

Who May Donate to Political Parties?

Before considering the mechanics and faults of the disclosure regime designed to implement this predominantly corruption rationale, it may be useful first to identify those who may lawfully make a donation to a political party. For this purpose, the PPERA introduces the concept of the permissible donor, though this

---

[11] It may also conflict with the need to ensure that parties are well funded if the only way a new or special interest party can get off the ground is to rely on the wealth of a generous benefactor. There are a number of parties which in the past (the Referendum Party) and more recently (the Pro-Life Alliance) are so dependent.

[12] PPERA, s 62.

[13] *Ibid*, s 63.

[14] Cm 4057–I, 1998, para 4.58.

[15] Representation of the People Act 1983, s 81.

is rather misleading for there are very few impermissible donors.[16] The mischief here, however, was foreign funding of British political parties, a matter which – as was discussed in chapter 1 – had proved to be controversial in the 1990s, with persistent allegations of large-scale foreign funding of the Conservative Party. It is difficult to know just how big a problem this was, for although some believed that as much as one-fifth of the Conservative Party income came from foreign sources, it was impossible to verify such claims because the Party refused to publish lists of donors. As was also discussed in chapter one, however, the Neill Committee reported that in the period between 1992 and 1997, the Conservatives accepted forty-seven foreign donations worth a total of £16.2m.[17] The Labour Party, in contrast, received no foreign donations, but the SNP is reported to have received two donations of between £40,000 and £50,000 from an individual who lived part of the time overseas. Plaid Cymru is said to have received less than £5,000 from foreign donors.[18]

Permissible Donors

By the time the Neill Committee reported, the problem of foreign donors was one that seemed to have largely disappeared, though the issue was revived in spectacular style in 2006 when it was revealed that the Conservatives had received unspecified loans from foreign sources. But in 1998, the Labour Party had for some time refused to accept foreign funding, while the Conservative Party had announced in the previous year that it would not accept foreign donations in the future.[19] It seems that only the nationalist parties were in favour, with the Scottish National Party (SNP) being particularly hostile to a ban, arguing forcefully in evidence to the Neill Committee that foreign funding of the SNP was the equivalent of the Scottish Labour Party receiving support from the national party in London:

> We are mindful of the fact that the Labour Party in Scotland in particular will (by their own admission) receive massive financial and other support from their London HQ to contest purely Scottish elections next year. It would be invidious if the SNP could not draw upon equally committed support from outside Scotland (often arising from the Scots Diaspora) and we see little difference in such support coming (at a time of globalisation), from London, Lisbon or Los Angeles.[20]

These arguments were dismissed by the Committee, which noted that there was a

---

[16] PPERA, s 54.

[17] Cm 4057–I, 1998, para 3.12. More recently, a former Conservative party treasurer has been reported as saying that it would be impossible to repeat today his achievement of raising £100m in donations between 1992 and 1997 'because you can't get foreign money, everyone has to declare their money': *Daily Telegraph*, 14 August 2006.

[18] Cm 4057–I, 1998, para 3.12.

[19] Conservative Party's Evidence to the Committee on Standards in Public Life, Cm 4057–I, 1998, pp 238–39.

[20] Cm 4057–I, 1998, para 5.15.

new climate of public opinion in relation to foreign donations, pointing out that it would be possible for the SNP also to raise money in England for use in Scottish elections.[21] The Committee endorsed the principle that those who live, work and carry on business in the United Kingdom should be the persons exclusively entitled to support financially the operation of the political process here.

To implement this latter principle, the Committee thought it easier to define what would be a permissible source rather than an impermissible source, and it is this approach which the draftsman has adopted. Nevertheless, the list of permissible donors is not without its difficulties, being very widely drafted. There are currently eight categories of permissible donor.[22] The first is individuals who are registered in an electoral register. This means two things: one is that a foreign national may donate; and the other is that it is not necessary to be resident in the United Kingdom to donate. So far as the former point is concerned, foreign nationals may be registered to vote in local government and European parliamentary elections, provided they are resident in this country.[23] The fact that they may not vote in general elections thus does not exclude them from donating. So far as the latter point is concerned, it is not necessary for a British citizen to be resident in this country in order to be on the electoral register. Following the Representation of the People Act 1985, a person who has not resided in the country for up to twenty years could still be registered to vote, though the twenty years was reduced to fifteen years by the PPERA.[24] This was a matter to which a considerable amount of time was devoted during the passage of the PPERA, with a number of Labour back-benchers taking the view that only British residents should be allowed to donate to a British political party.

Other Permissible Donors

The other permissible donors are organisations of one kind or another. So a political party may receive donations from a company, provided that the company is registered in the United Kingdom, incorporated in the United Kingdom or in another Member State of the European Community, and carries on business in the United Kingdom. This does not – of course – prevent what are in practice foreign-based companies from donating. A company that is registered, incorporated and trading in Britain may be a subsidiary of a foreign-based multinational, which may have its business headquarters in another country where strategic decisions are taken, and may be wholly owned by overseas investors.[25] So while it may be lawful for Ford Motor Company or McDonald's to make a

---

[21] *Ibid*, para 5.16.

[22] PPERA, s 54(2)(a)–(h).

[23] Representation of the People Act 1985, s 1.

[24] PPERA, s 141.

[25] According to one donor, a '100 per cent foreign-owned, but UK-incorporated, company that has only foreign directors, none of whom has ever been to Britain, let alone speaks English, yet because it is a holding company is therefore deemed to be doing business in the UK': *The Times*, 21 November 2005.

BOX 5.1
5th Avenue Partners

A major controversy arose following a series of donations totalling £2.4m to the Liberal Democrats in 2005 by a company called 5th Avenue Partners Ltd. This incident is discussed more fully in chapter 6. The director of the company, Michael Brown, was resident overseas and questions arose as to whether the company was a permissible donor.

The Electoral Commission took the view in October 2005 that it was reasonable for the party to regard the donation as having been permissible, a view based on the evidence available to the party at the time. However, the Commission indicated that this view was 'subject to any further information becoming available'. On 25 May 2006, the Electoral Commission posted a press notice that the matter may be revisited.

This followed 'an investigation by the City of London Police and separate legal proceedings concerning the financial affairs of 5th Avenue Partners Ltd and its director', as a result of which it 'is possible that further information will become available that may be relevant to the issue of whether these donations were permissible'. The Commission announced that it would await the outcome of these investigations before any further consideration of the matter.

---

donation to a British political party, not everyone would consider either Ford or McDonald's to be a British company. This was another controversial issue during the passing of the Bill. But in practice, few foreign-based multinationals now make political donations, and fewer still make donations of any significant size. For example, since 2001, US-based McDonald's have contributed £22,221 in three donations to the Liberal Democrats, while the Swiss-based drug company Novartis made one donation of £11,750 to the Labour Party in 2004. These donations were made by British based subsidiaries of global companies.

The remaining permissible donors give rise to less difficulty or concern. Donations may be made by one registered party to another. This may arise where two or more parties enjoy a close relationship, as in the case of the Labour Party and the Co-operative Party. Since 2001, the Co-operative Party has donated £1m to the Labour Party. Otherwise, donations may be made by a trade union entered in the list of trade unions kept by the Certification Officer for Trade Unions and Employers' Associations. The list covers all the trade unions that are known to fall within the statutory definition of a trade union, which is to be found in the Trade Union and Labour Relations (Consolidation) Act 1992.[26] But it does not include

---

[26] Trade unions may, however, only make donations if they comply with the separate obligations arising under the Trade Union and Labour Relations (Consolidation) Act 1992, discussed at pp 65–67 above and p 101 below.

the TUC, which although being a trade union is not on the Certification Officer's list. Apart from companies, political parties and trade unions, donations may also be made by building societies (within the meaning of the Building Societies Act 1986), partnerships such as law firms (registered under the Limited Liability Partnerships Act 2000), friendly societies (registered under the Industrial and Provident Societies Act 1965 or its Northern Irish equivalent), and other un-incorporated associations which carry on business or other activities wholly or mainly in the United Kingdom. Unlike in the case of companies, there is a requirement also in the case of unincorporated bodies that their main office should be in the United Kingdom.

The Mechanics of Reporting and Disclosure

Returning to the disclosure of donations from permissible donors, the corruption rationale for the obligation to disclose is evident not only in the arguments of the Neill Committee, but also in the substance of the law. Following the recommen-dations of Neill, the treasurer of a registered party must submit a quarterly donation report to the Electoral Commission, and this report must record all donations in excess of £5,000.[27] £5,000 is in fact rather high by comparative stan-dards,[28] and was deliberately chosen because donations of that size would trigger public interest concerns. According to the Committee, the relevant public interest is 'the need to know when a donation is made to a political party which is signifi-cant enough to prompt questions or to raise suspicion about its purpose'.[29] The report must be submitted within thirty days of the end of the end of the reporting period to which it relates.[30] Anything of £5,000 or less need not be reported, though if in the following quarter there is another donation of £5,000 or less, which together with donations in the previous period exceed £5,000, the combined amount must be disclosed.[31] Once the £5,000 limit has been reached for any one year – whether by way of a single donation or an aggregation of smaller donations – any subsequent donations of more than £1,000 must be recorded and reported. For this purpose there must be a reporting not only of any donation of more than £1,000, but also a reporting of a number of donations that in aggregate exceed £1,000.[32]

---

[27] PPERA, s 62.
[28] For Canada, see ch 9 below.
[29] Cm 4057–I, 1998, para 4.28.
[30] PPERA, s 65.
[31] *Ibid*, s 64(5)–(6).
[32] *Ibid*, s 62(6)–(7).

Donations at Local Level

The foregoing provisions apply to donations at national level. But it would not be appropriate – though it might be administratively convenient for the parties and the regulatory authority – to restrict reporting obligations to the national party organisation. As discussed in chapter nine below, this was a problem exposed by the Canadian system of reporting before the law was changed in 2004, where donations could be made to local party organisations and then transferred to the national party. These local donations would then be reported as an internal party transfer without the identity of the donor ever being revealed. This suggests the need for reporting local donations not only in order to prevent corruption at local level (for which purpose donations of much less than £5,000 would have to be reported),[33] but also as an anti-avoidance strategy to prevent the laundering of money through the outer reaches of party organisation. There are essentially two ways by which such reporting could take place. The first is by requiring each unit of party organisation (constituency party or association) to report donations to the Electoral Commission (as recommended by the Labour Party in its evidence to the Neill Committee). The second is by requiring each national party to be responsible for reporting to the Electoral Commission all donations to all units of party organisation (as is the case in Germany). The PPERA follows the German example, but it does so in very complex and impenetrable terms.

The treasurer of each party is thus responsible not only for reporting dona-tions to the central organisation of the party, but also to the accounting units of the party (in the case of those parties which have accounting units – which includes the three large parties). This is a formidable task in view of the number of accounting units in each of the major parties – the Conservatives have 683 and the Liberal Democrats 516. The task is made all the more formidable still by the content of the reporting obligation, with the Party treasurer to report quarterly any donation of more than £1,000 to any accounting unit, or any donations that in aggregate amount to more than £1,000 in any quarter, or in aggregate amount to more than £1,000 when added to other donations from the same source in previous quarters in the reporting year in question.[34] There is also the problem of the donation of £1,000 made locally and another of £5,000 nationally, by the same person. In neither case would the individual donation have to be reported, because in both cases it falls below the reporting threshold. Here the Act provides that any donation to a unit of party organisation which does not have to be reported (because it falls below the more than £1,000 limit) is to be treated as a donation to the central organisation of the party.[35] This means that it would have to be aggregated with donations made to the central party organisation, so that if in aggregate they exceed £5,000, they will have to be reported.

---

[33] A point made forcefully by the Neill Committee: see Cm 4057–I, 1998, para 4.35.

[34] PPERA, s 62(11).

[35] *Ibid*, s 62(12).

Table 5.1 Cash donations to Conservative leadership candidates 2006

Candidate	No. of cash donations	Total (£)
David Cameron	43	415,500
Kenneth Clarke	30	187,500
David Davis	28	301,000
Liam Fox	8	57,500
Sir Malcolm Rifkind	1	50,000

Source: Electoral Commission.

Table 5.2 Cash donations to Liberal Democrat leadership candidates 2006

Candidate	No. of cash donations	Total (£)
Sir Menzies Campbell	12	43,000
Simon Hughes	2	25,000
Chris Huhne	7	29,900

Source: Electoral Commission.

Donations to Individuals and Members' Associations

These are far-reaching requirements, which is not to say that they are perfect. But the Act goes further still in requiring reporting of donations not just in relation to units of party organisation, but also to (i) party members, (ii) what are described as members' associations and (iii) the holders of elective offices.[36] Some explanation may be needed as to why donations should be made to such people and bodies in the first place. So far as members are concerned, party members may seek selection as the party candidate for a parliamentary election; they may seek election to the party's executive or governing committee; or they may seek election as party leader in the event of a vacancy.[37] In all of these cases, and possibly others, the selection or election may be contested, and the different contenders may incur expense in seeking to persuade the party members that they should be preferred. A good example of this is the selection of party candidates for the London mayoral election in 2000 and 2004, and more recently the elections in 2006 of new leaders by the Conservative and Liberal Democrat parties respectively, on which see Tables 5.1 and 5.2. In the case of donations to individual members of parties such as these, the recipient must report donations

---

[36] *Ibid*, s 71 and Sch 7.

[37] These elections may be hotly contested and candidates may need to solicit donations for their campaign. £284,000 is said to have been spent by the five candidates for leader of the Conservative Party in 1997 (won by William Hague) to woo just 164 MPs: *The Guardian*, 21 November 1997.

Table 5.3 Donations to Conservative political organisations

Organisation	No. of donations	Total (£)
Conservative Christian Fellowship	4	43,000
Conservative Group for Europe	46	128,587
Conservatives for Change Ltd	14	189,000
Constituency Campaigning Services Board	16	1,219,043
Norris for London Campaign	33	493,400

Note: The nine cash and one non-cash donations to Constituency Campaigning Services Board were made by Midlands Industrial Council, while six non-cash donations were made by IM Properties (Coleshill) Ltd.
Source: Electoral Commission.

Table 5.4 Donations to Labour and Liberal Democrat political organisations

Organisation	No. of donations	Total (£)
Leeds Liberal Democratic Federation	1	3,000
Liberal Democrats Parliamentary Party	6	135,495
Socialist Environmental Research Association	2	10,155

Note: All four cash donations to the Liberal Democrats Parliamentary Party (£57,495) and both the donations to SERA were made by the trade union UNISON.
Source: Electoral Commission.

in excess of £1,000 within thirty days of acceptance of the donation. The application of the Act to the holders of elective office means that there is some overlap with other regulatory instruments, such as the House of Commons Register of Members' Interests,[38] and steps have been taken to remove the overlap by amending the PPERA.[39]

Members' associations are rather different. These are described in the Act as 'organisations' whose membership consists wholly or mainly of members of a registered party.[40] They do not include the party itself or any of its accounting units. But they might include organisations affiliated to or connected with a political party, such as the socialist societies affiliated to the Labour Party. These include the Fabian Society, the Socialist Education Association and the Socialist

---

[38] This requires MPs to register various forms of interests including (a) sponsorship prior to an election where to the member's knowledge the financial support exceeded 25 per cent of the election expenses in the election, and (b) any other financial or material support as an MP which involves any personal payment to the Member, or any material benefit or advantage. The latter is said to include any regular or continuing support from companies or organisations from which the Member receives any financial or material benefit in support of his or her role as an MP.

[39] Election Administration Act 2006, s 59.

[40] PPERA, Sch 7, para 1(6).

Environmental Research Association. In the case of the Conservative Party it would include bodies such as the Campaign for Conservative Democracy, and in the case of the Liberal Democrats it would include bodies such as the Peel Group. But it does not follow that all affiliated or connected bodies are to be regarded as members' associations, with an obvious exclusion being the trade unions affiliated to Labour; these do not consist wholly or mainly of members of the party. The definition would apply, however, to less formal groups working within a party, and presenting candidates for election in party ballots, provided that they could be said to be 'organisations'. Donations in excess of £5,000 to these bodies have to be reported in the same way that donations to members have to be reported, though as in the latter case there is no obligation to account for how the money is spent.[41] Remarkably few such organisations have reported donations, as revealed by Tables 5.3 and 5.4. This suggests that such bodies may not be as widespread as sometimes imagined and that those which do exist are not particularly well funded by large donors. There may also be uncertainty about the scope of the obligation. Does it apply, for example, to the growing number of think tanks which have various forms of association with political parties?

Who Does Donate to Political Parties?

Having considered who may donate to political parties and the obligation of parties to disclose donations, the next question for consideration is to determine who does donate. Information published by the Electoral Commission reveal that in the five-year period from 16 February 2001 to 30 June 2006, 13,685 donations were made to registered political parties. These donations amounted in total to £194,890,371. The great bulk of these donations (11,406) were provided as cash donations (£152,952,739 in total), with only a comparatively small number (1,755) being provided as donations in kind (£10,872,232 in total). The rest was accounted for by way of donations in the form of public funds (of which there were 302, accounting for £30,379,889), along with donations from impermissible donors (73 donations, accounting for £120,884), donations from unidentifiable donors (4 donations, accounting for £10,600), and donations from exempt trusts (145 donations, accounting for £554,025). Donations made by different categories of donor (individual, company, trade union, etc) are shown in Table 5.5, and the destination of the donations is shown in Table 5.6 and discussed more fully in chapter 6. As might be expected, the great bulk of the donations go to the three main national parties (Conservative, Labour and Liberal Democrat), with the nationalist parties trailing a long way behind.

---

[41] *Ibid*, paras 1(10)–(13).

Table 5.5 Donations to political parties by donor category

Donor	No. of donations	Total (£m)
Company	2,210	33.4
Friendly societies	366	3.6
Individuals	5,594	69.3
Partnerships	182	0.7
Political parties	418	1.1
Trade unions	3,640	52.6
Unincorporated associations	1,784	6.7
All	13,685	194.8

Note 1: All the donations by political parties were by the Co-operative Party to the Labour Party.
Note 2: Most donations by friendly societies were to the Co-operative Party.
Source: Electoral Commission.

Table 5.6 Total donations to political parties by party

Party	No. of donations	Total (£)
Conservative Party	4,056	83,107,911
Labour Party	5,987	82,048,261
Liberal Democrats	2,242	17,715,543
Plaid Cymru	85	559,676
SNP	188	1,999,774
Total	13,685	194,890,371

Individual Donors

The four largest sources of donation by some way are individuals, who account for 35 per cent of the total income, followed by trade unions which account for another 27 per cent, followed in turn by companies which account for 17 per cent, followed in turn by public funds which account for 15 per cent. Of these, the last is perhaps the most surprising, given the perception that there is no State funding in Britain. The £30m would be an even higher portion of the combined income of the parties who are its prime beneficiaries. The donations from the State accounted for here includes the money received by the Opposition parties at Westminster and Holyrood to help assist with their parliamentary

Table 5.7 Donations by individuals by size

Size of donation (£)	No. of donations	Value of donations (£)
0–25,000	5,157	20,267,071
25,000–50,000	166	7,145,078
50,000–75,000	29	1,678,993
75,000–100,000	49	4,758,547
100,000–250,000	40	7,369,836
250,000+	30	27,579,161

Note: There is a slight variation in the number and value of donations compared to Table 5.6. This is because Table 5.7 includes a number of donations excluded from Table 5.6 (such as donations from exempt trusts).
Source: Electoral Commission.

activities, and the money distributed to all the parliamentary parties for policy development under the PPERA.[42] But although the State is a significant source of donation income, it remains the case that individual donors are the largest category of donors in terms of numbers and amount. These donations break down as shown in Table 5.7. A striking feature of Table 5.7 is that the great bulk of the individual donors give £25,000 or less. But although representing 94 per cent of donations, these 5,157 donations account for only 29 per cent of the donation income received from individuals. This is because of the distorting effect of a few very large donations in excess of £100,000, of which there were forty, and the fewer still very large donations in excess of £250,000, of which there were thirty. Together these seventy donations accounted for more than half of the total donation income of the parties, despite accounting for only 1 per cent of donations.

In chapter 6, a fuller account is provided of the income of the parties. At this point, however, it is useful to identify where the individual donations go and which registered parties have most donations and most donation income. A striking feature of Table 5.6 above is that the Labour Party received many more donations than any other party. Nevertheless, the Conservative Party had the largest donation income, though a significant part of this (£22.3m) was accounted for by donations from public funds. Also striking is that despite the volume and value of donations, the Labour Party with 830 had many fewer individual donations than the Conservative Party and the Liberal Democrats, which had 2,486 and 1,497 respectively. Unsurprisingly, the value of individual donations to the Conservative Party at £36.7m greatly exceeded the value of individual donations to the Labour Party at £23.9m. However, although having many fewer individual donations than the Liberal Democrats, the Labour Party donation income from individuals greatly exceeded the £4,821,885 received by the former.

---

[42] These are considered more fully in ch 8 below.

The smaller parties did significantly less well, with 296 individual donations to the UK Independence Party (UKIP) yielding £1.5m, while only fifty and thirty-one individual donations respectively were made to the SNP and Plaid Cymru, yielding £511,313 and £220,428 respectively. The remaining 381 donations by individuals, accounting for £1.3m, were thus made to all the other parties.

Trade Unions and Companies

After individuals, the two other largest donors are trade unions and companies. So far as trade unions are concerned, we have seen that they are highly regulated in their political activity in sense that the union must have political objects which must be approved by the members every ten years in a secret ballot, political objects must be funded from a separate political fund financed by a separate political levy of the members, and each member has a right on giving notice to the union not to contribute to the fund. In 2005, some twenty-eight trade unions had political funds, but only some of these unions made donations to political parties. These are mainly the unions affiliated to the Labour Party and include Amicus, UNISON, the Transport and General Workers' Union, and the GMB (the so-called big four). The Fire Brigades Union and the RMT are no longer affiliated to the Labour Party though have given it money since 2001 before they disaffiliated, and at least one of these unions (RMT) has given money to the Scottish Socialist Party. The other unions with political funds generally do not give money to political parties and indeed may be forbidden by their rules from doing so. In these cases, the political fund is used for political campaigning on trade union-related issues. It is also the case that trade unions affiliated to the Labour Party do not donate all their political fund income to the party, but retain some for independent political campaigning as well. So although trade unions made donations of £52.6m over five years, total trade union political fund expenditure from 1999–2000 to 2004–2005 was £84.3m.

Companies, in contrast, are much less highly regulated than trade unions, though since amendments to the Companies Act 1985 introduced by the PPERA, they must now have shareholder approval for political donations and expenditures. The approval must be renewed at least every four years and the shareholder resolution must specify how much the company may spend annually for political purposes.[43] In the case of donations, however, shareholder consent is required only for contributions in excess of £5,000, though it would still be necessary to report to shareholders any donations below this sum that exceed £200. Few large public companies now make political donations, but some nevertheless seek shareholder approval, as in the case of the banking giant HBOS plc which has a policy of not making donations to political parties. The company is concerned,

[43] Companies Act 1985, s 347C.

Table 5.8 Company donations to political parties

Party	No. of donations	Total (£m)
Conservative Party	1,170	20.5
Labour Party	541	3.7
Liberal Democrats	299	5.8
UKIP	57	1.7
Others	143	1.7
Total	2,210	33.4

Source: Electoral Commission.

however, that the definition of political donations and expenditure in the PPERA 'could extend to routine activities undertaken by the company in the ordinary course of business'. For this reason, and in order to avoid 'inadvertent infringements' of the regulatory regime, HBOS sought permission to make donations to EU political organisations of up to £100,000 in total and incur EU political expenditure of up to £100,000 in total in the two years from 2005 to 2007.[44] There are in fact few household names among the donors to political parties, and those which are (such as Tesco, GNER and Scottish Power) give comparatively modest amounts.[45] The great bulk of the not insignificant corporate giving thus appears to come from the private companies, and most of it continues to go to the Conservative Party.

The Problem of Avoidance

Having thus identified the source of donations to political parties, how can we be sure that this is the whole picture? How can we be sure that there is no avoidance or evasion of the duty to disclose? If the principal aim of disclosure is the prevention of corruption, it is obviously essential that there are no loopholes through which donations may pass without having to be reported. Yet the risk of avoidance and evasion is a real one, as the experience of other countries makes clear. Both Australia and New Zealand introduced reporting and disclosure legislation before the United Kingdom. A problem in both countries is that most donations made to political parties are from front groups which hide the identity of the

[44] HBOS plc, *Annual Review 2005*, p 19.

[45] Since 2001, Tesco has given four donations totalling £42,269 to the Labour Party, and three donations totalling £13,642 to the Liberal Democrats, while Scottish Power has made ten donations totalling £41,000 to the Labour Party or Labour Party organisations (such as Scottish Labour and Labour Students. GNER has made seven donations totalling £24,639 to the Labour Party since 2004, and none to any other party.

donor. In Australia the groups in question include the Cormack Foundation and the Free Enterprise Foundation 'which funnel money straight to the [governing] Liberal Party'.[46] Although political donations over $10,000 must be disclosed annually in Australia, 'there is nothing preventing parties from setting up "associated entities" to protect the identities of political donors made uncomfortable by the public spotlight'.[47] A similar problem of 'faceless donations' exists in New Zealand where in the 1999 election year:

> Both of New Zealand's largest political parties received almost three – quarters of their declared funding from sources that it was impossible for the voting public to identify. These 'faceless' donations included both direct contributions from an 'anonymous' source, as well as indirect contributions that were made to the party via some conduit organisation (most notably the 'Free Enterprise Trust' which funnelled donations to the National Party).[48]

According to Andrew Geddis, such donations would not be so troubling if the candidates and political parties genuinely had no idea who was funding their campaigns. It was clear, however, that 'the donations received were not faceless in this sense', and that party fundraisers 'actively advise potential donors how to avoid being publicly identified as contributing to the party'.[49]

Concerns of the Parties

In their respective evidence to the Neill Committee in 1998, both the Conservative and Labour parties raised concerns about the possibility of the reporting obligations being avoided, as donors sought to protect their anonymity. For their part, the Conservatives highlighted a number of potential loopholes. These included:

- the making of payments disguised as trading items[50]

- donations to independent political institutes controlled by the parties

- donations to blind trusts to support the work of individual politicians

- the provision of facilities or payments in kind

- the spreading of donations across family members or companies controlled by an individual, and

- donations to constituency associations or other local bodies connected with national parties.[51]

---

[46] *The Australian*, 4 February 2003.

[47] *Ibid.* The Cormack Foundation 'poured' $4,059,196 into Liberal coffers.

[48] A Geddis, 'Regulating the Funding of Election Campaigns in New Zealand: A Critical Overview' (2004) 10 *Otago Law Review* 575, at p 590.

[49] *Ibid*, p 591.

[50] Examples include adverts placed in party magazines or party research papers bought at inflated prices.

[51] Conservative Party's Evidence to the Committee on Standards in Public Life, Cm 4057–I, 1998, p 239.

The Conservative Party was generally sceptical about whether it would be possible to address all the loopholes, without being 'overly complex and bureaucratic'.[52] A major concern, however, was with the support in kind which trade unions provided the Labour Party.[53] The Conservatives acknowledged that the question of trade union funding of parties was not a matter of its direct concern: not only did the Conservatives recognise 'the historic ties that bind the trade union movement with the Labour Party', it also did 'not believe that it is illegitimate for the trade union movement to provide support for political parties'.[54] Nevertheless, it was claimed that the trade unions provide 'substantially' more support for the Labour Party than appeared in the party's accounts: this was explained partly on the ground that donations in kind – in terms of staff, equipment, advertising and campaigning – 'are worth millions of pounds a year to the Labour Party'.[55]

The Labour Party also raised a number of concerns, though two principal concerns were to prove remarkably prescient. The first was the antipodean problem identified above, namely the use of intermediaries to protect the identity of donors. Thus, it was claimed that the Conservative Party were already engaging in a number of fund-raising activities of a dubious nature. Referring to a newspaper report,[56] it was said that

> company donations were solicited by membership organisations such as the Premier Club with an explanation that they would not have to be disclosed on the ground that the donor gives to the club not the party: 'the Premier Club donates to the party. It's a membership club. He's joining the club.'[57]

At the time these company donations were alleged to have been laundered in this way, companies were under a duty to report political donations in excess of £200 to their shareholders (as they still are).[58] The Labour Party thus invited the Committee to consider

- The extent to which funds are held by intermediaries for the purpose of benefitting the Conservative Party at least in part, who funds these accounts and how much they hold.
- The extent to which companies donate to these funds, in the knowledge that the money is then passed on to the Conservative Party, without disclosing the donation to shareholders.

The Labour Party was not proposing that this meant therefore that there should

---

[52] *Ibid.*
[53] *Ibid.*
[54] *Ibid*, p 238.
[55] *Ibid.*
[56] *The Observer*, 21 July 1996.
[57] Labour Party's Evidence to the Committee on Standards in Public Life, Cm 4057–I, 1998, p 235.
[58] This is a duty first introduced by the Companies Act 1967 which is now to be found in the Companies Act 1985.

be no transparency of party funding. Rather, it was suggested that active steps would have to be taken to anticipate ways by which a duty to report and disclose donations could be undermined by steps taken by donors to conceal their identity. The Labour Party therefore recommended that

> where money is donated to party by a club whose principal purpose is to raise money for a political party, the donation should be accompanied by a schedule of the donors to the club. These should be treated in the same way as donations directly to the party for the purposes of reporting and disclosure. Otherwise, donating money to an intermediary with a view to avoiding the obligation to disclose should be unlawful on the part of all those engaged in the transaction.[59]

Labour's other main concern was even more prescient in the light of subsequent developments. This related to donations in the form of loans which would be written off at a later date. The party therefore asked the Neill Committee to examine the nature of loans which had been made to the Conservative Party since 1979: by whom they were made, on what terms and when they were repaid.[60]

Legal Responses

Many of these concerns were addressed in one way or another by both the Neill Committee and the PPERA, though as we shall see not with unqualified success in all cases. The response begins with a wide statutory definition of a 'donation'.[61] This applies not only to cash donations, but also to aid in kind provided to the parties in lieu of cash.[62] In this latter case, the amount which is to be regarded as a donation is the commercial value of the services provided. This addresses the Conservative Party's concern about extensive trade union support in kind being provided to the Labour Party. In fact since 2001, trade unions have provided only 216 non-cash donations, these amounting to £428,562, in contrast to 268 non-cash donations to the Conservative Party from companies that in aggregate amount to £2.5m.[63] In the same period, the Labour Party received 192 non-cash donations from companies, amounting to £1.6m in total. The total number of non-cash donations to all parties from all sources was 1,755, and their total value was £10.8m. Apart from aid in kind, the Act also applies to commercial services (including loans) supplied to a party at a subsidised rate, as well as to services bought from a party at an inflated cost. In both cases, the subsidy is to be treated as the value of the donation.[64] It also covers the situation where any costs

---

[59] Cm 4057–I, 1998, p 220.
[60] *Ibid*, p 235.
[61] PPERA, s 50. See Box 5.2 below.
[62] *Ibid*, s 50(2)(f).
[63] For an argument that in-kind support by trade unions was greatly exaggerated, see S Ludlum and A Taylor, 'In Kind Donations to Labour by Affiliated Trade Unions: Revisiting the Neill Committee Evidence' (2002) 8 *Journal of Legislative Studies* 118.
[64] PPERA, s 53(4).

BOX 5.2
What is a Donation?

A donation is widely but not exhaustively defined. The key provision is section 50 of the PPERA, which defines a donation to mean:

- any gift to the party of money or other property, a gift defined to include a bequest

- any sponsorship provided in relation to the party

- any subscription or fee paid for affiliation to or membership of the party, a term which includes both individual and collective membership dues

- any money which is provided by way of a loan to the party, unless the loan is provided on commercial terms

- the provision otherwise than on commercial terms of any property, services or facilities for the use or benefit of the party (including the services of any person).[1]

Sponsorship is defined to mean the transfer of money to the party or to any person on behalf of the party with the aim of helping the party to meet defined expenses. These are defined in turn to mean conferences or other events organised by the party, the production of literature by the party, or any study or research organised by the party. But it is expressly provided that sponsorship does not include an admission charge to a conference or event or the purchase price of any publication. Nor does it include the cost of an advertisement in a publication, where the payment is made at the commercial rate for such an advertisement in such a publication.[2]

Although this is a wide definition there are a number of exceptions. Most of these are unexceptionable and apply typically to payments made to the parties from public funds (such as the policy development grants and the security costs at party conferences) or support provided by the broadcasters as party election and party political broadcasts. Otherwise a donation does not include anything which does not exceed £200, nor does it apply to the provision by any individual of his own services which he or she provides voluntarily in his or her own time and free of charge.[3] This last exception is an important provision which is to be found in the legislation of other countries and is designed to ensure that people are not discouraged from taking part in the activities of political parties.

---

[1] PPERA, s 50.
[2] *Ibid*, s 51.
[3] *Ibid*, s 52.

incurred by a political party are picked up by someone else, the act of generosity in this case being treated as a donation.

Other concerns related to blind trusts, and the the funnelling of money through local parties or through MPs and other individuals. The former are no longer permissible under the new regime, while the latter is addressed by requiring donations of £1,000 locally to be reported by the party nationally, even where there are autonomous local accounting units. So far as bundling money through intermediary individuals and organisations is concerned, this is addressed by section 50(8)(a) which provides that 'any reference to anything being given or transferred to a party or any person is a reference to its being given or transferred either directly or indirectly through a third person'. This would cover the situation where the individual gives money to family members or friends or employees to pass on to a party. In that case the donation would be made by the person using the third parties as his or her conduit. It would also cover the situation where the donation was given to an organisation to pass on to a party. Where, however, a members' association gives association funds to support a political party, there is no obligation to name the members of the association. Otherwise, the only major issue not to have been directly addressed by the Act relates to the donations to think tanks sometimes associated with political parties, though the point may be arguable in the case of those organisations (if any) which were to fall within the definition of a members' association under the PPERA. For this purpose, however, it would have to be shown at the very least that the membership of the association consists wholly or mainly of the members of a registered party.

Loopholes in the Regulatory Framework

Although serious attempts were thus made to anticipate and close loopholes in the regulatory regime, these have been only partially successful, and a number of well-publicised problems have emerged in the immediate aftermath of the legislation coming into force. These problems raise questions about the effectiveness of the Act to ensure full transparency by highlighting a number of ways whereby the flow of money can be concealed. Some of these problems were anticipated before the Act was drafted, and include what the *Sunday Times* has referred to as the range of 'controversial strategies that obscure the sources of funding'.[65] The most spectacularly public example of failure of the legislation relates to the use of loans to fund the parties. The identity of lenders does not have to be disclosed, provided that the loan was secured on commercial terms. In principle this ought not to give rise to any problem, with non-commercial lenders required to be identified. But there is uncertainty about what constitutes a commercial loan for

---

[65] 19 March 2006. See also *Sunday Times*, 20 November 2005.

BOX 5.3
A Regulated Loophole

A major loophole tailored into the Act applies to payments made for hiring a stand at a party conference.[1] The main party conferences are like trade fairs, and take place at large conference venues: in fact they are so large that there are now few places in the UK which can cater for the events. Outside the conference hall, the floor space in the lobbies and the corridors is be given over to companies, trade unions and charities which rent stalls to display their wares and draw attention to their activities and products in what is thought to be a very influential environment of political activists. The price of renting conference stalls varies from party to party (with the government party likely to be the market leader as the party that attracts the greatest attention), and from conference to conference (with national conferences likely to be more expensive than regional ones). This practice is now formally recognised by the PPERA, which also provides that the cost of hiring a stand does not constitute sponsorship for the purposes of the Act, and therefore does not constitute a donation. As such it does not have to be reported, reflecting the fact that most exhibitors do not regard themselves as making a political donation, but are using the conference as a platform to promote their goods and services to as wide an audience as possible.

The cost of renting stalls was already high when the Act was introduced, and would generally exceed the limit of £5,000 which has to be declared as a donation. In the case of the Labour Party (the market leader because it is the party of government), a stand in 2004 cost between £3,300 and £12,875. Indeed some parties may do season packages which enables an organisation to rent stalls at all the party's conferences over the course of a year. What is to stop the parties hiking up the cost of conference stands in order to channel donations through what would be a hidden route? The answer lies in the safeguard built into the Act which exempts the hiring of stands at a party conference only if 'the payment does not exceed such of the maximum rates which the [Electoral] Commission determine to be reasonable for the hire of stands at party conferences'. The Commission does not have a discretion to set reasonable rates: it is bound to do so. Any payment which exceeds the amount set would presumably fall to be regarded as a donation and would have to be reported in the likely event that it exceeds £5,000. The result is that although it will not be known exactly how much organisations are paying for conference stalls, it will be known which organisations have rented space (for it is a highly visible activity) and it will be known up to how much they have been prepared to pay.

these purposes, and there is concern that these loans could be converted into donations when it is expedient to do so. This is a matter which blew up spectacularly in 2006 and to which we return in chapter 6. Suffice it to say for present purposes that a loan thus allows both lender and recipient to maintain secrecy until it suits the interests of both that the matter should be placed in the public domain. This loophole has now been closed, with legislation in 2006 requiring transparency of loans as well as donations, though a number of other potential loopholes remain outstanding.

Intermediary Organisations

Apart from loans, the main issue that has arisen in relation to transparency concerns donations by what appear to be intermediary organisations, though this is by no means as great a problem as loans in lieu of donations. These intermediaries include unincorporated associations – 'effectively voluntary organisations that do not have to file public records in the same way as charities and companies, and therefore remain anonymous'.[66] The best-known organisation of this kind is the Midlands Industrial Council, 'registered to a terrace house in a Lincolnshire village'. The house is said to be owned by two individuals, one of whom apparently is a director of IM Trade Assist.'[67] The Council is said to be chaired by Mr Robert Edmiston, a multimillionaire 'active Christian and head of the IM Group, which imports and distributes cars'.[68] At the time of writing, it was not known who else was a member of the Council or where its money came from. Mr Edmiston – who was nominated for a peerage by the Conservative Party – is said to be a major Tory donor, and is recorded by the Electoral Commission as having made a donation of £250,000 to the Conservative Party in 2004. Although he is widely reported as a backer of the Council, it was not until late 2006 that other members were identified. By that time, the obscure Midlands Industrial Council had made fifty cash and two non-cash donations to the Conservative Party nationally and locally since 2001, these donations amounting to £955,789 and £12,900 respectively. Electoral Commission records show that since 2001, the same body had given another £1,118,140 in the form of ten donations to another obscure organisation called the Constituency Campaigning Services Board. The Conservative Party is reported as having said that: 'Donations by the Midlands Industrial Council have been registered in accordance with the Electoral Commission's rules',[69] and there is no suggestion of any impropriety in any of these arrangements.

The Midlands Industrial Council is by no means the only unincorporated

---

[66] *Sunday Times*, 20 November 2005.
[67] *Sunday Times*, 19 March 2006.
[68] *Sunday Times*, 20 November 2005.
[69] *Sunday Times*, 19 March 2006.

association that makes significant contributions to political parties. Although all three main parties receive donations from such bodies, the Conservatives receive significantly more than the other two. The Conservative Party had 297 cash donations amounting in aggregate to £3.3m from such bodies, while the Labour Party and the Liberal Democrats received 730 and 353 cash donations amounting to £1.3m and just under £1m respectively. The Conservative donors included the Carlton Club (seven donations, £356,600 in aggregate), Scottish Business Groups (one donation of £225,000), the United and Cecil Club (twenty-four donations, £146,865 in aggregate), the Leamington Fund (one donation of £93,000), the Primrose League (one donation of £69,700) and the London Scottish Tory Club (two donations, £58,478 in aggregate), as well as smaller sums from other groups such as the Magna Carta Club (£10,000) and the Portcullis Club (£15,200). Of these, the Leamington Fund has attracted most interest. According to the *Sunday Times*, this fund was established eighty years ago and is composed of local Conservatives who make donations to the fund for use by the party in the Midlands. It appears to have attracted controversy because it was managed by one of the country's senior freemasons, the individual in question being the grandmaster of the Warwickshire freemasons. There is no suggestion, however, that any Masonic lodges contributed to the fund or that Conservative party politics were discussed by lodges.[70]

Private Companies

The concern about unincorporated associations is that they allow money to be paid to political parties without knowing who is behind it. Similar problems can arise in the context of company donations, the issue having been highlighted by the *Sunday Telegraph*,[71] which drew attention to a number of companies. The first is Bearwood Property Services Ltd which was described on its website as a 'merger and acquisitions broker', providing 'a range of services to private and public companies'. By 2006, this company had donated over £1m to the Conservative Party nationally and locally, though its founder and managing director is reported as saying: 'We are not a company seeking publicity and we do not discuss our political donations.' According to research at Companies House by the *Sunday Telegraph*, Bearwood Corporate Services Ltd is 'owned by Bearwood Holdings which is itself 99 per cent owned by Astraporta UK, an investment firm entirely controlled by [Lord] Ashcroft', the multimillionaire Conservative. As we shall see, much of this money has been targeted at Constituency Associations, sometimes in marginal seats to support weak incumbents and sometimes to help candidates in winnable seats. According to the Parliamentary Commissioner for Standards, 'donations made by Bearwood . . . were part of a wider campaign of

---

[70] *Sunday Times*, 20 November 2005.
[71] *Sunday Telegraph*, 28 November 2004.

support by Lord Ashcroft for Conservative candidates in marginal constituen-cies'.[72]

In the words of the *Sunday Telegraph*, 'Bearwood is not the Conservatives' only mysterious corporate benefactor.' Reference was also made to Flowidea, 'a City-based investment company', which at the time of the *Telegraph* report had given £484,981 to the Conservatives since early 2001, a sum that had risen to £654,118 by early 2006. The *Telegraph* reported that Flowidea had 'no website, its telephone number is not registered with directory enquiries and when the *Telegraph* rang the office listed by Companies House as its registered address no-one had even heard of Flowidea'. 'In fact', the *Telegraph* report continues, Flowidea is a subsidiary of the investment bank Arbuthnot Securities, which is owned by Secure Trust Banking Group, a company listed on the London Stock Exchange. Another donor identified by the *Telegraph* was Meekland Limited, 'a holding company involved in areas as diverse as horse breeding, music and real estate', which has donated £175,000 to the Conservatives. Meekland was said not to 'pro-vide a UK trading address with Companies House but lists the address of its Surrey-based accountant'. Meekland '[was] actually owned by Brompton Invest-ments, which [was] registered in the Cayman Islands'. It must be presumed, however, to comply with the requirements of the PPERA and to be a permissible donor: for these purposes it is not necessary to provide a trading address. The concern is that as a private company – like some of the others – it is not obvious who is behind it.

Conclusion

Earlier in this chapter, it was suggested that the purpose of the disclosure regime is the prevention of corruption, taking a wider view of that term than simply the prevention of bribery. That being the case, any donation by any individual who receives some personal benefit of any kind is the proper subject of inquiry, and where such a coincidence of donation and benefit arises, there is legitimate need for an explanation. This focus on dealing with corruption by public account-ability means, however, that the disclosure regime has to carry an especially heavy burden. Any gap in the coverage – such as the undisclosed loans – is thus poten-tially fatal to the integrity of the scheme. This is because, paradoxically, the party-funding regime is actually very permissive despite its great technicality. There are few restrictions on who may donate to a political party, with the defini-tion of a permissible donor being extremely wide. In any event, the main parties had given up on foreign donations before the Act was passed, though this is not to say that the Act is without regulatory significance. The British National Party (BNP) courted controversy with funding from 'American Friends of the BNP'

---

[72] HC 420 (2005–06), Appendix 1, para 25.

which came to light in 2001,[73] the Liberal Democrats have encountered difficulties with a series of donations from 5th Avenue Partners Ltd, and the Conservatives are alleged to have taken foreign loans from unspecified sources.[74] The main source of restraint is thus not electoral law, but labour law and company law that indirectly impose restrictions on trade unions and corporations respectively, though trade unions and companies continue to provide 44 per cent of all the recorded donations to political parties.

The requirement that companies secure shareholder approval for donations has not prevented significant corporate funding of the parties, with 2,211 company political donations accounting for 16 per cent of all donations (13,686), and the £33.4m donated by companies accounting for 17 per cent of the value of all donations (£194.8m). It is also the case, as we shall see in the following chapter, that both the Conservatives and the Liberal Democrats have received corporate donations in excess of £1m from individual companies. This is not to deny that the requirement of shareholder consent can present difficulties. But the requirement of shareholder consent does not impose onerous obligations on companies, and the rules are certainly much less burdensome than the rules relating to trade union political funding. It is striking, nevertheless, that public limited companies account for only a small proportion of corporate political donations, and that the bulk is provided by private companies. It is likely, however, that the need for shareholder consent provides only a partial explanation for this development, at best. Many large companies (such as HBOS, Group 4 Securicor and BP) have decided as a matter of policy not to support political parties,[75] a form of political engagement that appears in some cases to be counterproductive.

Although not to be exaggerated, the role of private companies as donors has implications for the operation and effectiveness of the reporting and disclosure regime introduced by the PPERA. Total transparency is probably impossible, and indeed the 2000 Act does not purport to achieve this, with the reporting obligation beginning at over £5,000, a relatively high level by international standards. But even within the area where the law is designed to apply, total transparency is undermined by the use of a number of different strategies adopted by the parties, which have the effect of concealing the full identity of supporters, even if this is

---

[73] See *Evening Standard*, 31 August 2001; also *Searchlight*, November 2001. The donations were received before the Act came into force.

[74] See below, p 136.

[75] On BP, see J Browne, 'Why We Will No Longer Fund Political Parties', *The Independent*, 1 March 2002. Lord Browne was speaking in a Chatham House lecture as chief executive of BP, announcing that the company would no longer be making political donations anywhere in the world. The company would engage in policy debates, state its views and encourage the development of ideas, but would not fund any party or party activity. The lecture (parts of which were reproduced in *The Independent*) attracted world-wide attention: *New York Times*, 28 February 2002; *Toronto Star*, 18 March 2002. The impact of the decision was said to be most keenly felt in the United States where the company is said to have donated somewhere in the region of $1m to each of the Democrats and Republicans in 2000. The company denied that its decision had been influenced by the Enron affair: *The Guardian*, 1 March 2002.

not the intention. A number of problems identified before the PPERA was drafted have been shown to be fully substantiated since the Act was passed, these relating notably to loans and the role of intermediaries in the form of voluntary associations. The problem of loans – considered more fully in chapter 6 – has been addressed by more transparency, with the Electoral Administration Act 2006 requiring loans to be disclosed in the same way as donations. The difficulty with intermediary bodies, however, is that not all voluntary associations which fund political parties are the same, with many being engaged in other activities in relation to which political donations are purely incidental. If, however, there are associations which exist principally to raise money, and if the so far untested PPERA, section 50(8)(a) is not up to the task,[76] then the need for another legislative plug to block yet another legal loophole will be irresistible.

---

[76] As pointed out at p 107 above, the PPERA, s 50(8)(a) provides that 'any reference to anything being given or transferred to a party or any person is a reference to its being given or transferred either directly or indirectly through any third person'. But an unincorporated association is not a person. It may be enough to substitute 'third party' for 'third person'.

6

From 'Sleaze' to 'High-Value Donors' to Loans

Introduction

In the UK, we now have in place a detailed regime for the reporting and disclosure of political donations. But rather than restore public confidence in the political system after the indiscipline of the Major years, the new legislation has reaped a bitter harvest. If anything, the tawdry spectacle of political parties seeking business money to fund their expensive campaigns has revealed a situation that is just as bad. First, it has led to fresh allegations of 'sleaze', with the Labour Party on the end of yet more claims of cash for favours, and the like. Secondly, it has exposed political parties as being heavily dependent on a few million-pound donors, a dependence which is deeply ironic given that it was a £1m donation from Mr Bernie Ecclestone that was the immediate cause of the Neill Committee investigation in 1998 and the legislation that followed in its wake.[1] And thirdly, it has led to the continued funding of some of the parties by very rich people, without the identity of these people having to be revealed at the time the contributions were made. The principal way by which this last strategy was pursued was by way of loans, the legislation being drafted in such a way that in some circumstances loans do not fall within the definition of a donation. The aim of this chapter is to consider these different but closely related developments, and to conclude by beginning the process of contemplating the nature of the response that now needs to be made.

'Sleaze': The Continuing Problem of Political Donations

The ink was barely dry on the Political Parties, Elections and Referendums Act 2000 (PPERA) when a series of funding controversies erupted in quick succession. Two problems emerged around the time the Act was implemented, with

---

[1] See pp 13–16 above.

fresh allegations of 'sleaze' descending on British politics, providing an opportunity for the media to attack the government and the Labour Party, which was soon to learn about the downside of disclosure. The first problem is that some extremely large donations were made to the parties just before the commencement date on 16 February 2001. These include donations to Labour of £2m from each of Christopher Ondaatje (a retired financier who had previously funded the Conservatives), Lord Hamlyn (a publisher) and Lord Sainsbury (a government minister).[2] There was no obligation to disclose these donations as the Act was not retrospective, but the reluctance of Labour to identify the donors added to the unease about the donations, which were said to make the party 'unhealthily dependent on a few large gifts from a few rich men'.[3] The Conservative Party also reported a £5m donation from the spread-betting tycoon, Stuart Wheeler, making him the biggest one-off donor in British political history.[4] The other problem is a rather different one, which erupted in a frenzy of press excitement and indignation in the spring of 2002. This relates to allegations that a number of donors to the Labour Party (not those referred to above) appeared to benefit from government intervention or decisions in their favour, though it should be stressed that there is no evidence to link the intervention or decisions to the donations. In this latter case the donations were not huge, being in the region of £50,000–125,000. Three donations were particularly controversial, though there was no evidence of any impropriety in any of the three cases, by either donor or recipient, and no reason to believe that the support was given in return for any personal benefit. Each case appeared to reveal a series of badly timed coincidences.

Richard Desmond and Lakshmi Mittal

The first was the donation of £100,000 by Richard Desmond at the beginning of 2001, again before the legislation came into force, thus escaping the new disclosure rules by 'a hair's breadth'.[5] Apart from the timing of this donation, there were two reasons why it was controversial. The first was its source. Mr Desmond was reported in the press as a man who made his money trading in pornography.[6] This was thought by many to make him an improper source of funding for the Labour Party.[7] Senior Labour figures claimed in response, however, that there was no reason why the Party should not accept donations from the owner

---

[2] *The Guardian,* 5 January 2001. This was said to be a 'troublesome' donation, on the ground that 'it could be read as a form of insurance against dismissal': *The Guardian,* 3 January 2001. But the point is unconvincing.

[3] *The Guardian,* 3 January 2001.

[4] *The Times,* 18 January 2001.

[5] *Evening Standard,* 13 May 2002, accusing Labour of 'losing the moral high ground'.

[6] 'Porn magnate Desmond gives £100,000 to New Labour' (*The Independent,* 12 May 2002); 'Labour defends porn baron's donation' (*The Guardian,* 13 May 2002); 'How Blair's tea-time friend ran his porn empire' (*The Guardian,* 30 May 2002).

[7] See *The Times,* 13 May 2002; *The Guardian,* 13 May 2002.

of a leading national newspaper group. Indeed, the whole affair was condemned by the government as 'another over-ventilated piece of Sunday journalism'.[8] This response would apply equally to the other issue raised in the press about the donation, namely the circumstances in which it was made, only a few months after Mr Desmond purchased the *Daily Express* and its stablemate the *Daily Star*, and only a few months after Mr Desmond had taken tea with the Prime Minister in Downing Street. A particular focus of press attention, however, was the decision of the Secretary of State for Trade and Industry not to refer Mr Desmond's £125 million purchase of the *Express* to the Competition Commission. This decision was announced on 7 February 2001, with the press also reporting that the Labour Party secured Mr Desmond's donation shortly thereafter. It was made very clear, however, that in deciding not to refer the purchase to the Competition Commission, Mr Byers was acting in accordance with the policy announced on 26 October 2000 that he would accept the advice of the Office of Fair Trading (OFT) on takeovers 'save in exceptional circumstances'. In this case, the minister followed the advice of the Director-General of the OFT. This vigorous response was reinforced by equally vigorous denials of impropriety on all sides, and by Downing Street insisting that Mr Desmond had not discussed the donation with Mr Blair. Labour Party officials also denied any intention to defeat the reporting requirements of the new legislation coming into force on 16 February 2001.[9]

Similarly vigorous denials of impropriety were made in relation to the second controversial donation, the £125,000 donated by Lakshmi Mittal in June 2001, at a time when he was said to have been negotiating to buy a Romanian steel company. Press excitement was caused by claims that on 23 July 2001 the Prime Minister wrote to the Romanian Prime Minister in the following terms:

> I am delighted by the news that you are to sign the contract for the privatisation of your biggest steel plant Sidex, with the LNM Group. This represents an important step forward in the efforts you and your government are making to restructure and modernise your country's economy. I am particularly pleased that it is a British company that is your partner. This should send a very positive signal to investors and businessmen in Britain and more widely. Together with the other measures you are taking, I hope it will stimulate renewed interest by British business in Romania. And it will, I hope, set Romania even more firmly on the road to membership of the European Union, an objective of which the British government remains a staunch supporter.[10]

Not everyone was troubled by this letter, though claims were made that Mr Mittal's name had been deleted from an earlier draft, as had a reference to him as a friend of the Prime Minister. *Guardian* columnist Hugo Young took the view that 'the alleged service performed, writing a letter after a deal was done, was nugatory',[11] while others claimed that it was the attempt to cover up an

---

[8] *The Guardian*, 14 May 2002.
[9] *The Guardian*, 29 May 2002, *The Independent*, 13 May 2002, and *The Observer*, 19 May 2002.
[10] *The Guardian*, 14 February 2002.
[11] *The Guardian*, 12 February 2002.

embarrassment that caused more difficulty than the Prime Minister's actions themselves.[12] *Guardian* reporters, however, were not so sanguine, pointing out that 'the letter was sent at a crucial moment when the French had intervened, and Mittal had been forced to return to London empty-handed after a postponement of the deal on July 20'.[13] Apart from the timing of the letter, questions were raised about its content. Thus, although Mr Mittal was resident in the United Kingdom, his company was registered in the Netherlands,[14] and it was claimed in the press that the deal would 'bring no jobs and no profits into Britain',[15] although there was a small administrative staff in this country. So far as the Romanian plant is concerned, it was said to have been sold to an offshore-registered Dutch Antilles firm, LNM Holdings NV, a company said to have been privately owned by Mr Mittal. All this was said to call into question claims that Mr Blair was intervening on behalf of 'British business'. In addition to the foregoing, a crucial issue for the press was whether Mr Blair knew that Mr Mittal was a Labour Party supporter. When challenged about this in the House of Commons, the Prime Minister acknowledged that it was a matter of public record that Mr Mittal was a donor. But he also pointed out that the letter which he signed had mentioned not Mr Mittal but LNM, of which the Prime Minister said he had 'no knowledge'.[16] The Prime Minister continued by asserting boldly that had he known that 'Mr Mittal was a supporter of the Labour party, it would have made no difference whatever to the signing of the letter. That was entirely justified.' According to the Prime Minister the whole affair was 'not Watergate, it is Garbagegate'.[17]

Paul Drayson

The third controversy surrounded donations by Dr Paul Drayson (now Lord Drayson), the owner of a company called Powderject Pharmaceuticals. The reason why these donations (two of £50,000 each) gave rise to concern was that the company was awarded a £32m government contract to supply smallpox vaccine 'to protect Britain against a bio-terrorist attack'.[18] The second of these donations was said to have been given 'while the government was deciding who should be awarded the contract'.[19] Concerns were raised when it was suggested that the normal procurement procedures had been waived in the interests of national security. According to press reports, the government claimed that it was not in the public interest to draw attention to the preparations for terrorist

[12] *The Independent*, 14 February 2002.
[13] *The Guardian*, 14 February 2002.
[14] *The Independent*, 13 May 2002.
[15] *The Guardian*, 14 February 2002.
[16] HC Debs, 13 February 2002, col 198.
[17] *Ibid.*
[18] *Sunday Times*, 14 April 2002.
[19] *The Guardian*, 29 June 2004.

attacks by the use of biological weapons. Also according to press reports, the government claimed that Powderject was 'the only company that could quickly produce the millions of doses needed to protect the UK population', though it was further reported that 'other manufacturers say they could have met the requirements if they had been given the details'. For its part, however, the Government also claimed that Powderject was the only company that could supply the strain of the vaccine that had been recommended by the security and intelligence services.[20] An investigation by *The Guardian* tends to suggest that there was no impropriety in awarding the contract to Powderject. According to *The Guardian*, John Hutton the health minister 'appears to have been subsequently embarrassed' by the discovery that Drayson 'had been making party donations'.[21] But his request that the matter be reconsidered was overruled at the insistence of the Ministry of Defence, which wanted the strain that only Drayson could provide.[22] Any lingering doubts about impropriety were scotched by a National Audit Office investigation.[23]

Although the Drayson donations proved to be the last of the three most prominent cases, allegations and innuendos were made in the press about other donations. Apart from money from Enron, these included claims about donations from individuals and companies linked to the gambling industry, standing to gain from the government's policy of liberalisation.[24] This was followed by a claim that the Prime Minister used a trip to the Czech Republic 'to promote the sale of jet fighters made by a company [BAE systems] that donated money to Labour', in an affair that was said to have 'uncanny echoes' of Mittal.[25] The currency of claims that donations brought Prime Ministerial influence was, however, beginning to devalue with overuse. Thus:

> Tony Blair used his personal authority to save a £1bn deal to sell Hawk fighter-bombers to the Indian government. The company involved in the deal is British Aerospace Systems which is listed among companies who gave more than £5,000 in sponsorship in both 1998 and 2000.[26]

Nevertheless, other allegations about 'cash for favours' were also made. These included a claim that a law firm that had donated £6,100 was paid more than £8m by the government to look after miners' compensation claims.[27] But having made the claim under a 'cash for favours' headline, the newspaper also reported that there was 'no suggestion the donation was made in expectation of

---

[20] *The Guardian*, 13 April 2002.

[21] *The Guardian*, 29 June 2004.

[22] Other attempts have been made to link Drayson's donations to government benefits. But they too seem very thin and unconvincing: *The Observer*, 28 April 2002.

[23] Comptroller and Auditor General, *Procurement of Vaccines by the Department of Health* (HC 625, 2002–3).

[24] *Sunday Times*, 31 March 2002; *The Times*, 8 August 2002.

[25] *The Independent*, 15 April 2002.

[26] *The Independent*, 2 June 2002.

[27] *The Daily Telegraph*, 25 May 2002.

Government favours'. Several months later a new 'contracts for donors row' erupted following claims by a haulage company that 'it had lost government work during the foot and mouth crisis to a rival that had made a donation to the Labour Party'.[28] Here it was claimed that normal public procurement procedures were not applied, though in this case the £5,000 donation was made after the haulage contract had been awarded. But this was not the end of it. A millionaire Indian food entrepreneur had to insist that there was no connection between his £100,000 donation to Labour and his knighthood in the Golden Jubilee Birthday Honours' List.[29]

The Labour Party's Response

The introduction of the PPERA ought to have been a genuine cause for celebration. Instead, the Labour Party was mired in controversy because of donations and the circumstances surrounding them. Yet although these donations were controversial, transparency was working as it should, exposing the coincidence between donations by a number of individuals or companies on the one hand, and alleged benefits or support of various kinds on the other. As already suggested,[30] these coincidences need to be explained and assurances given that there was nothing untoward in the conduct of either donors or politicians. That was done in all of the cases discussed above. The lesson of these episodes, however, is that reporting and disclosure also require the parties to adapt to the new legal regime unless they are prepared to be mocked and embarrassed by what is revealed. The Labour Party was particularly stung by the donation from Mr Richard Desmond. Apart from the concerns raised about the coincidence between the donation and Mr Desmond's acquisition of the *Daily Express*, as we have seen concerns were also expressed about the Labour Party's judgement in accepting money from people with business interests such as those of Mr Desmond. Those concerned about the latter could hardly have been impressed by the response of the then Chairman of the Labour Party (Dr John Reid) who is reported as having said that the party would not sit in moral judgement of those who want to make gifts.[31] The concerns expressed in the spring of 2002 led to a number of calls for a fresh round of controls on the funding of the parties, as well as the introduction of State funding. These are matters to which we return.

---

[28] *Sunday Times*, 4 August 2002.
[29] *Independent on Sunday*, 16 June 2002.
[30] See p 111 above.
[31] *The Guardian*, 13 May 2002; *Tribune*, 17 May 2002. One Member of Parliament – described as 'one of Labour's leading feminist MPs' – is also reported as rejecting criticism: 'If society thinks making money from pornography is legitimate, I think it is legitimate for a political party to take money from pornographers, so long as there is no evidence of influence over policy.'

Adapting to the New Regime

The Labour Party was sufficiently chastened by the increasingly adverse publicity surrounding its donations that it moved to introduce a number of safeguards to avoid any repetition of such controversies. Transparency may thus help to alter behaviour, though it is unfortunate that the Labour Party was not better prepared. Nevertheless, the party in the recent past has a good record on self-regulation: before there was any obligation to do so, it published the names of donors of more than £5,000 and refused foreign donations. That legacy finds more contemporary expression with the announcement in May 2002 of changes in the way that the Labour Party would deal with donations and donors.[32] One of the key features of the new arrangements is the adoption of a *Statement for Donors*, whereby it was declared that 'donors to the Labour Party provide support because they are broadly committed to the Aims and Values of the Labour Party', and accept that they provide this support 'without seeking personal or commercial advancement or advantage for themselves or others'. Quite what rich donors make of this is unknown, given that the *Statement* reproduces clause IV of the party constitution which makes clear that the Labour Party 'is a democratic socialist party'. The *Statement* also makes clear that 'by supporting the Labour Party with donations, it is understood that this should not of itself disadvantage anyone, whether personally or in terms of business activities'. In addition to this new *Statement*, another important initiative was the setting up of a fund-raising committee to 'have oversight in the area of major donors'. This was referred to in the press as an ethics committee, and was expressly stated by Labour to be designed to build on the legislation.

Yet despite winning plaudits from the right-wing press for its ethical initiative,[33] eyebrows were raised about the composition of the committee, with difficulty caused in particular by the fact that it included the Labour Party's chief fund-raiser. In some ways, however, any such reservations were unfortunate, given that the initiative was accompanied by a willingness on the part of Lord Levy to speak to the press and to explain his role and his *modus operandi*. In this sense, there was also a greater measure of public accountability, as Lord Levy sought to provide reassurance that there was no question of cash for access. One interview is reported in the following terms:

> But whereas he might take a potential charity donor to a project, he will introduce prospective Labour backers to senior ministers, and even the prime minister, usually at private gatherings at his north London home. 'It's showing the goods. If someone is a serious donor you want to say: 'Well, hear from the leadership directly, I can share with you what I feel their vision is, but you know, you need to hear it from the leader in order to make that commitment.' It's done on a fairly personal basis. Come over for dinner, I'm having a few people.'

---

[32] See C Clarke, 'Committed to a Funding Re-think', *Tribune*, 31 May 2002.
[33] *Daily Telegraph*, 22 May 2002: 'a step in the right direction'.

Gatherings like these should not be confused with the kind of access that uncharitable journalists mean when they write about cash for access. 'If someone basically has an agenda in any way commercial or anything like that it's a no-no, absolute no-no. If you are talking about meeting on a social occasion, with ministers or even a dinner with the prime minister that is a social occasion, where one is talking about political vision for the leader, political vision for the party – I wouldn't really call that access.'[34]

Nevertheless, it would not be difficult to persuade a hardened public that the person who raises the money should not also be involved in judgements on whether to receive it. For his part, Lord Levy is reported at a press conference announcing these initiatives as being amazed that 'people cannot understand that you can put various areas of your life into different boxes and deal with them accordingly'.[35] The more sceptical, however, saw Lord Levy's presence as raising doubts about whether the committee would make tough decisions,[36] though what evidence there is of the work of the committee suggests that it was robustly independent and that Lord Levy's work was closely examined.[37]

The Response of Donors

It is not only the parties that were adapting to the new regime. There are suggestions that donors went cold, as the press became interested in who they were and questioned their motives for making donations. The press interest can be sustained and intrusive, and indeed one of the issues raised in the Labour Party's self-regulatory initiative was to condemn much of this coverage, and to assert 'the democratic right of individuals and organisations to make political donations', said to be 'vital to the existence and quality of our democracy', while accepting that 'donors should not be treated differently, positively or negatively, because they are donors'. But it may have been too late. According to Lord Levy, 'the big donors are running scared, and it is becoming increasingly difficult to raise money'.[38] Big donors have become quasi-public figures whose conduct is newsworthy on matters quite unrelated to their donation, as in the report that 'Labour donor cuts workers' pensions'. The story was reported in April 2002; the donation referred to in the article was made in 1997.[39] All of which is to suggest that transparency was beginning to operate to restrict the number and size of donations to political parties, though it is not to be overlooked that in the second quarter of 2006 the Conservatives received 183 donations with an overall value of £5.8m, including two donations of £1m or more. Nor is it to be overlooked that potential donors found other ways to be generous, with the reluctance to be publicly

[34] *The Guardian*, G2, 2 December 2004.
[35] *The Times*, 22 May 2002.
[36] *The Guardian*, 23 May 2002.
[37] *Sunday Times*, 19 March 2006.
[38] *Daily Telegraph*, 25 May 2002.
[39] *The Guardian*, 22 April 2002.

identified being a factor leading some supporters of the party to offer loans rather than donations.[40]

Although some may lament the shyness of the donors, it is not necessarily to be deprecated. Indeed, it might be argued that the Labour Party procedures did not go far enough in this regard. Thus, it is possible to argue that alongside the category of 'permissible donors' in the PPERA, it may be appropriate – especially for a party of government – to develop a category of 'impermissible donors', that is to say classes or categories of people or companies from whom it may not always be desirable to accept donations. Such an idea in embryo is to be found in the Honours (Prevention of Abuses) Act 1925, which prohibits the acceptance of donations from those seeking to purchase a knighthood or a peerage.[41] The other side of this coin is the question whether a donor should be disqualified from receiving certain public benefits, again in order to avoid the appearance of a conflict of interest. This is a question that requires attention to be given to the propriety of political honours, government contracts or other benefits being awarded to donors. Although it may be difficult – and perhaps inappropriate – to have a firm rule prohibiting eligibility for such benefits in all circumstances, this is a matter which may require more detailed consideration in a regulatory environment where significant personal donations continue to be permitted. It is perhaps only by more precise rules of this kind – whether of a voluntary or statutory nature – that any appearance of a conflict of interest will be eliminated. Moreover, it is perhaps only by more precise rules of this kind that the cloud of suspicion (however unjustified it may be) will be finally removed from the philanthropy of those who financially support the democratic process, and political parties in particular.

'High-Value Donors': The Labour Party

One reason why the flight of the donors is a problem for the parties is that they rely on them very heavily, and indeed rely very heavily on so-called high-value donors who now play a more prominent part in the funding of all the parties. It would be wrong to say that these are the main source of finance of any of the parties. But at a time when party memberships are in decline, they have become a crucially important source of funding, the loss of which could be financially catastrophic. One of the consequences of disclosure is that it has required these donations to be disclosed along with the amount of the donation, and in the process has revealed the full extent to which the parties depend on this form of financial support. It has to be stressed that such donations are perfectly lawful and do not necessarily give rise to any conflict of interest in the way that others

[40] *Sunday Times*, 16 July 2006.
[41] In other countries, such as the United States, it is to be found in rules that prohibit government contractors from making donations to political parties.

are alleged to have done. Quite apart from issues of conflict of interest, however, such donations raise other questions about their desirability, questions arising from a symbiosis between personal wealth and politics which is not only tolerated but is encouraged, and indeed by its public disclosure is given legitimacy, as well as approval by the State, to the extent that this legitimacy derives from a statutory obligation (an act of the State). It is conduct open to question in the sense that it violates the first principle of democracy (equality), by enabling some citizens to engage in a form of political participation not open to many others, and open to very few on the same scale.[42]

As we saw in chapter 5, donations to the Labour Party amounted to £82m in the period from 16 February 2001 to 30 June 2006. Given the history, membership arrangements and constitution of the Labour Party, it will be no great surprise that the bulk of the Labour Party's income derives from trade union sources. It is true that trade unions no longer contribute as great a portion of party funds as in the past, for reasons considered below. Nonetheless, of the £82m donated to the Labour Party between 2001 and 2006, £51.9m was by way of affiliation fees or other donations from trade unions, accounting for 63.3 per cent of donation income. The bulk of trade union funds were donations by the so-called 'big four' unions (AMICUS, UNISON, TGWU and the GMB), as shown in Table 6.1. The total number of donations from each of these unions was 790, 488, 505 and 300 respectively, many of these from union branches to Constituency Labour Parties (CLPs), as well as head office affiliation fees and election donations. Between them the four large unions accounted for 45 per cent of the Labour Party's donation income. Other large union contributors included the CWU (communication workers), USDAW (shopworkers) and Community (the merged union of steelworkers and textile workers). With the exception of Connect (which has made seventeen donations, amounting to £84,160), all the union

Table 6.1 Trade union donations to the Labour Party

Donor	Total cash and non-cash (£)
UNISON (public service union)	9,842,317
GMB (general workers' union)	8,050,534
TGWU (transport workers' union)	7,187,469
AMICUS[a] (manufacturing workers' union)	11,937,112
Total 'Big Four' donations	37,017,432

[a] This includes donations by the two constituent unions (AEEU and MSF) prior to the amalgamation to create AMICUS in 2002. It also includes donations from GPMU which subsequently merged with AMICUS.
Source: Electoral Commission.

[42] See ch 2 above.

supporters were affiliated to the Party, at least at the time the donations were made.

Although trade unions are thus a major source of Labour Party funding, trade union membership levels are in decline, having fallen from around 13 million in 1980 to around 6 million today, and the decline has been particularly significant in a number of unions (such as the mineworkers and steelworkers) which historically have been great stalwarts of the Labour Party. The number of trade unionists paying the political levy of their union has also declined in consequence, as has the number of trade unionists now affiliated to the Labour Party, now approaching a quarter of its strength in 1980. Trade unions are thus no longer in a position to fund the Party to the extent of its need, and it is any event part of the New Labour project that trade union funding should be balanced and displaced by other sources of funding. These latter sources are largely wealthy individuals, and it is the assiduous courting of these potential donors that has led to the Labour Party to be less dependent on the Labour movement than in the past.[43] Although it is true that the Labour Party received fewer large personal donations than the Conservative Party, that gap appeared to be shrinking. The Labour Party could also thus claim – perhaps incongruously – to be the party of ostentatious wealth. In the period under review, Labour received thirteen donations in excess of £250,000 from six people, as shown in Table 6.2.

Table 6.2 Personal donations to the Labour Party in excess of £250,000

Donor	Date	Donation (£)
Lord Sainsbury	13.01.02	2,000,000
Lord Paul Hamlyn	20.12.02	500,000
Lord Sainsbury	01.03.03	2,500,000
Mr William Haughey	05.12.03	330,000
Lord Paul Hamlyn	19.12.03	500,000
Sir Christopher Ondaatje	19.12.03	1,000,000
Lord Paul Drayson	17.06.04	505,000
Mr William Haughey	12.11.04	330,000
Lord Paul Drayson	21.12.04	500,000
Sir Christopher Ondaatje	27.12.04	500,000
Lord Sainsbury	10.03.05	2,000,000
Lakshminiwas Mittal	13.07.05	2,000,000
Mr William Haughey	21.10.05	330,000
Total		12,995,000

Source: Electoral Commission.

[43] See *The Guardian*, G2, 2 December 2004.

In addition to the million-pound donations, and the other donations in excess of £250,000, another eleven individuals gave eighteen donations of between £100,001 and £250,000, as shown in Table 6.3. The thirty-one donations from seventeen donors in Tables 6.2 and 6.3 amount to £16,741,351, which represents 20 per cent of total donation income, which rises to 55 per cent if trade union income is excluded. This, however, may significantly underestimate the dependence on the large donors. Apart from the donations listed in Table 6.3, at least another two individuals (Mr Charles Peel and Sir Frank Lowe) gave multiple donations that exceed £100,000 in total (£300,000 and £300,000 respectively), while four of those named in Tables 6.2 and 6.3 gave ten additional donations in £100,000 parcels, amounting to £1,000,000 in aggregate. This, however, is not the end of the story. An earlier study of the period from 16 February 2001 to 31 March 2005 found that if donors whose contributions over the period total more than £100,000 *in aggregate* are taken into account, a further twenty-one donors emerge, contributing in that period another £3.32m. This category of donations accounted for 5 per cent of donation income and 14 per cent of donation income

Table 6.3 Personal donations to the Labour Party between £100,001 and £250,000

Donor	Date	Donation (£)
Alan Sugar	09.06.01	200,000
Lakshmi Mittal	28.06.01	125,000
Sir Ronald Cohen	14.02.02	200,000
Bill Kenwright	13.06.02	200,000
Sir Ronald Cohen	17.02.03	250,000
Sir David Garrard	23.05.03	200,000
Sir Ronald Cohen	12.05.04	250,000
Ms Denise Gleeson	23.08.04	119,967
Sir Sigmund Sternberg	05.11.05	101,384
Mr William Bollinger	14.01.05	250,000
Mr Nigel Doughty	10.02.05	250,000
Mr Derek Tullett	16.03.05	200,000
Mr Jon Aisbitt	13.04.05	250,000
Sir Ronald Cohen	26.04.05	250,000
Mr William Bollinger	16.01.06	250,000
Mr Michael Watts	26.03.06	150,000
Mr Nigel Doughty	02.05.06	250,000
Sir Ronald Cohen	06.06.06	250,000
Total		3,746,351

Source: Electoral Commission.

if trade union income is excluded. That earlier study found that high-value private donations (defined as donations above £100,000, or donations from a single source which exceed £100,000 in aggregate) accounted for 25 per cent of Labour donation income, although that figure rises dramatically to 71 per cent of donations if those of trade unions are filtered out.[44]

Although the balance of Labour Party funding is thus changing, the Party's dependence on large subscribers does not find a parallel dependence on corporate money, even though it is likely that almost all of the high-value donors contributing to the analysis above made their money in business. But as the PPERA makes clear, there is a difference between corporate donations and donations from private individuals, with each operating under a very different regulatory framework.[45] According to the Electoral Commission, the Labour Party has received 541 donations from companies, totalling £3,711,922, which represents 4.5 per cent of the Labour Party's donation income. In comparison to the scale of donation given by individuals, the average business donation to Labour is a relatively modest £6,861. Only one cash donation was over £100,000 (Sterling Capitol plc, £160,000), and only two in kind (Video Meeting Company, £131,930 and Picture Production Company Ltd, £131,600). Further, all but seven cash donations were £25,000 or less – of which two were donations of £30,000 from Manchester Airport that had to be returned for reasons which are unclear.[46] Taking aggregate corporate contributions into account does not significantly alter the picture, adding as it does only KPMG's nine non-cash donations of £257,500 and TBWA's mixed donations of £737,343. Although sizeable, neither alters the fact that corporate money has a decidedly tertiary role in Labour's income streams.

'High-Value Donors': The Conservative Party

For obvious reasons, donations to Opposition parties are never likely to be as newsworthy as donations to the governing party. Nonetheless, the (mis)perception of the Conservative's reliance on the largesse of a single donor (Lord Ashcroft), and the questions raised about the Conservative-nominated peers in 2004, indicates that the Opposition parties are not immune from scrutiny and criticism. (More recently, revelations that as much as half of the Liberal Democrats' donation income issued from a single individual proved to be one of the major talking points after the 2005 election.[47]) For much of the post-1997 period, there seemed to be a crisis in the Opposition parties, insofar as it seemed

---

[44] K D Ewing and N S Ghaleigh, 'Donations to Political Parties in the United Kingdom' (2006) 6 *Election Law Journal* (forthcoming).
[45] Ch 5 above.
[46] BBC News, 22 October 2003.
[47] *The Guardian*, 27 May 2005.

that they had fallen badly behind Labour in terms of financial security, though the difficulties of the Conservatives may have been exaggerated, and in any event may now be changing rapidly. Labour's traditional trade union base has weathered well, providing financial security by way of a large and reliable income stream. This has remained true, despite strategic attempts by the Conservative governments of the 1980s both to undermine the trade union movement generally and by more discrete obstacles to their donating to political parties.[48] To the extent that such measures sought to undermine the financial link between the Labour Party and trade unions, they have largely failed.

Between February 2001 and June 2006, the Conservative Party received 4,056 donations, which is significantly fewer than Labour's 5,987, though more than Labour's 2,498 donations if trade union donations are deducted from the total. The first striking feature of Conservative funding is the party's heavy reliance on the State. Of the £83,107,911 in donations reported by the Conservative Party, some £22,385,544 was in the form of sixty-five donations from public funds, such as Short money[49] and Policy Development Grants.[50] Accordingly, the party for a long time most strongly opposed to State funding nevertheless depended on public funds for over a quarter (26.9 per cent) of its donation income. A more striking (albeit not a surprising) feature of Conservative Party funding is that like the Labour Party, it too is heavily dependent on large private donations. In the period under review, the Conservatives received seventeen donations in excess of £250,000 (including one bequest), as shown in Table 6.4. In terms of very large donations (that is, single donations over £250,000), there is thus a rough parity between the two major parties, both in terms of number of donations (thirteen Labour and seventeen Conservative), and their combined value (an extra £1.5m for the Conservatives), with the Conservatives having a slight edge.

Apart from the million-pound donations and the donations in excess of £250,000, the Conservatives also received nineteen cash donations of between £100,001 and £250,000 from fourteen people, as shown in Table 6.5. There were also two donations in kind by Corin Graeff (£128,353) and Edward Haughey (£119,816), accounting for another £248,169. Total donations between £100,001 and £250,000 thus amounted to £3.4m. Overall then, the total sum that the Conservatives received in high-value donations was just under £18m, deriving from twenty-seven people and representing 30 per cent of all donations from private sources. This compared with Labour's seventeen donors providing over a fifth of donation income. As with Labour, however, this does not take account of additional donations from any of the foregoing donors for £100,000 or less, or donations from individuals not named above whose combined donations exceed £100,000 in aggregate. For example, Mr George Magan has given ten donations in

---

[48] The Trade Union and Labour Relations (Consolidation) Act 1992 requires that ballots be undertaken every ten years for the continuance of trade unions' political fund. See ch 5 above.

[49] Introduced in 1975, the quantum of Short money was tripled in 1998. See ch 8 below.

[50] This scheme, introduced by PPERA, s12, annually distributes £2m to parties to enable policy development.

Table 6.4 Personal donations to the Conservative Party in excess of £250,000

Donor	Date	Donation (£)
Mr John Wheeler	03.05.01	2,450,000
Sir Paul Getty	11.06.01	5,000,000
Mr John Wheeler	27.11.03	504,000
Mr George Magan	24.02.04	400,000
Mr Maurice Bennett	16.07.04	450,000
Ms Ruth Beardmore	05.11.04	396,409
Mr George Magan	23.12.04	325,417
Mr Maurice Bennett	04.01.05	500,000
Mr Joseph C Bamford	05.01.05	1,000,000
Ms Diana Van Neivelt Price	01.03.05	440,000
Sir Tom Cowie	15.04.05	500,000
Mr Kenneth Richards	15.11.05	452,512
Mr Roger Gabb	31.03.06	500,000
Mr Peter Harrison	31.03.06	259,945
Lord Steinberg	31.03.06	530,876
Mr Thomas Scott	03.04.06	500,000
Mr George Magan	11.04.06	375,000
Total		14,584,161

Source: Electoral Commission.

total, with an aggregate value of £1.3m (of which only £1.1m is accounted for above), while Sir Stanley Kalms has given twenty-eight cash and non-cash donations of £626,551 in total (of which only £280,500 is accounted for above). Those who have not given single donations in excess of £100,000 but whose donations in aggregate exceed this amount include Mr Michael J Stone, with two donations of £100,000 each. Indeed, the study of donations received referred to above suggests that at the time the study was conducted, the Conservatives' reliance on large donations individually or in aggregate in excess of £100,000 amounted to 43 per cent of donation income from private sources.[51]

Apart from the heavy reliance of the Conservative Party on the State and the heavy dependence on large personal donations, the Conservative Party also receives more donations from companies than does the Labour Party, and these donations are of a significantly higher average value (£17,564) than the comparable donations to Labour (£6,861). 1,170 corporate donations yielded £20,550,119, this accounting for 34 per cent of party income from private sources. Of these

[51] Ewing and Ghaleigh, *supra* n 44.

Table 6.5 Personal donations to the Conservative Party between £100,001 and £250,000

Donor	Date	Donation (£)
Mr Robert Fleming	15.05.01	206,000
Mr Roderick Fleming	15.05.01	200,000
Mr Leonard Steinberg	03.01.02	110,000
Sir Stanley Kalms	04.03.02	120,500
Sir Stanley Kalms	24.06.02	160,000
Dr Hans Rausing	01.07.04	198,000
Mr John Wheeler	02.07.04	236,000
Mr Robert Edmiston	10.09.04	250,000
Mr Frederick Catlin	22.10.04	150,000
Mr John Wheeler	22.12.04	200,000
Dr Hans Rausing	21.02.05	145,000
Mr John Wheeler	10.03.05	190,000
Mr Michael E Slade	23.03.05	102,000
Mr Ernest Neathercott	12.09.05	104,568
Mr Mahomed Galadari	11.11.05	150,000
Lord Steinberg	23.12.05	250,000
Sir Martyn Arbib	23.03.06	109,231
Mr David Instance	31.03.06	211,559
Mr George Pinto	31.03.06	107,203
Total		3,200,064

Source: Electoral Commission.

donations, ten were over £250,001, as shown in Table 6.6, while another fourteen were between £100,001 and £250,000, with a combined value of £2,192,865. Several of those in the latter category were made by companies that appear in Table 6.6, including six worth an aggregate of £783,615 from IIR Ltd. These twenty-four donations by just twelve corporate donors thus account for £9,340,222 of Conservative income in total, this representing 45.4 per cent of income from company donations and 15.3 per cent of all private donation income. (But again, this may understate the position because some of these twelve companies have given additional donations of less than £100,001, while there are other companies whose aggregate donations exceed £100,000, in some cases by a large amount). When individual and company donations are combined, the Conservatives relied on high-value donations from both sources for 45.3 per cent of their private donation income, a figure that rises to over 47 per cent if seven donations in excess of £100,000 from four unincorporated associations (such as the Midlands Industrial Council) are taken into account.

Table 6.6 Company donations to the Conservative Party in excess of £250,000

Donor	Date	Donation (£)
Norbrook Laboratories	02.04.01	1,000,000
IIR Ltd	26.03.02	520,000
IIR Ltd	31.12.04	267,500
Intercapital Private Group Ltd	14.01.05	350,000
IIR Ltd	30.03.05	303,720
Harris Ventures Ltd	23.03.06	307,438
Cringle Corporation	31.03.06	267,931
International Motors Ltd	31.03.06	2,110,767
IPGL Ltd	06.04.06	1,000,000
RF Trustee Co	13.04.06	1,020,000
Total		7,147,357

Note 1: Norbrook Laboratories is a Northern Ireland-based company associated with Ulster Unionist peer, Lord Ballyedmond. As Edward Haughey, he was elevated to the peerage in 2004.

Note 2: IIR Ltd is a large conference company sold by Lord Laidlaw for £768m in 2005. Lord Laidlaw, who was elevated to the peerage in 2004, made a loan of £3.5m to the Conservatives reported in 2006. See Table 6.8 below.

Note 3: International Motors is associated with Robert Edmiston, who also has links with the Midlands Industrial Council encountered in chapter 5 above. Mr Edmiston is not a member of the House of Lords, though he was nominated (*The Guardian*, 30 March 2006).

Source: Electoral Commission.

It is important to emphasise that within this group of forty-three donors (twenty-seven individuals, twelve companies and four unincorporated associations), there are some who are more significant than others, in the sense that some have given only one-off donations, whereas others are regular contributors of smaller sums as well as the high-value donations already referred to. The point has already been illustrated by the donations from Mr George Magan and Sir Stanley Kalms. Another example is IIR Ltd, which made nine donations accounted for above, but which in fact made fifteen donations in total with an aggregate value of £1,951,820. It is also important to emphasise that the role of large donors may be understated further by virtue of the fact that the high-value donations have all gone to Conservative Central Office, whereas the Electoral Commission registers record all donations to all parts of the party organisation. This means that these donors will account for a higher proportion of Central Office income than the donation income of the party as a whole. Indeed, it has been calculated by the Labour Research Department that Conservative Central

BOX 6.1
Donations to the Liberal Democrats

In the period under review, the Liberal Democrats received 2,242 donations, raising £17,715,543 in the process. Of these donations, slightly more
than 35 per cent (£6,028,565) took the form of donations from public
funds, though the whole nature of Liberal Democrat funding has been
skewed by a series of large donations from 5th Avenue Partners Ltd. In the
period from 2001 to 2006, the Liberal Democrats received no personal
donations in excess of £250,000, and only one in excess of £100,000, which
was a bequest. The party did, however, have a number of corporate donations in excess of £100,000, in addition to the combined donations (five in
total) of £2.45m from 5th Avenue Partners Ltd. These other companies
included Carrousel Capital Ltd (£290,000) and the Joseph Rowntree
Research Trust (eighteen donations of £1.5m in aggregate) These three
companies are the only ones to have made individual donations in excess of
£100,000. Other notable donations include two donations from Alpha
Healthcare Ltd (£160,000 in aggregate), and three donations from UNISON
totalling £93,441.41. The donations from 5th Avenue Partners accounted for
41 per cent of Liberal Democrat corporate donations and just under a fifth
of all donations from private sources. (In the quarter in which they were
given [first quarter of 2005], they accounted for more than half of the total
donation income of the party (£4,164,970).) For more than one reason, the
donations by 5th Avenue Partners Ltd were by far the most controversial,
the money having been 'transferred from a parent company in Switzerland
to London-based 5th Avenue Partners UK Ltd in order to be handed over
to the Liberal Democrats'.[1] An investigation by the Electoral Commission
concluded that the company was a permissible donor, but was reportedly
critical of the party's failure to make better checks on the source of the
donations.[2] This did not end the matter, with fresh controversy arising
following the arrest in Spain of Michael Brown (the owner of the company),[3] who was later extradited to the United Kingdom,[4] where he stood
trial and was imprisoned.[5] These proceedings have provoked fresh claims
that 5th Avenue was not a permissible donor,[6] and the possibility as a result
that the Liberal Democrats could forfeit the money. This was described as a
'nightmare', which could 'force the party into bankruptcy'.[7]

[1] *The Guardian*, 27 October 2005.
[2] *Ibid.*
[3] *The Times*, 26 April 2006.
[4] *Daily Telegraph*, 26 May 2006.
[5] *Ibid.*
[6] See pp 92–94 above.
[7] *The Times*, 26 April 2006, *Daily Telegraph*, 26 May 2006.

Office may depend on high-value donors for more than three-quarters (76.1 per cent) of its income (in the period from February 2001 to March 2006). Finally, however, it is important to recognise too that some substantial donors have not appeared above, or have not appeared to any significant extent, because they have chosen to spread a large number of smaller donations across various parts of the party organisation. Bearwood Corporate Services Ltd, whom we encountered in chapter 5, donated some £1,182,154 but in 145 separate donations mainly to Conservative Associations, of which the largest was £30,000, though almost all the others were for a significantly smaller sum.[52]

The Loans Affair: A New Problem Erupts

Closely related to the dependence of the parties on large donations is the issue of undisclosed loans. There had been suggestions for some time in the media that the Conservative Party had been funding its activities in part by commercial loans rather than by donations.[53] As we shall see, there may be good reasons for doing this, but one of the consequences of doing so is that it undermines the transparency obligations of the PPERA. Although a donation is widely defined in the legislation, it is expressly provided to apply to money lent to the party 'otherwise than on commercial terms'.[54] This means that commercial loans do not have to be disclosed, and it also means that political parties can be sustained by foreign nationals who are not permitted to make donations to political parties, as well as by companies that do not have shareholder approval for making donations. Yet the dependence on secret loans has been said to be more damaging and more challenging to the independence of parties than reliance on secret donations. This is because loans 'leave the party in hock to the lender', and make them very vulnerable to lenders should they demand the return of their money.[55]

The Problem Erupts

The fresh controversy that engulfed the British political parties in 2006 was tangled with the funding of the new city academies – state schools that rely on business sponsorship.[56] It was also tangled with allegations that some large donors to both the city academy programme and to the Labour Party were

---

[52] Similarly, although the Midlands Industrial Council made two donations of over £100,000, these amounted to only £352,500, in contrast to fifty-two donations with an aggregate value of £968,689 (as well as another £1m or so to a Constituency Campaigning Board).

[53] *Sunday Times*, 19 March 2006.

[54] PPERA, s 50(2)(f).

[55] *Sunday Times*, 19 March 2006.

[56] *Sunday Times*, 15 January 2006.

BOX 6.2
Donations to the Nationalist Parties

The **Scottish National Party** (SNP) received 188 donations in the period under review, these amounting to £1,999,774. Public funds from the House of Commons, the Scottish Parliament and the Electoral Commission accounted for 119 of these donations, totalling £1,446,025 – over 72 per cent of the SNP's total donation income. The SNP received only fifty cash and sixteen non-cash contributions, amounting to £455,378 and £27,882 respectively. The SNP received only twenty-two cash donations of £5,000 or more, five of which were bequests (£10,000; £10,829.09; £62,945.16; £80,234.46; £296,834.60).

Apart from bequests, only eleven donations were for £10,000 or more, of which the largest by some way was for £50,000. Corporate largesse has not then troubled the SNP greatly, with only five small company donations, though four were from the same source (Flagship Media Group Ltd). There were also thirteen non-cash contributions of £23,806 donated by South of Scotland Power Ltd in the form of staff secondment and accommodation costs. Although modest compared with the other parliamentary parties, the SNP is still more generously funded than other nationalist and minor parties.

Plaid Cymru (the major Welsh nationalist party) has reported eighty-five donations of £559,676. Of these, fifty-two have been provided by public funds (Short money and the Electoral Commission), these accounting for £308,598. This means that substantially less than half of the party's donation income derives from a non-state source. Only £251,078 was provided by private donors of which £29,450 was provided as a non-cash donation by a company (Splitside Ltd) by way of a computer software system. The Party's highest cash donation was £16,000, and it received only two cash donations of £10,000 and another of £6,000. All other donations were less than £6,000 save six bequests, the highest of which was £56,737.

---

recommended for honours in the form of knighthoods and peerages. The story about secret loans to political parties broke when three of the Labour Party's lenders were turned down for a peerage by the House of Lords Appointments Commission – the body which vets nominations to the upper house – after having been nominated by the Prime Minister.[57] According to press reports, the Commission disapproved of the nominations for reasons other than the fact that

---

[57] *Sunday Times*, 5 March 2006. Three people (identified in the press at the time as donors) were mentioned as having been blocked by the Commission. At this stage the loans were unknown. The press reports suggested that the three had been blocked not because of their financial support.

BOX 6.3
Donations to Small Parties

The **United Kingdom Independence Party** (UKIP) received 356 donations with an overall total of £3,286,332, the majority (£2,529,916) of which were non-cash donations. Cash donations accounted for £731,416. UKIP's biggest benefactors were Mr Alan Bown, Alan Bown (Margate) Ltd and Highstone Group Ltd. Alan Bown and Alan Bown (Margate) Ltd contributed 174 cash and non-cash donations, totalling £1,025,413, and representing 31 per cent of all donation income. Highstone Group Ltd contributed four non-cash donations worth £885,199.18, the majority of which was in the form of billboard and media advertising during the 2004 European elections. Donations from these three sources accounted for almost 58 per cent of all donation income.

The **Green Party** received 158 donations, amounting to £382,366; 158 cash donations accounted for £321,538 and fifteen non-cash accounted for £32,796. The Green Party received one donation of public funds of £15,139 from the Electoral Commission. Their biggest donor is Snack Dragon Catering, an unincorporated association which donated £35,417 (fourteen donations). Geoffrey Norman Syer also donated £33,237.33 in three bequests. The biggest single donation, excluding the above bequest, was £20,000 donated by Ben Goldsmith. Most donations were under £5,000. The **British National Party** received seventy-four donations, amounting to £140,531; fifty-eight cash donations accounted for £128,811. Excluding bequests, almost all donations were less than £5,000, the largest being for £6,850.

---

the individuals had made loans (of which – as we shall see – the Commission had not been informed). One of those who had been vetoed took the unprecedented step of raising his rejection publicly, claiming that he had never been told why he had been rejected by the Commission, or given an opportunity to respond to any concerns that it might have.[59] It was while these concerns were being raised in public that the same nominee also revealed that he had given money to the Labour Party and that he had been asked to provide the money not as a donation but as a commercial loan, for reasons that are not clear.

One reason why a party may seek loans from private individuals is that the banks may be unwilling to lend because of the financial situation of the party in question. In the case of Labour, the bank was said to be 'squeezing the party' and unwilling to lend any more money.[59] Another reason is that an individual may be

[59] *Sunday Times*, 12 March 2006.
[59] *Ibid.*

willing to help but may not want any publicity that would be associated with a donation or its amount, though it does not follow that a supporter of a political party seeking anonymity for his or her financial support would do so for reasons that are by any means improper. Yet another possible reason is that the party may want to keep the support secret, either from its rivals or from other third parties, perhaps to gain some tactical advantage at an election. But whatever the explanation, the Labour Party was eventually forced to reveal that it had received just under £14m by way of loans from twelve 'wealthy businessmen' (see Table 6.7). The Conservatives were then forced to reveal that they too had received loans of just under £16m from twelve individuals and one company (see Table 6.8), while the Liberal Democrats admitted to loans on a much smaller scale from three supporters. In the case of the Conservatives it has been reported that the Party had repaid another £5m to a number of other lenders – including foreign nationals – who wanted to remain anonymous. Their identity is still not in the public domain.

The Nature of the Problem

The use of loans to fund parties was especially controversial for the Labour Party, which was seen to be evading the spirit if not the letter of its own legislation, even if it resorted to the practice because the Conservatives were doing the same.[60]

Table 6.7 Loans to the Labour Party 2005

Name	Amount
Sir David Garrard	£2.3m
Richard Caring	£2m
Lord Sainsbury	£2m
Dr Chai Patel	£1.5m
Rob Aldridge	£1m
Professor Sir Christopher Evans	£1m
Nigel Morris	£1m
Andrew Rosenfeld	£1m
Barry Townsley	£1m
Gordon Crawford	£500,000
Derek Tullett	£400,000
Sir Gulam Noon	£250,000
Total	£13,950,000

Source: Electoral Commission.

[60] *Ibid.*

Table 6.8 Loans to the Conservative Party 2005

Name	Amount
Lord Ashcroft	£3.6m
Lord Laidlaw	£3.5m
Johan Eliasch	£2.6m
Michael Hintze	£2.5m
Raymond Richards	£1m
Lady Victoria de Rothschild	£1m
Henry Angest	£550,000
Cringle Corporation	£450,000
Lord Steinberg	£250,000
Dame Vivien Duffield	£250,000
Alan Lewis	£100,000
Charles Wigoder	£100,000
Graham Facks-Martin	£50,000
Total	£15,950,000

Source: Electoral Commission.

What appeared to be even more controversial, however, was the fact that although a number of the party's lenders had been nominated for a peerage, their loans had not been made known to the House of Lords Appointments Commission, which as we have seen is responsible for vetting nominations to the upper House. This is despite the fact that the Prime Minister not only authorised the use of loans by the Party General Secretary to raise money for the 2005 general election, but – unlike the Party Chairman and the Party Treasurer – was aware that the four nominees had made loans to the Labour Party.[61] It is despite the fact also that the nomination of one of the lenders was made – according to press reports – only weeks after his loan was secured, though both the lender and the Labour Party are at pains to emphasise that the loan was neither given nor secured in return for the promise of an honour.[62] While three of the nominees were rejected by the House of Lords Appointments Commission before they knew about the loans, the failure to disclose this information at the time the nominations were made led the Commission to withdraw its approval for a fourth Labour nominee, once his loan was publicly disclosed.[63] This particular nominee subsequently claimed to have been advised that he was not required to mention the loan in his dealings with the Commission.[64]

[61] The party Chairman (Ian McCartney) is reported as not knowing about the 'secret-backers', as is the Party Treasurer (Jack Dromey) – see *Sunday Times*, 19 March 2006.
[62] *Sunday Times*, 12 March 2006 where any such suggestion was 'vehemently denied'.
[63] *Sunday Times*, 19 March 2006.
[64] *The Guardian*, 11 July 2006.

The Labour Party's funding was such that it was already attracting unwanted publicity about donors and honours. Indeed it was claimed that 'nearly all Labour donors who have given the party more than £1m since 1997 have been given a knighthood or a peerage',[65] and that 'the government has bestowed honours on 12 of the 14 individuals who have given Labour more than £200,000'.[66] Similar concerns had been raised in the past about the Conservatives and honours to the executives of companies that had made donations to the party. On this occasion, however, new ground was opened when a complaint about the Labour Party was made to the police by the SNP and Plaid Cymru.[67] The complaint alleged a breach of the Honours (Prevention of Abuses) Act 1925, whereby it is an offence to seek or to offer an honour in return for money or other valuable consideration, though the last conviction is thought to have been in the early 1930s when Maundy Gregory was jailed for two months.[68] To the evident surprise of many commentators, these allegations appeared to be the subject of a thorough investigation by the police, though the Labour Party denied that there had been any wrongdoing and insisted that all the Labour nominations for membership of the House of Lords had been made only on the basis of individual merit.[69] At the time of writing, the investigations have not been completed, though 48 people are reported as having been interviewed by the police. A number of arrests have been made in connection with inquiries under the 1925 Act and the PPERA, but no one has been charged.[70]

Implications and Consequences of the Loans Affair

Apart from the fact that these loans breached the spirit of transparency in the legislation (even though this may not have been the intention), they also cause us to review and revise the financial support for the parties. If we add donations and loans together, the Labour Party received £95.9m in the period from 2001 to 2006, while the Conservatives received £104m (including public funding), assuming in both cases that details of all the loans received by the parties since 2001 have been published. The main effect of the loans is to make the parties even less dependent on other sources of funding and more heavily dependent on wealthy individuals than was previously thought to have been the case. In the case of the Labour Party, personal donations and loans in excess of £100,000 (from twenty-six people) accounted for 32 per cent of total donation and loan income,

[65] *Sunday Times*, 19 March 2006.

[66] *Sunday Times*, 15 January 2006.

[67] See M Pinto-Duschinsky, *British Political Finance 1830–1980* (1981), p 106.

[68] *The Guardian*, 12 July 2006; *Sunday Times*, 16 July 2006. See page 1 above.

[69] For an account of the police investigation and the nature of the inquiries being pursued, see *The Independent*, 20 July 2006.

[70] For fresh allegations that a Labour nominee was nominated for an honour, see *Sunday Times*, 16 July 2006.

rising to 69 per cent if trade union donations are filtered out. In the case of the Conservatives, the £21m in loans meant that the party depended on personal and company donations and loans (from fifty sources) in excess of £100,000 for 46 per cent of total donation and loan income, rising to 58.5 per cent if public funding is filtered out. These figures need to be slightly adjusted, in the light of the additional loans disclosed in August 2006 which are dealt with below. They increase still further the dependence on large donors and lenders.

The Electoral Commission's Response

Following the eruption of the loans crisis, the Electoral Commission wrote to the parties on 20 March 2006 to ask them to confirm that they had complied with their reporting obligations in relation to loans, and to ask them if they were prepared to adhere to a voluntary code of conduct about the reporting and disclosure of loans. In its letter to the parties, the Commission specifically asked the registered treasurer to confirm that he or she was 'entirely satisfied that any loans that the party has received and not so far reported are on fully commercial terms and that they involved no benefit to the party which should have been declared and has not been declared'. The Commission also drew attention to earlier guidance given about interest paid on loans, as follows:

> Where a loan is made available to a political party and the difference between the following is positive
>
> • the interest that would have been paid had that loan been made on commercial terms;
>
> • and the interest actually accrued during the financial year,
>
> this difference should be recorded as notional expenditure in the income and expenditure account.

The Commission also drew attention to matters other than interest which was said to be 'not the only term of a loan'. In determining whether any loans were commercial or not, party treasurers were also invited to consider matters such as 'any requirement for security, the repayment terms and flexibility – including a clear understanding that a loan may be converted into a donation at a later stage'. Finally, the 'overall test' was said to be 'the extent to which similar terms would have been available at the time of the loan from a commercial lender'.

The parties were invited to report any loans which in the light of these points they felt ought now to be reported. In responding to the Commission, the Conservative Party said that after having reviewed its files with the benefit of legal advice, it was satisfied that loans made to the party were made on 'commercial terms falling within the scope of the relevant legislation'. Similarly, the General Secretary of the Labour Party replied by saying that the Party was satisfied that 'all the loans were made on a commercial basis and as such there is no requirement in law to declare them'. The response by the Liberal Democrats was in the same terms, though rather more explicit, pointing out not only that the party was satisfied that it had complied with all the requirements of the PPERA, but that it had reported the notional interest foregone by its three loan providers in the appropriate quarterly donation return to the Commission. These responses were mirrored by the responses of a number of smaller parties who had also been written to, with the SNP stating bluntly that 'there is no benefit to the party which should have been declared which has not been declared'. A selection of other parties – the English Democrats, the Green Party, Respect, the Scottish Socialist Party and UKIP – formally acknowledged that they had received loans of various kinds, though these tended to be relatively small. There was no indication of any failure to comply with appropriate reporting obligations, though enquiries by UKIP 'identified a loan of £20,000 made to the West Midlands region and which was subsequently converted into a donation before 31 December 2005'. The party was verifying the position so that 'late notifications of the donation and any applicable notional interest for the period before it became a donation, can be made as soon as possible'.

From Code of Practice to Legislation

The Electoral Commission did not appear to be fully satisfied with the parties' responses and wrote to them again asking for a 'more detailed explanation of the rationale' that they used 'in coming to the view that all loans accepted by the party were on commercial terms'. Rather menacingly, the Commision also asked for 'supporting evidence' to help clarify its understanding, and indicated that it may be necessary to consider information that the parties would normally be required to provide under the PPERA. Moreover, the Commission indicated that it might want to consider expert advice from outside the Commission 'on the question of the terms of the loans' in order to say publicly that it agreed with the parties that all the loans received since the Act came into force had been secured on commercial terms. This particular menace was, however, postponed in the light of an even greater menace, namely the related police investigation sparked by the loans affair. In the meantime, it appears that at least the main parties agreed to be bound by the Electoral Commission's voluntary code of conduct on the reporting of loans, under which 'political parties would report to the Commission all loans they have received above a certain threshold (£5,000 for loans to head office and £1,000 for loans to accounting units), including details of the lender, the amount of the loan and the period of the loan'. This would be done pending the implementation of a statutory obligation to disclose such donations introduced by the Electoral Administration Act 2006, but not due to come into force until 11 September 2006. Under the terms of the code, the parties submitted details of loans with their second quarterly reports for 2006, covering the period from April to June.

It appears that only the three large parties submitted loans to the Commission, presumably because only they had something to report. The Conservatives reported four loans obtained in the reporting period, amounting to £2,812,000, the bulk being provided by way of two loans from a company based in Northern Ireland called AIB Group (UK) Ltd. This particular company provided two loans of £2.5m and £300,000 respectively. The Labour Party adopted a more generous construction of its obligations under the code and appeared to include all outstanding loans, not just those obtained during the reporting period. So in addition to the twelve loans referred to in Table 6.7, the Labour Party disclosed another six loans, and it was also revealed that at least six of those referred to in Table 6.7 were understated. Of the six new loans disclosed, one was another from Sir David Garrard for £300,000, and the other five were from the Co-operative Bank and Unity Trust Bank for a combined £13.5m. The aggregate reported loans was thus a whopping £28,200,693. The Liberal Democrats also appeared to report all outstanding loans, revealing nothing quite on this scale. They included three loans already in the public domain, accounting for £475,000 in total from three Liberal Democrat peers, as well as twenty-three much smaller loans mainly from individuals, ranging from £1,248 to £20,000. The total amount of these twenty-three loans was £109,237. It remains to be seen if yet more loans will be reported in the next quarter under this voluntary procedure, covering the period from 1 July to 11 September, at which point there will be a statutory obligation to report loans and other credit facilities made available to political parties, as well as a prohibition on receiving loans from those who would not be permissible donors. The first report of party loans under the new statutory procedure was published by the Electoral Commission on 28 November 2006, too late for inclusion in this volume.

Conclusion

The transparency requirements of the PPERA have had extraordinary consequences. They have fuelled rather than dampened allegations of 'sleaze', they have exposed political parties as being heavily dependent on large donors (who are becoming more reluctant to donate), and they led the parties to raise money in ways that coincidentally would protect supporters from unwanted publicity (in the process contributing still further to the problem of 'sleaze'). At the heart of the matter, however, is the failure of the parties to accept that transparency requires a change of practice rather than provide a justification of existing practice. In particular, it requires the parties to show restraint in terms of who they accept money from, how much they accept from any particular donor, and how far they seek and exploit loopholes in the legislation. In fact, the undisclosed loans are only one of two major loopholes to have been identified in the PPERA, the other being the channelling of large sums of money by donors to constituency associations which are largely unregulated in terms of their spending. This practice was considered in chapter 5, but it has major implications for the election spending limits considered in chapter 7 below.

In a sense we are now back to where we started with the Neill Committee in

1997, but with compound interest, and the added problem of what to do about it. The government's immediate response was for more transparency, with parties now required to register loans, credit and other regulated transactions, and permitted to receive loans only from people or organisations which fall within the definition of permissible donors.[71] In this way two loopholes are closed, with the new measures applying to loans and other benefits in excess of £5,000 (or £1,000 in the case of loans or benefits to accounting units), and requiring weekly reporting during an election campaign to match the comparable regime relating to donations. But this is clearly not enough, with the case for further measures to address large donations now being irresistible, the only question being the strategy by which this should be done. One approach – which was rejected by the Neill Committee[72] – would be a limit on the amount that any donor may give to a political party in any one year. Such a measure would serve at least one of the regulatory objectives identified in chapter 2, in the sense that it addresses corruption concerns and specifically what has been identified as a corruption of principle caused by the presence of multimillion-pound donations.

But a contribution cap would not necessarily deal with issues relating to 'sleaze' or conflict of interest or the appearance of conflict of interest, it being sobering to reflect that the donations that gave rise to so much grief after the 2001 general election were for comparatively small amounts. Nor would it necessarily meet other regulatory objectives, notably the need to ensure that the parties are adequately funded, or the need to ensure that there is fair electoral competition, or the need to respect the autonomy of internal party organisation. These problems – which are more fully considered in chapter 10 below – arise in part as a result of the asymmetrical nature of party structure which makes regulation difficult to introduce in a way that does not have partisan consequences. But before considering these matters in greater detail, it is necessary first to look at the extent to which other regulatory strategies have been adopted in party-funding regulation, and to what extent there is room for developing these strategies to reduce the need for large donations and to wean the parties off the large donors, for what may be cold turkey for some in the light of recent problems. These are the demand side initiatives – limits on the levels of permitted spending by political parties on the one hand, and the role of the State in providing resources on the other.

[71] Electoral Administration Act 2006, s 61.
[72] Cm 4057–I, 1998, ch 6.

7

Spending Limits in Election Campaigns

Spending controls are an important form of party-funding regulation. They have been adopted (and retained) by a number of countries, for one of two reasons: first as a strategy for dealing with political corruption, and secondly as a way of promoting equality of electoral opportunity. So far as the first of these reasons is concerned, the spending limits assist by reducing the money available to spend, thereby containing the money which needs to be raised, thereby in turn relieving the parties of the need to seek larger and larger donations from more and more people. So far as the second of these reasons is concerned, spending limits assist by helping to create a level playing-field on which campaigns can be fought, without either side having an unfair advantage based on financial resources alone. It is true that spending limits will not eliminate all unfairness in a campaign, but it is also true that they address the concern that economic power should not translate into direct electoral advantage. Spending controls apply with variations and qualifications to all British elections,[1] that is to say local government, devolved bodies, parliamentary and European. Nevertheless, the main focus of this chapter is parliamentary elections. These are the most important, the most hotly contested, and the most expensive.

Regulatory Challenges

As a regulatory device, spending limits may take a number of different forms. In their purest form they will apply to *all* items of expenditure incurred by a political party and its representatives, and so control all forms of political activity. As we saw in chapter 3, however, regulation on such a scale is unusual, and almost without precedent. Otherwise, spending limits may apply to particular events or

---

[1] For example, there are no national spending limits in local government elections, though there are in the other elections. But there are candidate spending limits in local government elections, as there are in all other elections. Also there are no limits on third-party national spending in local elections, but there are limits on third-party support for or attacks on local government candidates. There are both national and local limits on third parties in parliamentary elections. See below.

activities, most obviously elections, though here two questions arise. The first is to consider to which electoral participants the limits should apply: should they apply both to candidates and political parties, and should they apply to other actors whose role might also have to be considered, such as companies (including newspapers), trade unions and pressure groups? Having determined to whom the limits are to apply, the second question is to determine to which items of expenditure they should apply: should they apply to all items of election expenditure (if elections are targeted for spending limits), or should they apply only to segments of expenditure (such as electoral advertising)? If the strategy is to be effective, the control of election expenses has to apply as widely and as deeply as possible, for a number of reasons.

Political machines will always seek a competitive advantage over their rivals. If only candidates are restricted as to how much they can spend, the money will flow to the parties to spend on national campaigns, or will be retained by interest groups to spend independently. If, on the other hand, only the parties are subject to restrictions, the money will inevitably flow to the candidates, for spending in key seats where there is real competition, or will be retained for interest group campaigns. But if both candidates and parties are restricted and interest groups are not, there will be a tendency for high spending by interest groups, which might otherwise have donated money to candidates and parties to help with their campaigns. All of which is to suggest that the dam has to apply to candidates, political parties and interest groups if it is to be effective. In terms of whether it should apply to all election expenditures or segments thereof, there are obvious problems if the latter route is to be adopted at the expense of the former. Apart from the uncertainty about which expenditures to include (though some will be obvious), segmental limits create the obvious risk that the limit will be evaded by large-scale expenditures on unregulated items and the development of new campaign techniques which fall beyond the reach of regulation.

This last point is nicely illustrated by British experience, where unlike most countries there is a ban on political advertising on radio and television. Indeed, the ban applies not only to political parties but also to other political organisations and purposes.[2] And it does not apply only at election time, but at all times. Provision is made for free party political and party election broadcasts for the political parties, but there is no comparable provision for other organisations, which remain excluded from this means of communication. Yet although the ban has no doubt played an important part in controlling expenses in national election campaigns, it did not stop the massive escalation of costs in the 1990s as the parties found other ways to spend money. We saw in chapter 1 that while the two main parties spent £10m (Labour) and £11m (Conservative) in 1992, this rose to an estimated £26m (Labour) and £28m (Conservative) in 1997. Although extremely modest by US standards in particular, nevertheless this increase invites

---

[2] Broadcasting Act 1990, s 8. See T Gibbons, *Regulating the Media* (2nd ed, 1998). Also, A Scott, '"A Monstrous and Unjustifiable Infringement"? Political Broadcasting and the Broadcasting Ban on Advocacy Advertising' (2003) 66 *MLR* 224.

the question of how the parties are able to spend so much money. Between 1992 and 1997, major items of expenditure that increased significantly include newspaper and outdoor advertising, direct mailing, and staff hired for the election campaign. In the case of the Conservatives, for example, expenditure on 'outdoor advertising' rose from £4m in 1992 to £11.1m in 1997.[3]

The Victorian Legacy: Candidate Limits

Spending limits have been employed as a regulatory device in Britain since being first introduced by the Corrupt and Illegal Practices Act 1883. The law has been changed and consolidated on several occasions since, and now is to be found in the Representation of the People Act 1983, which has been amended by the Political Parties, Elections and Referendums Act 2000 (PPERA) and the Electoral Administration Act 2006. The modern purpose of the legislation was expressed in the courts in the following terms:

> The object, plainly, is to achieve a level financial playing field between competing candidates, so as to prevent perversion of the voters' democratic choice between competing candidates within constituencies by significant disparities of local expenditure.[4]

In promoting this purpose, the 1983 Act (as amended by the PPERA) now provides that the 'election expenses incurred by or on behalf of a candidate at an election must not in aggregate exceed the [permitted] maximum amount'.[5] It is still the case that the permitted maximum amount varies according to the number of electors in a constituency, and according to whether the constituency is a borough or a county constituency; a higher permitted expenditure operates in the latter case on the assumption that it is more difficult to reach the voters in remote areas.[6] But as a rule of thumb, a sum of around £10,000–12,000 per candidate would be close to the mark, given the size of the typical constituency.[7] A candidate's election agent is required to file a return of the candidate's expenditure to the returning officer within thirty-five days of the election,[8] and both candidate and agent must make a statutory declaration attesting to the accuracy of the return.[9] It is an illegal practice for a candidate or agent knowingly to exceed the limit.[10]

---

[3] See Fifth Report of the Committee on Standards in Public Life, *The Funding of Political Parties in the United Kingdom*, Cm 4057–I, 1998, Table 3.6.

[4] *R v Jones* [1999] 2 Cr App R 253.

[5] Representation of the People Act 1983, s 76(1), as amended by the PPERA, s 132.

[6] Representation of the People Act 1983, s 76.

[7] The precise formula at the time of writing is £7,150 plus 7p per elector in a county constituency, and £7,150 plus 5p per elector in a borough constituency: SI 2005 No 269.

[8] Representation of the People Act 1983, s 81.

[9] *Ibid*, s 82

[10] *Ibid*, s 76(1B), as inserted by PPERA, s 132.

Undermining the Limits

Despite its grand objectives, the integrity of the legislation on candidates' spending limits was undermined for many years by parliamentary neglect. One problem was knowing what kind of expenditure was covered by the limits. True, the term 'election expenses' has always been defined in the Act, but the original draft was in the most circular terms to mean 'expenses incurred, whether before, during or after the election, on account of or in respect of the conduct or management of the election'.[11] Some guidance was provided by Schedule 3 of the Act which specified the information which had to be provided in the candidate's return of election expenses: if the matter had to be returned, it would not be difficult to argue that this was because it was presumed to arise in respect of the conduct or management of the election. But the list was said to be 'comically out of date',[12] having been re-enacted on several occasions since 1883 without being seriously revised. Admittedly the criticism seems harsh given that the Schedule called for information about printing, advertising and stationery, as well as the hiring of rooms, postage and miscellaneous matters. Nevertheless, it was the requirement to report expenditure on clerks and telegrams that gave the Schedule a distinctly Victorian smell. The same was true of the failure to address more contemporary campaign methods involving the use of such modern instruments as the motor car and the telephone, though these might well have been caught as miscellaneous matters.

The fact that the Act was badly out of date was not simply a matter of aesthetic concern. Whole areas of candidate expenditure were completely unregulated, as was revealed by the case of Fiona Jones, the Labour MP for Newark, who (together with her agent) was prosecuted after the 1997 general election for filing a false return and making a false declaration.[13] This was the first case of its kind in Great Britain since 1924, though there had been a case in Northern Ireland in 1993.[14] The complaint in the Fiona Jones case related principally to a failure to declare the cost of renting an office in the constituency during February and March 1997 before the election in May of that year, as well as the cost of compiling a voter database which had been produced by telephone canvassing conducted in 1996 and 1997. The conviction was overturned on both counts. Not only did the appeal court doubt whether the rental of the property before the latter part of March had to be disclosed as an election expense, there was no evidence of dishonest intent on the part of the candidate: under section 82 of the 1983 Act it is only an offence 'knowingly' to make a declaration 'falsely'. This was an area where there was a lot of confusion, said the court, not only about when an election was deemed to start for the purposes of section 76, but also about what items of expenditure should count towards election expenses and what

---

[11] *Ibid*, s 118.
[12] Fifth Report of the Committee on Standards in Public Life, above, para 10.12.
[13] *R v Jones* [1999] 2 Cr App R 253.
[14] *McCrory v Hendron* [1993] NI 177.

should not. The voter database was not an election expense, and although the candidate might be expected to be charged to use it during the election, there was no evidence to say that the charge of £100, which the defendants had put in the return for the use of the database, was too low.

Revising the Limits

Some of the problems identified in the *Jones* case are addressed by the amendments to the 1983 Act introduced by the PPERA and more recently by the Electoral Administration Act 2006. The amendments clarify matters in a number of respects. One important step is to identify clearly the trigger from which expenses begin to run. A new section 118A of the 1983 Act now provides that a person becomes a parliamentary candidate on the date of the dissolution of Parliament if he or she has already declared as a candidate. Otherwise the candidature commences from the date after dissolution when the nomination is made. In the Fiona Jones case, the candidature would be deemed under the new rules to have begun on 8 April 1997. The Prime Minister (Mr John Major) announced the date of the general election on 17 March 1997, Ms Jones was formally adopted as the Labour candidate on 19 March 1997, Parliament was dissolved on 8 April, and Mrs Jones was formally nominated on 14 April. It does not follow, however, that expenditure incurred before that date on items to be used during the election will not count as an election expense under the revised rules. Thus, the new definition of election expenses introduced by the 2006 Act applies to any item of expenditure 'which is used for the purposes of the candidate's election after the date when he becomes a candidate at the election'. And should there be any doubt, it is further provided that any reference to 'election expenses' includes expenses incurred 'before the date' when the individual becomes a candidate, but which 'fall to be regarded as election expenses'.

Greater clarity about what counts as an election expense was also provided by the new section 90A of the 1983 Act, and more recently by the Electoral Administration Act 2006. As a result of the 2006 amendments, election expenses are now defined to mean expenses on specified matters where these are incurred for the purposes of the candidate's election. The items in question are the costs of advertising, unsolicited material to electors, transport, public meetings, the services of an election agent or any other person, and accommodation and administration. But these combined changes will not necessarily affect the position in the *Jones* case where expenditure is incurred in the constituency before the date the meter starts to run for the spending limits, and the expenditure does not relate to materials to be consumed after the election is deemed to start. Some of the expenditure of this nature may be caught by the national spending limit on political parties which the PPERA introduced, to the extent that it is covered by Schedule 8 of that Act (which is considered below), but only if incurred by the local party rather than the candidate. But potential loopholes which have been closed relate to the provision of goods and services at less than their market value, and the secondment of staff to help in the campaign.[15] In the former case the candidate must regard the full market rate as an election expense, and in the latter case the salary costs of the seconded employee are to be treated as an election expense. However, volunteer labour in the volunteer's own time is not an election expense.

The Problem of Third Parties

As already suggested, one of the problems associated with limits on candidates is that these limits can be rendered pointless if other electoral actors are not also regulated. These other actors include interest groups, which may seek to influence the outcome of an election in a particular constituency, as part of a national co-ordinated campaign to secure the election of as many candidates of a particular party as possible. Trade unions might have an interest in promoting the election of Labour candidates, while the Countryside Alliance might have an interest in promoting the election of Conservative candidates. An election may also provide a platform for the national campaigns of groups concerned about single issues that cut across political parties and candidates. In these latter cases, the interest groups may wish to provide information about candidates to electors and may seek to promote the election of candidates of any party who are closest to their own positions on the political or ethical issue concerned. In addition to these national campaigns which spill into individual constituencies, there are also any number of local causes which could motivate local interest groups to intervene in an election: the closure of a hospital, the building of a new road, or even the financial plight of a local football team.

Restraining Local Expenditure by Third Parties

The response to this problem is to be found in the Representation of the People Act 1983, section 75, which contains a provision first introduced in 1918.[16] This imposes restrictions on third parties by providing that only candidates and their agents may incur or authorise expenses of the kind set out in the Act 'with a view to promoting or procuring the election of a candidate at an election'. The expenses to which the Act applies are those incurred by holding public meetings, issuing advertisements, circulars or publications, or 'otherwise presenting to the electors the candidate or his views or the extent or nature of his backing or

---

[15] Representation of the People Act 1983, ss 90A–C, as amended by the PPERA, s 134. Further amendments have been made and much greater clarity introduced by the Electoral Administration Act 2006, s 27, not yet implemented at the time of writing.

[16] Representation of the People Act 1918, s 34.

disparaging another candidate'. In the unlikely event of a candidate or agent authorising expenditure of this kind to be incurred by a third party, the expenditure in question counts towards the candidate's maximum permitted expenditure. An exception is made in the case of the last of the items of regulated expenditure referred to, which does not restrict the publication of material relating to the election in a newspaper or other periodical, or in a television or radio broadcast. This means that there is an exception for newspaper editorialising but not advertising, which would otherwise be caught by section 75. In these cases (newspaper editorialising), the authorisation of a candidate or agent is not required, and the expenditure does not count towards anyone's permitted maximum expenditure.

In this way, section 75 maintains a balance between protecting the integrity of the electoral process and the freedom of the press, though it is arguable that the balance tilts too heavily in the favour of the latter, to the extent that newspaper coverage is wholly unregulated. The result is that companies which own local newspapers have a potentially disproportionate influence that cannot be balanced even by advertising in the newspaper. The position of other non-candidate interests is very different, in the sense that a second exception to the restraints imposed by section 75 allowed individuals to spend up to 50p on the regulated expenditure without having the authority of a candidate or agent and without this counting towards a candidate's maximum permitted expenditure. But even in 1983, 50p did not go a long way (a first-class stamp cost 16p), particularly as it could not be 'incurred in pursuance of a plan suggested or concocted with others'.[17] So the individual or interest group could spend up to 50p on his or her own campaign to promote or procure the election of a candidate. The only surprise is that it took so long for the restriction to be challenged as violating the right to freedom of expression in Article 10 of the European Convention on Human Rights (ECHR). The fact that the 50p had been raised to £5 by the time the successful challenge took place in *Bowman v United Kingdom*[18] was hardly likely to make much difference to the outcome of the legal proceedings.

Relaxing the Restraint

Mrs Bowman had been prosecuted (but not convicted) for offences under section 75 of the 1983 Act. As the executive director of the Society for the Protection of the Unborn Child, she had distributed voter information leaflets to electors in Halifax during the general election in 1992, with details about the views of parliamentary candidates on abortion and human embryo experimentation. In upholding her complaint alleging a breach of Article 10 of the ECHR, the European Court of Human Rights (by a majority) had no hesitation in saying that section 75 of the 1983 Act 'amounted to a restriction on freedom of expression'.

---

[17] Representation of the People Act 1983, s 75 (1)(c)(ii).
[18] (1998) 26 EHRR 1.

That, however, does not end the matter, for not all restrictions on free speech are prohibited, with the Convention permitting restraints if they are 'prescribed by law' and are 'necessary in a democratic society' on a number of grounds listed in Article 10(2). These include the protection of the rights and freedoms of others, and on this point, the government's case seemed very strong, it having been submitted that

> the spending limits in section 75 of the 1983 Act pursued that aim of protecting the rights of others in three ways. First, it promoted fairness between competing candidates for election by preventing wealthy third parties from campaigning for or against a particular candidate or issuing material which necessitated the devotion of part of a candidate's election budget, which was limited by law, to a response. Secondly, the restriction on third-party expenditure helped to ensure that candidates remained independent of the influence of powerful interest groups. Thirdly, it prevented the political debate at election times from being distorted by having the discussion shifted away from matters of general concern to centre on single issues.[19]

The Court accepted that these powerful arguments pointed to a legitimate aim of the legislation, but a majority concluded nevertheless that the legislative provisions could not be justified as being 'necessary in a democratic society', and that a restriction of £5 was disproportionate to the aim of achieving equality between candidates.

The government responded to *Bowman* by bringing forward an amendment to section 75 of the 1983 Act.[20] It is now possible for individuals and interest groups to spend up to £500 promoting or procuring the election of a candidate without the need for approval by the candidate or his or her agent. No one knows whether the £500 is higher than required to meet the requirements of the *Bowman* judgment, or too low. It is based on the recommendations of the Neill Committee which was concerned that if the limit was set too high, third parties cumulatively 'could spend a significant proportion of the candidate's own spending limit of [what was then] around £8,000'. The Committee was also concerned, as was argued in *Bowman*, that a candidate could be forced to devote part of his or her limited resources to 'rebutting the attacks made by the third parties'.[21] The figure of £500 was proposed by the Committee on the ground that it 'would provide an allowance sufficient to cover, for example, the production and distribution of a leaflet throughout a constituency or the publication of an advertisement in a local newspaper'.[22] But this does not wholly meet the concerns of some candidates who may have to hold back limited resources in order to respond to attacks from interest groups (which must still be uncoordinated) in the closing stages of a campaign. Nor are there any restrictions on third-party

---

[19] *Ibid*, at p 16.
[20] PPERA, s 131. Further amendments were made by the Electoral Administration Act 2006, s 25, though these do not affect the substance of the law.
[21] Fifth Report of the Committee on Standards in Public Life, above, para 10.62.
[22] *Ibid*, para 10.64.

expenditure before someone formally becomes a candidate at the election, that is to say before the dissolution.

Spending Limits on Political Parties

One of the most innovative features of the PPERA is the extension of expenditure limits to apply to the national election expenditures of the political parties. The provisions of the Representation of the People Act 1983 applied only to candidate spending, but not also to national party spending. This extension of the law follows the recommendation of the Neill Committee, which proposed party spending limits for a number of reasons, though – as we saw in chapter one – not all of the members of the Committee 'were as persuaded as some of [their] witnesses were by the "equality" or "level playing field" argument'.[23] It seems that the Committee was driven principally by concerns about the acceleration of campaign spending by the parties, and a worry that this brought with it 'the need to raise even larger sums to pay for the spending'. According to the Committee, 'limits on campaign spending are necessary to prevent undue concentration on fund raising'.[24] The Neill Commitee thus appears to have adopted what might be described as an anti-corruption rather than an equality rationale for spending limits. This is despite the fact that it is the latter that has been accepted by the courts both in Britain and Canada,[25] and the former that has been rejected by the courts in the United States, which also rejected equality arguments.[26]

Campaign Expenditure

The PPERA applies to 'campaign expenditure',[27] defined as expenditure listed in Schedule 8 of the Act which is incurred for 'election purposes'.[28] It also applies to what is called 'notional expenditure', which is expenditure on regulated matters incurred by others on behalf of the party. Schedule 8 applies to eight listed items, and was drafted in consultation with representatives of the parties, as the Neill Committee proposed. The items in question are as follows: (1) party political broadcasts, (2) advertising, (3) unsolicited material addressed to electors, such as leaflets and handbills, (4) any manifesto or other document setting out the party's policies, (5) market research or canvassing 'conducted for the purpose of ascertaining polling intentions', (6) the provision of any services or facilities in connection with press conferences or other dealings with the media, (7) the

---

[23] *Ibid*, para 10.28.
[24] *Ibid*, para 10.29.
[25] *R v Jones* [1999] 2 Cr App R 253 and *Libman v Quebec* (1998) 151 DLR (4th) 385.
[26] *Buckley v Valeo*, 424 US 1 (1976), at pp 55–57.
[27] PPERA, s 72.
[28] *Ibid*, s 72(2).

transport of people (such as the party leaders) to any place or places 'with a view to obtaining publicity in connection with an election campaign', and (8) rallies and public meetings organised to obtain publicity in connection with an election campaign. In many cases, the Schedule indicates in greater detail the type of activity that falls within the scope of these different items. So, for example, the first includes the expenses incurred in respect of these broadcasts, such as agency fees, design costs, and other costs incurred in preparing or producing the broadcasts; the second and third include costs 'in connection with preparing, producing, distributing or otherwise disseminating such advertising'; and the last includes the costs of hiring premises for the event.

There are a number of important exclusions in Schedule 8, so that expenditure that might otherwise fall within the above list of matters is exempt, and does not count as part of a party's election expenses. These include party newsletters which are designed to inform the electors in a particular electoral area about the opinions or activities of their elected representatives or existing or prospective candidates. It does not follow, however, that such expenditure will be unregulated, for if incurred during the period when the candidates' spending limit is active, it could be caught by the limits on candidates' expenses already considered.[29] The exclusions also apply to unsolicited material addressed to party members, which would cover party newspapers and magazines, as well as other material directed specifically at the election. A third exemption applies to property, services or facilities made available to a party from public funds. But although these are important exclusions, they are eclipsed in significance by another, which applies to expenses incurred in respect of the remuneration or allowances payable to any member of the staff of the party, whether permanent or temporary. This is important because it means not only that the cost of existing staff does not count towards the total spending limit, but also that the cost of hiring staff to work on the election does not count either. There is also an exception for the personal expenses (including travel) of 'an individual' where these are met from his or her own resources and are not reimbursed.

'Election Purpose' and 'Notional Expenditure

Schedule 8 expenses must be incurred for election purposes in order to fall within the scope of the Act.[30] So any expenditure that is not for an election purpose is not covered, and may be incurred without restraint. An 'election purpose' is defined to mean for the purpose of 'or in connection with' promoting or procuring electoral success for the party at an election. By this is meant the return of candidates standing in the name of the party, or included in the list of candidates submitted by the party.[31] Otherwise, an election purpose means

---

[29] See pp 145–148 above.
[30] PPERA, s 72(2).
[31] *Ibid*, s 72(4)(a).

enhancing the standing of the party or its candidates with the electorate 'in connection with future relevant elections (whether imminent or otherwise)'.[32] The Act also makes clear that negative campaigning against one party may constitute promoting, procuring or enhancing another party,[33] and that an expenditure may fall within the definition even though there is no express mention of a party or candidates.[34] Unlike the Representation of the People Act 1983, the term 'candidates' is widely defined to include 'future candidates, whether identifiable or not'.[35] So a leaflet which said 'vote for our candidate', before Parliament was dissolved or before a candidate was selected, would be a campaign expenditure under PPERA, but not an election expense under the Representation of the People Act 1983. This is important because it means that campaigning by constituency parties in the 365 days before the election may involve conduct to which the national limits apply, even though the limits on the candidate himself or herself have not yet been activated.

Other possible loopholes are addressed by the concept of 'notional expenditure'.[36] This arises where goods, services or facilities are provided to a party at less than their true commercial value. This could be the use of premises, cars or other transport, printing or copying facilities, accounting or legal services, or a phone bank and the staff to operate it. Under the Act this all counts as an expenditure by the party, where it is provided at a discount of more than 10 per cent of the market rate. In the case of staff seconded to a party, the commercial rate is treated as being 'the amount of the remuneration or allowances payable to the employee by his employer in respect of the period for which his services are made available'.[37] But not all notional expenditure is to be regarded as a campaign expenditure by a party: it applies only to goods, services or facilities which if actually incurred by the party would be campaign expenditure for the purposes of the Act.[38] So if staff are seconded to a party, the cost will only count as a campaign expenditure if they are engaged on work which falls within Schedule 8 of the Act. Indeed it is open to question whether staff seconded to a political party can ever be regarded as a campaign expense, notional or otherwise. This is because under Schedule 8 staff costs are expressly stated not to be campaign expenses, leading to the question of just precisely what the inclusion of staff costs in the definition of notional expenditure is designed to cover. The Electoral Commission takes the view, however, that seconded staff must be accounted for, as must agency staff (but not directly employed temporary staff).[39]

---

[32] *Ibid*, s 72(4)(b).
[33] *Ibid*, s 72(5)(a).
[34] *Ibid*, s 72(5)(b).
[35] *Ibid*, s 72(9).
[36] *Ibid*, s 73.
[37] *Ibid*, s 73(5).
[38] *Ibid*, s 73(1)(b)
[39] Electoral Commission, *Campaign Expenditure: Guidance for Political Parties* (2004), p 11.

Calculating and Enforcing the Limit

In these ways, the legislation adopts a relatively narrow definition of campaign expenditure, which is confined mainly to the different forms of direct contact between the parties and the electorate. Campaign expenditure is widely defined in this narrow area (to include assistance in kind), but there are a number of excluded expenditures, emphasising that considerable sums of money can be spent on a campaign without it having to be recorded as a campaign expense, or without it counting towards the maximum expenditure permitted by the Act. This is one of the United Kingdom's soft money loopholes, in the sense that the parties are free to spend on infrastructure and staff without this being fully covered by the legislation. In terms of how much campaign expenditure the parties may incur, the amount is based on the number of candidates a party presents for election. But it is important to make clear that the money which may be spent by the party is additional to the amount which may be spent by each of its candidates.[40] The limits applicable to parties and candidates are calculated in different ways: while the amount the parties may spend depends on the number of candidates it fields in the election, the limit on candidates depends on the number of voters in the constituency contested by the candidate.

Limits on Campaign Expenditure

The limits on campaign spending by a political party are set out in some detail in Schedule 9 of the PPERA, where different limits are set for different elections (parliamentary, European Parliament, Scottish Parliament, Welsh Assembly and Northern Ireland Assembly). Special provisions are also made where more than one election takes place at the same time. But to take the straightforward case of a parliamentary election, the position here is that the maximum permitted campaign expenditure is determined by the number of seats that the party contests. So the maximum permitted expenditure of the large national parties is greater than that of small parties contesting only a few seats, whether in a particular locality or peppered throughout the country. Under the Act, the maximum amount of campaign expenditure is based on a formula of £30,000 multiplied by the number of seats that the party contests. In the case of the large parties, this gives a sum of £18,810,000, if they contest every constituency (excluding the Speaker's) in England, Scotland and Wales.[41] At the general election in 2001 (the first under this new regime) the amount of permitted expenditure was less, being closer to £15m, with parties permitted to spend up to £24,000 multiplied by the number of seats their candidates were contesting. That is to say, the parties were

---

[40] PPERA, s 72(7): campaign expenditure does not include anything that falls to be included in the election expenses return of a candidate at an election.

[41] All parties are permitted to spend up to £1m regardless of the number of candidates they field.

permitted to spend up to this amount in the period between the day the relevant parts of the Act were brought into force (16 February 2001) and polling day (7 June 2001).[42] In fact, the spending of the two main parties was well within the limit, as we shall consider below. But there was no regulation of what they may have spent before the Act came into force, following the principle that legislation bearing criminal penalties should not normally be retrospective.

This limit on expenditure by registered parties applies during what the Act refers to as the 'relevant period'.[43] The relevant period is defined to mean the period of 365 days before polling day, which is much different from the formula used to determine when the spending limits for candidates begin to take effect.[44] It is also different from the position in Canada where the national spending limits apply only in the period between the issue of the writ and polling day.[45] The 365-day period is a recognition of the fact that the campaign starts before the election is announced; but it also creates uncertainty for political parties which must exercise care that any expenditure incurred in the closing years of a Parliament does not inadvertently have to be drawn from their campaign budget. Indeed, it may be argued that these arrangements give the governing party an important strategic advantage in a system where there are no fixed parliamentary terms. This is because only the Prime Minister will know when the election is likely to be called, with the result that the governing party will be able to plan its strategy and budget accordingly. But on the other hand, events may conspire to frustrate even the best-laid plans, as in 2001 when the government's preferred date for the election had to be postponed because of the foot-and-mouth epidemic that swept across the country. It may indeed be the case that any perceived advantage of the governing party is exaggerated. Election dates are usually fairly predictable, and an unpredicted election date may be as big a surprise to the governing party as to the opposition.

Strategies for Compliance with the Limits

It is one thing to set limits, but something else to enforce them. Apart from any other consideration, what can be the sanction if there is proof of overspending? In the case of the candidate who overspends, it is possible to annul that particular election and have it re-run.[46] But in the case of over-spending by a party, it is thought impossible to have the general election result invalidated.[47] The solution settled upon in the PPERA is to impose criminal penalties on party officials and

[42] See SI 2001 No 222.
[43] PPERA, Sch 9, para 3(7).
[44] Representation of the People Act 1983, s 118A, as inserted by the PPERA, s 135.
[45] Canada Elections Act 2000, s 2.
[46] See Representation of the People Act 1983, ss 160, 164, 173 for the circumstances in which an election may be rendered void.
[47] See the exchange in the course of the Labour Party's oral evidence to the Neill Committee in 1998: Cm 4057–II, paras 1039–48. See also Neill Committee Report, above, at para 10.123.

on the party itself in the event of a conviction for overspending.[48] But the Act also provides that no campaign expenditure is to be incurred by or on behalf of a registered party unless incurred by the treasurer or deputy treasurer or a person authorised by the treasurer.[49] These are also the only people who may make a payment for a campaign expenditure, and any payment over £200 must be supported by an invoice or a receipt.[50] It is further provided that all claims for payment must be made within twenty-one days of the end of the campaign period, and must be paid within forty-two days.[51] All of these restraints are supported by criminal sanctions: it is an offence for anyone other than those specified to incur an expenditure or make a payment, or for anyone to make a payment outside the permitted time without the leave of a High Court or county court judge.[52]

Apart from these controls on who may incur an expense and the time when expenses must be paid, there are obligations on party treasurers to submit a return of campaign expenditure after the election.[53] Similar obligations have existed for parliamentary candidates for many years, though it is likely that the party returns will be pored over more carefully than those of the candidates in each of the 646 parliamentary constituencies, and indeed the national newspapers on 25 April 2006 were full of detail about the parties' 2005 election returns which had been released the previous day. The return by the party treasurer must contain a statement of payments made in respect of campaign expenditure,[54] and where the party has spent more than £250,000 the return must be accompanied by an auditor's report, the auditor to be appointed under regulations approved by the Electoral Commission.[55] In the case of the large parties (those spending more than £250,000), the return must be submitted within six months of the end of the campaign period, and in the case of the other parties it must be submitted within three months. The party treasurer must take personal responsibility for the return, and must sign a declaration that it is 'a complete and correct return as required by law'.[56] It is an offence to make a false declaration,[57] and any return submitted to the Commission must be made available by the Commission for public inspection for at least two years.[58]

---

[48] PPERA, s 79.
[49] *Ibid*, s 75.
[50] *Ibid*, s 76(2).
[51] *Ibid*, s 77(1) and (2).
[52] *Ibid*, s 77(4). In Scotland the application is to the Court of Session or the sheriff court.
[53] *Ibid*, s 80.
[54] *Ibid*, s 80(3). It must also be accompanied by invoices: s 80(4).
[55] *Ibid*, s 81.
[56] *Ibid*, s 83(2)(b)(i).
[57] *Ibid*, s 83(3).
[58] *Ibid*, s 84.

Spending Limits and Third Parties

One of the problems of spending limits already identified in relation to the candidate limits in the Representation of the People Act 1983 is the position of third parties. As considered earlier this chapter, there is little point in seeking to control spending by parties if there are no limits on other electoral participants. It would be an easy way to evade or undermine the limits if restricted spending by political parties could be accompanied by a cacophony of noise from unregulated interest groups. It is true that third-party spending has not been a major feature of British elections to date, though we should not underestimate the extent to which it has occurred, or underestimate the extent to which it may occur. Although there has not been an active or vibrant third-party competition in the past, there have been elections in which there has been a keen presence by specific third-party interests. Different third parties have been concerned at different times about particular aspects of policy of one or other of the parties, and as a result have sometimes been prepared to spend considerable sums of money. The most notorious of these examples is the general election of 1959 when the iron and steel companies outspent all the political parties in their campaign of opposition to their nationalisation proposed by the Labour Party,[59] which proceeded to suffer a third successive electoral defeat.

Controlled Expenditure

The PPERA deals with third parties by regulating what is described as 'controlled expenditure'.[60] A third party for this purpose is any body or person other than a registered party.[61] This would include trade unions, companies and single-issue interest groups such as the Countryside Alliance, the Society for the Protection of the Unborn Child, and the organisations that emerged to campaign for and against the single European currency. Controlled expenditure in turn means 'expenses incurred by or on behalf of the third party in connection with the production or publication of election material which is made available to the public at large or any section of the public (in whatever form and by whatever means)'.[62] So there are two major qualifications here: controlled expenditure applies only to 'election material', and only to election material that is addressed to the public. So far as the former is concerned, election material includes material that 'can reasonably be regarded as intended to promote or procure electoral success for one or more parties or candidates', or otherwise enhance the standing of any particular parties or candidates with the electorate in connection with

---

[59] See D Butler and R Rose, *The British General Election of 1959* (1960), pp 252–253.
[60] PPERA, s 85.
[61] *Ibid*, s 85(8).
[62] *Ibid*, s 85(2).

future elections (whether imminent or otherwise).[63] The width of this definition is underlined by the fact that such material can be election material even though it can reasonably be regarded as being intended to achieve other purposes as well, by the fact that it applies to negative campaigning material in addition to that expressly promoting a party or candidate, and by the fact that the material need not expressly mention the name of any party or candidate.[64] Yet although the scope of the restriction is thus widely defined, there are a number of important loopholes and exceptions, ensuring that this width may be circumvented.

Two such loopholes or exemptions may be noted here. The first relates to the absence of any definition in the Act of 'the public' or 'a section of the public' for the purposes of section 85 above. The question arising here is whether communications between a third party and its members fall within the definition of controlled expenditure, or whether they are exempt because a restricted circulation is not to the public or a section thereof. That is to say, newspapers or circulars published by a body such as a trade union or a company or an NGO advising its members to vote for a particular party or against another. The Act is surprisingly silent on this, though it does make clear that communications between a political party and its members do not fall within the definition of campaign expenditure as it applies to political parties. In the absence of a similar provision relating to third parties (such as trade unions), the Electoral Commission has taken the view that such communications do not fall within the statutory definition of controlled expenditure, which means as a result that the control on third-party spending applies only to their external communications.[65] In addition to the foregoing, the other notable loophole or exemption is the publication of anything – other than an advertisement – in a newspaper or periodical or a broadcast on BBC or commercial television or radio. Although in some respects quite unexceptional, this is another extremely generous exemption for the corporate press. So if the *Sun* carries a front page imploring its readers to vote Conservative because Mr Murdoch thinks that this will best serve his commercial interests, there is no offence. Yet while the newspaper proprietors can spend an unlimited sum at an election in the editorial columns and front pages of their newspapers promoting or opposing a particular party or candidate, there are financial limits that apply to others, including those who advertise in the same newspapers.

Spending Limits

Third parties are subject to limits on the amount they may spend in an election. All third parties can spend £10,000 in England and £5,000 for each of Scotland,

---

[63] *Ibid*, s 85(3).

[64] *Ibid*, s 85(4). For a critique of this provision on the ground that it is too wide, see C Feasby, 'Issue Advocacy and Third Parties in the United Kingdom and Canada' (2003) 48 *McGill L J* 11.

[65] Electoral Commission, *Guidance for Recognised Third Parties: Controlled Expenditure and Donations* (2004), p 21.

Wales and Northern Ireland.[66] If a third party wants to spend more than this, it must become a recognised third party, which means in effect that it must register with the Electoral Commission.[67] Once recognised, there is no obligation to spend more (and some do not), though the various financial accountability procedures discussed below will nevertheless apply. On becoming recognised, however, a third party may spend in the relevant period £793,500 in England, £108,000 in Scotland, £60,000 in Wales and £27,000 in Northern Ireland.[68] As in the case of party campaign expenditure, the relevant period is the period of 365 days before polling day, which means that recognised third parties are subject to the same uncertainties as the political parties. Crucially, only UK electors or organisations can become recognised third parties, and in the latter case this means only those organisations which may make donations to political parties.[69] Recognised third parties thus may be companies, trade unions, building societies, partnerships, friendly societies, or unincorporated associations, provided in each case they are registered or have their principal business in the United Kingdom. Curiously, only 'listed' trade unions may become recognised third parties: this covers all the individual unions, but it does not include the TUC, which could not lawfully repeat the campaign it undertook at the time of the 1997 general election to raise awareness about workers' rights (even though it did not directly or expressly urge the electors to vote one way of the other). But there is no legal objection to the TUC becoming listed with the Certification Officer for Trade Unions and Employers' Associations.

The Electoral Commission maintains a published register of recognised third parties. Entry on the register must be renewed annually, and at the time of writing there are only nine organisations on the register, of which four are trade unions. Apart from the spending limits, there are a number of other financial controls that apply to recognised third parties. Reflecting similar controls on the political parties, expenditure by a recognised third party can be incurred only by a 'responsible person'.[70] At the time the third party registers with the Commission, it must notify the Commission of the name of the person who will be 'responsible' for compliance with the Act on behalf of the body in question.[71] Claims for payment must be submitted to the responsible person within twenty-one days of the end of the campaign period, and must be paid within forty-two days of the end of the same period, subject to the power of the courts to authorise late payment.[72] After the election, a recognised third party is required to submit an election return to the Electoral Commission. The return should include a statement of all payments, as well as a statement of 'relevant

---

[66] PPERA, s 94(3)–(5).
[67] *Ibid*, s 88.
[68] *Ibid*, Sch 10, para 3.
[69] *Ibid*, s 88(2).
[70] *Ibid*, s 90.
[71] *Ibid*, s 88(3)(c)(ii).
[72] *Ibid*, s 92.

donations received by the third party in respect of the relevant election'.[73] A relevant donation is one that has been given 'for the purpose of meeting controlled expenditure incurred by or on behalf of that third party'.[74] (There are restraints on who may donate to a recognised third party, similar to the restraints on who may give to political parties.[75]) In some cases (where the controlled expenditure exceeds £250,000), the election return must be professionally audited,[76] and in all cases the returns must be submitted to the Commission. Where the accounts are to be audited the return must be submitted within six months of the election, but in other cases within three months.[77]

Spending Limits in Practice – The First Cycle

These measures relating to political party and third party spending came into force on 16 February 2001. This means that they have been in force through a full parliamentary cycle which has seen elections to the European Parliament, the Scottish Parliament and Welsh Assembly, as well as local authorities. The initial impression from the 2001 general election and these subsequent elections is that the Act had little regulatory impact, as the parties appeared to be spending much less than the law permitted, perhaps suggesting that the spending limits had been set too high. So far as candidates are concerned, the Electoral Commission has calculated that at the general election in 2001, the average amount spent per candidate was £3,581, and that only 21 per cent of all candidates spent more than 80 per cent of the permitted maximum, while more than half (53 per cent) spent less than 30 per cent of their permitted expenditure. Predictably, candidates representing the larger parties spent more than those representing smaller parties, with Conservative and Labour candidates in particular being more likely to spend closer to the legal maximum. But even so, only 37 per cent of Conservative and only 23 per cent of Labour candidates spent more than 90 per cent the permitted maximum (compared to 9 per cent of Liberal Democrats), while only 70 per cent of Conservatives and 68 per cent of Labour candidates spent more than 50 per cent of the maximum permitted. Low levels of expenditure were also recorded for the elections to the Scottish Parliament and Welsh Assembly in 2003: only 9 per cent and 13 per cent of candidates respectively spent more than 80 per cent of what was permitted; in the case of the Scottish Parliament elections only 25 per cent of candidates spent more than half of what they were entitled to spend.[78]

[73] *Ibid*, s 96(2).

[74] *Ibid*, Sch 11, para 1(4).

[75] *Ibid*, s 95 and Sch 11. Relevant donations may only be accepted from permissible donor, as defined by s 54(2). See ch 5 above,

[76] *Ibid*, s 97.

[77] *Ibid*, s 98.

[78] Electoral Commission, *The Funding of Political Parties* (2004), pp 55–57.

Political Parties

The difference between what could be spent and what was spent was more clearly illustrated by the election spending of the political parties. In none of the elections between 2001 and 2005 (the general election of 2001, the Scottish Parliament and Welsh Assembly elections in 2003, and the European Parliament election in 2004) did the parties spend anywhere near the maximum permitted. Table 7.1 shows that at the general election in 2001, the Conservative Party was the largest spender at £12.75m, but this accounted for only 83 per cent of the maximum permitted. This compared with Labour's £10.94m which amounted to 71 per cent of the maximum permitted. None of the other parties spent more than 13 per cent of their maximum permitted expenditure: the SNP managed 13 per cent, Plaid Cymru 9 per cent and the Liberal Democrats 9 per cent. Indeed the six UK parties that won seats at the election (the foregoing plus Independent Kidderminster Hospital and Health Concern) were entitled to spend £48,774,000, but managed to spend only £25,371,633, that is to say only 52 per cent of what was permitted. There was also expenditure by thirteen parties in Northern Ireland, though much of this was modest, the biggest spenders being the Ulster Unionists (£167,495) and the SDLP (£155,565).

The difference between what the parties could spend and what they did spend is more marked still in the three elections that took place after the general election in 2001. In the election for the Scottish Parliament in 2003, Labour incurred the highest expenditure at £726,702, followed by the SNP (£473,107), the Conservatives (£323,279), the Liberal Democrats (£130,360), the Scottish Socialist Party (£74,362), the Scottish Green Party (£63,864) and the Scottish Senior Citizens' Unity Party (£3,672). All of these parties won seats at the election,

Table 7.1 Political party expenditure at the general election 2001

(1) Name of political party	(2) Campaign expenditure limit (£)	(3) Campaign expenditure incurred (£)	(4) Per cent of limit incurred
Conservative and Unionist Party	15,360,000	12,751,813	83
Labour Party	15,360,000	10,945,119	71
Liberal Democrats	15,336,000	1,361,377	9
Scottish National Party	1,728,000	226,203	13
Plaid Cymru	960,000	87,121	9
Independent Kidderminster HHC	30,000	0	0
Total	48,774,000	25,371,633	52

Source: Electoral Commission.

despite spending only 48 per cent, 31 per cent, 21 per cent, 8.5 per cent, 4 per cent, 10 per cent, and 1 per cent respectively of their permitted maximum. Total permitted expenditure by these parties was £8.4m in total, whereas total actual expenditure was £1.7m, the latter representing only 21.4 per cent of the former. The experience of the Welsh Assembly election held on the same day is much the same. Here again Labour incurred the largest expenditure of £265,009, followed by the Liberal Democrats (£249,339), the Conservatives (£80,716), Plaid Cymru (£72,976) and the John Marek Independent Party (subsequently Forward Wales) (£9,633). Again, all of these parties won seats at the election, spending respectively only 44 per cent, 42 per cent, 13 per cent, 12 per cent and 16 per cent of their permitted maximum. The total permitted expenditure of these five parties was £2.4m, whereas the actual expenditure was only £677,673, the latter representing only 27.5 per cent of the former.

Third Parties

At the general election in 2001, the spending limits had been in force for less than four months before the election. As a result, the amount that recognised third parties were permitted to spend in this period was reduced from the full amount that would have applied had the Act been in force for a full year before the election date. They were permitted to spend £634,800 in England, £86,400 in Scotland and £48,000 in Wales. But there was no regulation of how much the third parties could spend before 16 February 2001 (the commencement date).[79] There was only one recognised third party for which this would operate as a restraint on spending, namely UNISON, which spent £774,796 (including £19,422 spent in Northern Ireland). As shown by Table 7.2, no other recognised third party spent more than Charter 88's £180,868, with the Yes Campaign Ltd spending only £185. UNISON spending can be accounted for the fact that uniquely among trade unions, it has two political funds, the Affiliated Political Fund which is used for Labour Party activities (including donations), and the General Political Fund which is used for independent campaigning. The existence of the two funds came about because UNISON is a merger of three unions: NUPE and COHSE had been affiliated to the Labour Party, and NALGO had had a political fund which it used for general political purposes. UNISON was thus the only third party to spend more than £250,000, the point at which, as we have seen, audited accounts must be provided under the Act. The combined expenditure of the other eight third parties was only £398,681, about half the expenditure of UNISON.

As in the case of political party spending, recognised third-party spending was also fairly light at the Scottish Parliament, Welsh Assembly and European Parliament elections in 2003 and 2004. At the Scottish Parliament election on

---

[79] See SI 2001 No 222.

Table 7.2 Third Party expenditure at the general election 2001

Name of recognised third party	Total controlled expenditure (£)
Charter 88	180,868
Campaign for an Independent Britain	1,694
Democracy Movement	104,128
Manufacturing, Science & Finance Union	4,726
Tacticalvoter.Net Ltd	4,615.75
The South Molton Declaration	18,185
UNISON	774,796
Union of Shop, Distributive and Allied Workers (USDAW)	84,280
Yes Campaign Ltd	185
Total	1,173,477.75

Source: Electoral Commission.

1 May 2003, there were only two third parties reporting controlled expenditure, namely UNISON and USDAW (both trade unions), these spending £55,973 and £2,478 respectively. At the Welsh Assembly election on the same day, the same two trade unions were two of the only three recognised third parties incurring controlled expenditure, this time £24,263 and £1,457 respectively. The other third party in the Welsh Assembly election was the Society for the Protection of the Unborn Child, which spent only £233. UNISON again incurred the largest third-party expenditure at the European Parliament election held on 10 June 2004, on this occasion recording £167,704. The only other two recognised third parties reporting controlled expenditure at this election were anti-racist groups, namely Unite against Fascism (£62,923) and Searchlight (£78,774), the former receiving two donations from trade unions (£13,500 from the Communication Workers Union and £8,500 from the Transport and General Workers' Union).

The General Election 2005

The main point to emerge for the first cycle of spending regulation is that the legislation appeared to have little regulatory impact, with the spending limits set at a level which the political parties could not reach. The experience of the 2005 general election, however, suggests that there is now a different story to tell. Although there is no evidence to suggest any significant change in the levels of spending by candidates, there is evidence to suggest higher levels of spending by both the national parties. As a result, initial assessments about the impact of the legislation may have to be revised. Rather than impose a restraint on the parties, the legislation may have imposed a target level of spending which the parties felt they had to reach for competitive reasons, which in turn led to new ways of funding the expense as traditional methods (large donations) were unavailable. The need for money and the reluctance of donors in an era of transparency appears to have thrown the parties in the direction of lenders. The other development noted in the 2005 election is the 'bulking up' of spending at local level, not by candidates but by local parties. This is a development most notable in the case of the Conservative Party, a development reflected in the annual accounts of local associations published on the Electoral Commission website. These refer to the local parties having been engaged in a 'two year campaign', which had a 'very high profile', and which in one case was acknowledged to have led to an increase in expenditure of 50 per cent on the previous year (2004).

Political Parties and Third Parties

A striking feature of the 2005 general election – as shown in Table 7.3 – is that for the first time ever, the Labour Party was the highest-spending party in terms of national spending, and that for the first time ever it spent more than the Conservative Party. As we shall see, however, this may not tell the whole story, as there was significant spending by the Conservatives locally. A second striking feature of

Table 7.3 Political party expenditure at the general election 2005

(1) Name of political party	(2) Campaign expenditure limit (£)	(3) Campaign expenditure incurred (£)	(4) Per cent of limit incurred
Conservative and Unionist Party	18,810,000	17,852,240	94.9
Labour Party	18,810,000	17,939,617	95.3
Liberal Democrats	18,780,000	4,324,574	23
Scottish National Party	1,770,000	193,987	10.9
Plaid Cymru	1,200,000	38,879	3.1
Respect – The Unity Coalition	780,000	320,716	41
Independent Kidderminster HHC	30,000	1,756	3.3
Total	60,180,00	40,671,769	67.5

Note: Expenditure of over £100,000 was also recorded by three parties that contested the election but did not win any seats: UKIP ((£648,397) (496 seats contested), the Green Party (£160,224) (183 seats contested) and the BNP (£112,068) (118 seats contested).
Source: Electoral Commission.

the 2005 general election is that the spending levels of the two parties increased, and did so quite dramatically in the case of the Labour Party. It should be pointed out, however, that comparisons between 2001 and 2005 are to be treated with caution in view of the fact that the 2001 figures apply only from the commencement of the Act on 16 February 2001 to the election on 7 June 2001, whereas the 2005 figures apply to the full period of 365 days before the election. Nevertheless, the comparisons are not without validity, as most spending is likely

Table 7.4 Third-party expenditure at the general election 2005

Name of recognised third party	Total controlled expenditure (£)
Amicus	656.00
British Declaration of Independence	12,775.98
Campaign for an Independent Britain	225.00
Community	20,662.65
Conservative Rural Action Group	550,370.00
Evershed, Patrick	48,546.99
Gilpin, Mr Zaccheus	405.00
GMB	53,164.00
Howard's End Ltd	8,400.00
League Against Cruel Sports Ltd	20,943.00
Musicians' Union	0.00
Muslims Friends of Labour	21,449.65
National Autistic Society [The]	15,099.00
Searchlight Information Services	42,761.00
Society for Protection of the Unborn Child	3,362.00
TMVO Ltd	24,157.00
Transport & General Workers' Union	20,128.00
Transport Salaried Staffs' Association	9,255.00
Uncaged Campaigns Ltd	12,051.00
Unite Against Fascism	20,343.00
Union of Shop, Distributive & Allied Workers	71,810.62
UNISON	682,115.00
Vote-OK	36,207.00
Waging Peace	30,340.00
Working Hounds Defence Campaign	470.00
Total	1,705,696

Source: Electoral Commission.

to be incurred in the period closer to the election. The third – and perhaps the most – striking feature of the 2005 election is the extent to which spending by the parties is now much closer to the limit, with Labour Party and Conservative Party spending 95.3 per cent and 94.9 per cent respectively of what is permitted. Although a long way behind, even the Liberal Democrats significantly increased the level of their permitted spending to 23 per cent. There are, however, exceptions, with the nationalist parties spending less in 2005 than in 2001.

Turning to third-party spending, Table 7.4 reveals evidence of rising levels of activity here as well, there being three times as many recognised third parties at the 2005 general election than at the general election in 2001. However, recognised third-party spending remains very modest, with only two organisations (Conservative Rural Action Group and UNISON) each spending more than £500,000, with the highest being UNISON's £682,115 (less than what the same organisation spent in 2001). Although UNISON is still the highest spender, it did not dominate third-party spending in the way that it did in 2001 when its £774,796 alone accounted for two-thirds of all third-party spending. A striking feature of the recognised third-party spending at the 2005 general election (and at all the other elections since 2001) continues to be the absence of any significant business presence, with recognised third parties being mainly trade unions, and single-issue groups such as those concerned with animal welfare, voting reform, hunting and racism. The main business intervention in elections (by means of the privately owned press) is – as we have seen – exempt from the legislation. There are no reported donations by companies (other than the Joseph Rowntree Trust) to recognised third parties, and the four large donations to the Conservative Rural Action Group were each from individuals. Trade unions, in contrast, donated to two recognised third parties, namely Searchlight and to Unite against Fascism, with UNISON's donation of £19,500 to the former being the largest of five trade union donations to these two organisations.

A Spending Loophole?

Apart from the rising levels of national party spending, the other feature of the 2005 general election already indicated was the apparent channelling of money on a large scale by donors to Conservative Associations to spend at local level. This came to light officially in a report of the Parliamentary Commissioner for Standards published in July 2005. The Commissioner had conducted an investigation into a failure by two Conservative MPs to report payments received by their Constituency Associations from Bearwood Corporate Services Ltd, a company associated with Lord Ashcroft which we encountered in chapter 5. In the course of correspondence with the Commissioner, one of the MPs in question revealed that in 2004 he 'became aware that Lord Ashcroft was making donations to Conservative Associations in marginal seats'. Thinking that his Association might qualify, the MP in question contacted Lord Ashcroft who indicated that he would 'match' any funds raised by Association 'and spent on campaigning pound for pound up to a maximum of £10,000'. In fact, the Electoral Commission reveals that sixty-three Conservative Associations benefited from donations from Bearwood Corporate Services Ltd between April 2004 and the end of May 2005. The amounts varied from Conservative Association to Conservative Association, from £1,020 to Ilford South on the one hand, to £42,333 to Hammersmith and Fulham on the other. Of these sixty-three donations, twenty-two were for £5,000 or less; sixteen were between £5,001 and £10,000, nineteen were between £10,001 and £20,000, four were between £20,001 and £30,000, and two were in excess of £30,001. But it was not only Bearwood Corporate Services Ltd that was providing money in this way, with the Midlands Industrial Council doing the same. In this case, twenty-one Conservative Associations enjoyed support, a few of these supported also by Bearwood.

Support from the Midlands Industrial Council also varied, from £2,246 to the Hereford Association on the one hand, to £58,565 to Burton Conservatives on the other. Of these twenty-one recipients, eight received £5,000 or less; four received between £5,001 and £10,000; six received between £10,001 and £20,000; and three received more than £30,000. Apart from Burton, the last included Halternprice and Howden Conservatives, given a donation of £35,000 by Midlands Industrial Council, and another £35,000 from Bearwood just after the election. Such funding coincides with significant spending by local parties, as indicated by Table 7.5 (though not all these parties were supported by either of

Table 7.5 Campaign expenditure by selected Conservative Associations

Conservative Association	Relevant spending 2004 (£)	Relevant spending 2005 (£)
Aylesbury	41,647	52,536
Bedford and Kempston	64,355	73,788
Burton	21,971	35,571
Eastleigh	0	24,545
Folkestone	12,707	30,737
Kensington and Chelsea	10,886	28,604
South Thanet	20,012	28,384
Wealden	34,716	63,779
Wokingham	7,373	12,226
Wrekin	41,045	26,342

Note: The campaign expenditure documented here is reported in different forms, including 'election expenses', 'other (campaigning expenses, meetings, travel and sundry)', 'campaign costs', 'campaign and development', 'campaigning costs', and so on. These costs do not necessarily relate exclusively to the 2005 general election.
Source: Electoral Commission.

the afore-mentioned donors). This activity reflects the change of the law in 2000 about the triggering of a candidate's expenses, the regulated period running only from the date of dissolution at the earliest. There was previously no such temporal limitation, and one effect of the clarification of the law in 2000 was to create a possible loophole that some parties have quickly spotted and exploited. This expenditure, from which a candidate will benefit, will not have to be accounted for by the candidate as part of his or her election expenses, as it is likely to be incurred before the candidate limits formally apply. It is only if it is incurred after the candidature begins that it will need to be authorised by the candidate (to the extent that it exceeds £500) and be treated as part of his or her expenses. It does not follow, however, that this expenditure is wholly unregulated. If it falls within the definition of campaign expenditure in the PPERA, section 72 and within the list of qualifying expenses within Schedule 8 of the Act, it is arguable that it will therefore count as part of the national spending of the party. But section 72 is so unclear and the exemptions to Schedule 8 so wide that it is unlikely that much (if any) campaign expenditure incurred by local parties would be caught by their terms.

Conclusion

The spending limits in British electoral law are more wide-ranging and far-reaching than in almost any other comparable democracy. They apply to candidates, political parties and third parties. The only other parliamentary democracy with anything quite like this is the federal election regime in Canada. There, the limits are lower than those in the United Kingdom, though they apply for a much shorter period, from the time the writ is issued for the election until polling day. Nevertheless, the evidence of two general elections in the United Kingdom (2001 and 2005) suggests that the UK spending levels are too high. This was reflected by the inability of the parties in 2001 to raise enough money for the legislation to have any significant regulatory impact, and by the inability of the parties in 2005 to raise enough money to meet the spending limit without resorting to undisclosed loans. The spending limits ordained by the PPERA were set following the recommendations of the Neill Committee, which had acted on the basis of spending patterns at the 1997 election. But that was an unusual election in terms of spending, which the parties have been unable to repeat. It is also the case that party fund-raising must now be conducted in a more difficult and more transparent environment than in 1997. The evidence of the 2005 election is that a high spending limit will undermine the benefits of transparency in restraining large donations.

Apart from the level of spending which continues to be permitted, the other concern relates to the areas of unregulated expenditure under PPERA. The first is that by no means all national expenditure is covered. The amount spent on capital and infrastructure is excluded, as is the amount spent on existing and temporary staff recruited for the election period. This is all the more striking for the fact that the costs of hiring staff by a candidate fall within the new definition of an election expense at local level. There is also the question of people who volunteer their services, which in principle is hardly unexceptionable. But the problem arises where the volunteers are self-employed (perhaps designers, lawyers or other professionals), or where the volunteers take paid holidays more generously provided by some employers than by others. The second concern relates to local expenditure where the limits do not apply before Parliament is dissolved, and mean that there is now a significant period in which spending can be incurred at local level by the candidate without having to be accounted for. We have also seen the growth of local party spending in the pre-election period. This has emerged as a contentious area of largely unregulated activity, depending on the timing and purpose of the expenditure. This means that resources can be ploughed into local campaigns, for spending that does not have to be declared.

So far as the future of spending controls is concerned, the Electoral Commission has recommended that the national limit for the parties should be reduced to £15m at general elections. It is not clear, however, whether this goes far enough, particularly as it is accompanied by a recommendation that the campaign period should be reduced from 365 days to four months. More controversial, however, is the proposal that candidate spending limits should be doubled to allow candidates to spend more 'in order to engage with the electorate'.[80] Yet, as we have seen, only a few candidates currently get near to the existing maximum. So why would candidates want to spend more money that they do not have or incur expenditure that is unnecessary? According to the Commission, the fact that so few reach the current limits 'may well reflect cautiousness in ensuring that the limit is not breached, which, in the case of the winning candidate, would run the risk of the result being overturned'. Raising the limit 'would provide the opportunity for candidates to run more effective campaigns to ensure that their messages reach more voters', and would encourage parties 'to channel more of their funds into local campaigns'. But this would wholly negate the point of reducing the national spending limit if the parties were to feel obliged to raise an amount equivalent to the reduction in permitted national spending in order to fuel local campaigns.

---

[80] Electoral Commission, *The Funding of Political Parties* (2004), p 61.

8

The Role of the State:
Supporting Candidates and
Political Parties

Introduction

Following the controversies surrounding some of the donations to the Labour Party in 2001 and 2002, State funding was widely proposed as a solution to the problems these controversies revealed. Newspapers reported that 'Downing Street is giving ministers rare freedom to express a personal view in an attempt to see if a political consensus can be created for State funding.'[1] A number of ministers or former ministers were reported to be in favour, including Prescott, Byers, Blunkett, Hain, Cook and Mandelson. According to the late Robin Cook, 'the Government could have avoided the latest "silly season" of donor rows if politicians had "grasped the nettle" years ago and introduced State funding for parties'.[2] The call for State funding was supported by a leading businessman,[3] and had some cross-party support. Although the Conservative Party at that time remained opposed,[4] some Conservative MPs came out in favour. Mr Andrew Tyrie claimed that 'taking tainted donations has brought a stench into the nostrils of the electorate. We must act decisively to quench the impression that parties can be bought and that influence in government is for sale.'[5] Other Conservative support was demonstrated by Mr John Maples's Political Parties (Funding) Bill which enjoyed cross-party support, including from Home Office minister Mike O'Brien.[6]

---

[1] *The Guardian*, 17 April 2002.

[2] *The Times*, 17 April 2002.

[3] *The Independent*, 20 May 2002. The businessman in question was Sir John Egan, the president of the CBI.

[4] *The Times*, 5 August 2002, quoting the Chairman of the Conservative Party. The Conservative Party now appears to be in favour of State funding.

[5] *The Guardian*, 23 May 2002. See also A Tyrie, 'Only Clean Money Can Stop the Stink in Politics', *The Times*, 17 April 2002, and now A Tyrie, *Clean Politics* (2006).

[6] *The Guardian*, 23 May 2002. See also M O'Brien, 'There's Only One Way to Take the Sleaze Out of Politics – Let the Taxman Pay', *The Times*, 16 May 2002.

Regulatory Challenges

This support was reinforced by widely reported recommendations for State funding by the Institute for Public Policy Research (IPPR),[7] though by the time the IPPR reported, the temperature was beginning to cool, and interest in the idea was much less intense. But in any event, not everyone was impressed, notwithstanding the context. Apart from the Conservative Party, a number of prominent commentators expressed scepticism or opposition to the idea of State funding. These included Peter Riddell of *The Times*, who claimed that State support 'is no guarantee of probity, as the German experience shows'. Moreover, 'substantial State support risks ossifying the existing party structure and deterring new parties'.[8] Alan Watkins of the *Independent on Sunday* defied what appeared to be the editorial line of his employer by proposing that there is 'not the slightest reason' why the taxpayer should get the government 'out of trouble of their own making'.[9] Here we are beginning to encounter the first problem for those proposing State funding for the parties, namely that there is a lack of consensus for the idea even when the political conditions seem most propitious. Despite the efforts of Downing Street, the consensus proved to be elusive, just as it had almost thirty years earlier when the last Labour government found itself lacking the support to implement the recommendations of the Houghton Committee on *Financial Aid to Political Parties*.[10] The Committee had recommended that an annual grant should be made to the parties based on votes at the immediately preceding general election.

The Houghton Committee had recommended wide-ranging support for the parties, despite the objections of four of its twelve members. But then as now, opposition to State funding is to be found on both the left and the right of the political spectrum. Apart from the concerns already expressed, there are also concerns of principle, about whether it is 'right' that political parties should be dependent on the State, and in particular whether the taxpayer should be forced to pay for political parties to which he or she may be opposed. This is a concern felt all the more keenly if State funding were to be made available to extremist parties such as the British National Party (BNP). There are also concerns about the consequences of any move towards greater State funding of the parties, and in particular the effect on the relationship between the trade unions and the Labour Party. At the time of Houghton in the 1970s, the concern was whether State funding would create a source of autonomous revenue that would dilute the influence of trade unions in a party heavily dependent on trade union money and resources. As it happens, alternative sources of revenue have been opened up

---

[7] IPPR, *Keeping it Clean* (2002).
[8] *The Times*, 17 April 2002.
[9] *Independent on Sunday*, 26 May 2002.
[10] Cmnd 6601, 1976. See below, pp 185–188.

by the Labour Party, and it is a matter of great regret that Houghton was not implemented. In the current climate, however, the concern is rather different. It is not so much a concern that the trade union influence will be diluted so much as banished, particularly if State funding is associated with contribution caps (which was not on the agenda of the Houghton Committee).

But the challenge to the regulator lies not only in overcoming resistance to the idea of State funding. The other problem lies in determining precisely what State funding means. Here there is a range of options, and it is unclear whether those who support State funding are always proposing the same thing. Apart from the large-scale funding of the parties by the State, some of those who were proposing State funding were proposing a range of different initiatives. As Riddell pointed out, there was a 'variety' of partial reforms, including tax relief for small donations, and 'matching finance for small contributions and membership subscriptions (to encourage parties to broaden their bases of support)'.[11] But even this does not begin to capture the complexity or subtleties of what is involved here. Before deciding how money should be allocated or funds distributed, there are two other matters to be considered. First, are we thinking about State funding of the parties, or State support for the parties? It would be possible to have a system of total State funding, but also possible to have a system of mixed State and private funding, and possible as well to have a system in which the State supported or aided the parties but did not fund them. Secondly, there is the question of which activities of the parties it is proposed should be funded by the State. Here again there is a range of options, from total funding at one end of the scale to support for specific activities at the other.

Responsibility of the State

Political parties first and foremost are private organisations that exist to promote the views of their members. In the case of the larger parties, the members may hope to see their party elected to office, and to see their views reflected in the policies of the government. In the case of the smaller parties, members may hope to have influence on the development of public affairs, and in this way indirectly to influence the policies of the government. To the extent that the parties are serving the personal interests and enthusiasms of their members and supporters, it is appropriate that the members and supporters should make their own contribution to sustain the parties to which they belong. In this way, political parties are like other private organisations, which are also sustained principally by their members and supporters, whether they be trade unions, churches or clubs of various kinds. But although political

---

[11] *The Times*, 17 April 2002.

parties should be sustained principally by their members and supporters, this does not exclude a role for the State, provided there is a State interest in supporting political parties financially or otherwise, and provided there are acceptable ways by which that support can be provided.

The Public Function of Political Parties

The case for supporting political parties is that they are different from other civil society organisations of the kinds identified, in the sense that they are an essential part of the democratic process, and part of the *informal* constitutional infrastructure of the State. Indeed, in some countries with written constitutions political parties are part of the *formal* constitutional infrastructure of the State. As suggested in chapter 2, political parties thus perform two functions. One is a private function already referred to. But a second is a public function, in the sense that political parties exist to serve a public interest, which is greater than the interests of their members or supporters collectively or individually. Political parties are thus private bodies, which provide channels for public participation and political representation. There is, as a result, a public interest in ensuring that such organisations are able to perform their public functions, on which the operation of our system of constitutional government depends. So, to the extent that parties promote the interests of their members, they should be sustained by them. But to the extent that the parties or the party system provides a benefit to the public, so the public should be prepared to make a contribution, to the extent that the private sector (the party members and supporters) is unable adequately or properly to meet a public need.

This does not, however, answer the question about how much money political parties need to perform their functions, an issue that is controversial in view of the fact there is no settled view of what political parties are for. We can say, nevertheless, that there are a number of core activities that are performed by political parties in the public interest, without which constitutional government would be impossible. These core activities are activities of an electoral, parliamentary and governmental nature. So in the first place, we expect the parties to develop policies to be presented to the electorate, policies which will reflect a vision of society and a programme for office. The programme needs to be coherent and intellectually robust. Secondly, we expect the parties to recruit and train candidates, and to present us with a choice at a wide range of elections from local government to European, as well as parliamentary. In presenting us with a choice, we expect the parties and candidates to inform us about their policies and to be persuaded to vote for them. And thirdly, we expect the largest party to govern the country in accordance with the mandate that we have given it, and the Opposition parties to hold the government to account, in a sense to act not only in their narrow party interests, but as a public watchdog. For these purposes, parties need to be nourished and sustained.

Reinforcing the State's Responsibility

The public function of political parties thus creates some public responsibility to ensure that parties are able adequately to perform these functions. That responsibility is reinforced where the State by its conduct makes it difficult for parties to perform these functions from their own resources, or imposes additional burdens on the parties, which stretch their capacity to meet them. In other words, the responsibility is reinforced where the public sphere invades the private space. This may happen in one of two ways. The first is by increasing the regulatory burden of the parties as private associations, and the second is by increasing the range of activities the parties are expected to perform. So far as the former is concerned, one reason why the parties are facing financial difficulty is partly because of the increased burdens placed upon them by the Political Parties, Elections and Referendums Act 2000 (PPERA). As we have seen, this imposes new requirements of transparency and accountability, as well as new administrative obligations. These not only add to the expenses of the parties directly, but have also had the indirect effect of turning off the tap of funds, as more donors are shy of the publicity that their donations might attract. It might be argued that where State intervention is having an adverse impact on the funds and funding of the parties, there is an obligation on the part of the State to make good any shortfall. All the more so when these measures restricting the flow of money to the parties come at a time when other initiatives have increased the obligations on the parties and the costs which they will inevitably have to bear. Particularly important in this respect is the great flood of constitutional reform since 1997. In addition to the Westminster elections, there are now direct elections to the European Parliament, elections to the Scottish Parliament and the devolved assemblies, as well as to the Greater London Authority (GLA).

But the responsibility of the State is reinforced not only where it adds to the difficulties of parties as private bodies to comply with their public duties. That responsibility is reinforced further by the need to protect the parties as public bodies from being captured or compromised by private interests. In other words, the responsibility is reinforced further in order to stop the public space from being invaded by the private sphere. This is a responsibility that arises independently of any regulation of the parties by the State, but it is a responsibility that may be reinforced by such regulation if the effect of the latter is to force the parties to seek lawful funding of doubtful propriety. It may be argued that this is part of the background to the loans affair in 2006, with the parties encouraged to solicit loans rather than donations, as a result of the legislation requiring transparency of donations and the growing reluctance of donors to be identified. Whatever the explanation of the loans affair, it remains the case that, as a general principle, a party – with a mandate from the people and a duty to govern in the public interest – should not be compromised by the need to secure funding from private interests, whether these interests are corporations seeking, or seduced by, the offer of policy favours, or individuals seeking, or seduced by, the offer of personal favours in the form of honours, contracts or licences. So the case for public funding is not just about meeting the needs of the parties; it is also about the need of the community to be protected from corruption and conflicts of interest. Parties without money are easy prey for the corrupt and the influence seeker and parties can quickly be placed in compromising positions. Yet a system of private funding of the parties means that they must inevitably rely on large private donors for their funds, if their needs are to be met.

Meeting the State's Responsibility

In determining how best to meet what might be described as 'the constitutional responsibilities of the State', there are two issues for consideration. The first is to determine the activities for which the State will provide support. Here there are several different activities of the parties which invite some such support.

- *Electoral activities*, in the sense that the State may be called upon to support the parties and their candidates at election time to ensure that they are able to communicate with the electors.
- *Representational activities*, in the sense that the State may be called upon to ensure that elected members of a political party are properly equipped while in office to discharge the responsibilities of office.
- *Organisational activities* necessary to sustain the party as an organization, including the costs of accommodation, policy development, political training and education, and the costs of internal democracy.

Having determined the purposes for which State support may be provided, it then becomes necessary to determine the form that support will take. It may take the form of (i) aid in kind by the State or others, or (ii) the acceptance by the State that it has to absorb costs that in the past have fallen to the parties, or (iii) the making of cash subsidies to the parties. Unlike the practice in many other countries, however, the distinctive British approach has been one of State aid rather than public funding, which has concentrated on the electoral and representational but not the organisational activities of the parties.

Assistance for Candidates: Enhancing Access

Since 1918, candidates in parliamentary elections have had the right to send one electoral communication free of charge to every voter in their constituency.[12] This was estimated to cost somewhere in the region of £17.6m at the 2001

---

[12] Representation of the People Act 1983, s 91.

general election,[13] this being a real cost which in the case of parliamentary elections is met by a reimbursement to the Royal Mail from the Treasury.[14] Assuming an electorate of 70,000 people, it would cost each candidate over £16,000 to mail-shot every elector. Although it is true that there are substantial discounts for bulk mailing, nevertheless this alone would consume a significant portion of the permitted expenditure of most candidates if they had to pay for it themselves, assuming a spending limit in the region of £10,000–12,000. Free mailing is thus a considerable benefit not to be underestimated. Although the right to send election addresses post-free does not apply to local elections, it has been extended to European elections and the elections to the devolved bodies, as well as the GLA. In some of these cases (such as the European elections), the right is a right of the party, not the candidates, and in this sense it is a right adapted to new electoral procedures. The only formal condition in the legislation is that the material must not weigh more than 60 grams, and that the entitlement is subject to Post Office regulations.[15] These require material to be submitted to the Royal Mail for checking before it is printed, and provide that the communication should relate to the election only, contain no advertising (other than the candidate) and include no sign, words, marks or designs which are offensive or indecent.

There are three important features of this initiative, the first being that it has the effect of ensuring that all candidates have the right to a minimum level of access to the electorate. That is to say, all candidates have the right to ensure that their message reaches every home, though it does not guarantee that every candidate will do so on equal terms. The better-equipped candidates will be able to send better-quality material, and may be able to make other distributions at their own expense. But it does mean that electors have an opportunity to form a judgement on the basis of the message of each of the candidates. The second and related point is that there are no qualifying conditions in terms of eligibility for this facility: it is available equally to so-called serious and so-called frivolous candidates. The only restraint is whether the candidate has enough money to produce the materials: it is the postage costs that are met by the State, not the production costs. It is not necessary to demonstrate a prescribed level of support, and there is no question of funding having to be reimbursed by candidates who perform badly in the election. A third point is that there is no right on the part of the Royal Mail to censor the message. There may, however, be management problems for the Royal Mail given the existence of a conscience clause in the contracts of employment of postal workers: it has been claimed that this has provided the basis for members of the Communication Workers Union to refuse to deliver material from extremist parties such as the BNP.[16] The Royal Mail's own operational requirements also provide that the material should not infringe legislation, including legislation that prohibits the incitement to racial hatred.

---

[13] Electoral Commission, *The Funding of Political Parties Background Paper* (2003), p 16.
[14] Royal Mail, *Elections in the United Kingdom. Operational Requirements for Election Mail* (2004).
[15] Representation of the People Act 1983, s 91(1).
[16] *Scotland on Sunday*, 30 May 2004.

Assistance to Candidates: Free Use of Meeting Rooms

The other principal way by which candidates are assisted by the State was also introduced in 1918.[17] This is the provision of local authority halls or school rooms for public meetings at election times. Although applied initially to parliamentary elections, this too has been extended to European elections as well as to elections to the devolved bodies (with the exception of the Northern Ireland Assembly). Like the postal subsidy, this facility does not apply to local elections; nor does it apply to the GLA elections. Although the facility provides an important opportunity for candidates to meet electors, its significance has declined in recent years, given the reduction in the practice of holding election meetings.[18] In any event, this is a facility that may not be without costs to a candidate. The legislation provides specifically that the local authority may charge for the costs of 'preparing, warming, lighting and cleaning the room', as well as the cost of 'providing attendance for the meeting and restoring the room to its usual condition after the meeting'.[19] Moreover, the candidate may be called upon to pay for any damage to the room, the premises in which it is situated or the furniture, fittings and apparatus in the premises.[20] Nor is it an absolute right: a candidate is not entitled to use school-rooms during times when they are needed for educational purposes, or other rooms where these are being used for other purposes.[21]

However, the same principles apply here as apply to the postage facility. It applies to all candidates, it seeks to ensure that all have the same minimum level of access to the electorate, and there is no power of censorship vested in the local authority. The local authority may not prevent the holding of such meetings because it is opposed to the political party the candidate represents. When in the past local authorities have refused access to this facility by BNP candidates, the candidates in question have taken legal action to force the authorities to yield.[22] But obviously a candidate may be unable to obtain a hall or a room for an event if it has already been booked, and the police may intervene to prevent an event from being held if they anticipate a breach of the peace. On this last point, however, the hitherto largely unconstrained discretion of the police will now have to be exercised in accordance with the Human Rights Act 1998 which pushes freedom of expression and assembly slightly further up the agenda, as well as the State's duty to conduct free elections 'under conditions which will ensure the free expression of the opinion of the people in the choice of the legislature'. Yet although the activities of extremist parties in particular have made the exercise of

---

[17] Representation of the People Act 1983, s 95.
[18] Electoral Commission, *supra* n 13, p 17.
[19] Representation of the People Act 1983, s 95(4)(a).
[20] *Ibid*, s 95(4)(b).
[21] *Ibid*, s 95(6).
[22] *Webster v London Borough of Southwark* [1983] QB 698.

this right at times controversial, the principles by which it is underpinned never-theless remain important and continue to have contemporary significance.

Party Political Broadcasts: Transferring the State's Obligations

The foregoing provisions are designed to provide benefits principally for candi-dates rather than parties. Nevertheless, the parties will benefit to the extent that they will be relieved of the need to provide financial assistance to candidates to enable them to distribute their message: it reduces mail costs and the costs of hiring rooms. The other form of electoral support is provided to the parties rather than the candidates, and again is designed to ensure that the parties are able to communicate with electors. As with free postage and the free use of build-ings, it is about the State providing an opportunity to the parties without directly subsidising their efforts. This is the provision of free broadcasting time, which is not provided directly by the State, but under an obligation imposed on third parties by the State. The cost must be borne by the broadcaster, in the sense that there is no rebate paid to the broadcasters by the Treasury for the broadcasting time that is lost. In the case of the independent broadcasters, this would be not insignificant if it were to be quantified in lost advertising revenue. It has been estimated that during the 1997 election, the party election broadcasts were worth £20m to each of the two main parties and £16m to the Liberal Democrats.[23] It is thus clearly a very important facility, which according to the Electoral Com-mission contributes to

> the fairness of the election campaign as, to some extent, it compensates for the parties differential ability to attract campaign funds, offsetting the ability of one party heavily to outspend its rivals in other advertising.[24]

It is trite to point out, however, that broadcasting is a scarce and expensive resource, even with the multiplicity of channels now available. Unlike the free postage and the free access to meeting rooms, not everyone can have access, and not everyone who does have access can do so on equal terms.

Party Political Broadcasts

There are two types of free broadcasting traditionally provided by British tele-vision and radio: party political broadcasts and party election broadcasts. The former are carried outside the period of an election and will be used by the parties generally to encourage support for their platforms. The latter are carried

---

[23] Committee on Standards in Public Life, Fifth Report, *The Funding of Political Parties in the United Kingdom*, vol 1, Cm 4057-I, para 13.18.
[24] Electoral Commission, *Party Political Broadcasting: Report and Recommendations* (2003), p 12.

during election campaigns: they are made available by the broadcasters for general elections to the Westminster Parliament, the European Parliament, as well as the devolved legislatures, though in the last case the broadcasts will be carried only in Scotland, Wales or Northern Ireland, where the elections in question are held. Since 1998 the annual series of party political broadcasts has been reduced following a review by the broadcasters, in order to move the focus to election broadcasts. This was done in light of the increased number of elections in the United Kingdom and the increased coverage of political matters in news and current affairs programmes throughout the year. Nevertheless, a small number of party political broadcasts continue to be held at other times of the election cycle to coincide with events such as the Budget, the Queen's Speech and party conferences, so that the parties have access to the electorate throughout the year.[25] Party political broadcasts are (and always have been) available only to parties that have parliamentary representation; but party election broadcasts may be allocated to other parties as well.[26] The Communications Act 2003 requires all licensed public service television channels and all national radio services to carry party political broadcasts (a term which includes party election broadcasts). The BBC is not bound by this statutory obligation but has traditionally carried such broadcasts as part of its public service obligations.

Under the Communications Act 2003, the independent sector must carry party political broadcasts in line with rules laid down by OFCOM (the broadcasting regulator).[27] The allocation of broadcasts to each party was a task previously undertaken by the (non-statutory) Committee on Political Broadcasting, on which sat representatives of the parties and the broadcasters. This Committee fell into disuse, and the allocation of broadcasts was left to the broadcasters and the broadcasting regulators, though 'by convention these bodies put proposals to the major parties represented in Parliament with a view to reaching a consensus'.[28] It is now the responsibility of the BBC and OFCOM to determine the eligibility criteria for broadcasts and the amount of time any party is to be allocated. The Electoral Commission has recommended that the criteria for allocating broadcasts should be made more transparent, to include a reference to allocation on the basis of proven electoral support.[29] In performing its duty, OFCOM must have regard to the views of the Electoral Commission, as must the BBC.[30] At the general election in 2001, the arrangements were altered to reflect the distribution of the parties thoughout the United Kingdom, which led the broadcasters to have separate broadcasts in the four 'nations' where this was possible. The Labour Party and the Conservative Party were each allocated five broadcasts, and the

---

[25] O Gay, *Party Election Broadcasts: Standard Note* (2001).

[26] See L Klein, 'On the Brink of Reform: Political Party Funding in Britain' (1999) 31 *Case Western Reserve Journal of International Law* 1.

[27] Communications Act 2003, s 333.

[28] Electoral Commission, *Election 2001: The Official Results* (2001), p 60.

[29] Electoral Commission, *Party Political Broadcasting: Report and Recommendations, supra* n 24.

[30] PPERA, s 11(3).

Liberal Democrats four broadcasts in England; whereas in Scotland each of these parties was allocated four broadcasts, as was the Scottish National Party (SNP).

The Small Parties

The arrangements relating to the small parties have always been controversial.[31] In order to qualify for a party election broadcast in the past, a party had to have at least fifty candidates at an election. This was a not inconsiderable burden, given that electoral law requires each candidate to pay a deposit of £500, which will be returned if the candidate in question secures at least 5 per cent of the vote; otherwise the deposit will be lost.[32] The small parties can generally expect to lose almost all their deposits. Nevertheless, at the general election in 2001, the bar was raised: the broadcasters decided that only those parties which stood in more than one-sixth of the parliamentary seats would qualify for a broadcast. This means that to qualify for a broadcast in England, it was necessary to put up eighty-eight candidates; to qualify for a broadcast in Scotland it was necessary to put up twelve candidates; and to qualify for a broadcast in Wales it was necessary to put up six candidates. A party standing in one-sixth of the seats across Great Britain would qualify for a GB-wide broadcast. At the general election in 2001, six small parties qualified for an election broadcast under these rules. Of these six parties, the UK Independence Party (UKIP), the Socialist Labour Party and the Socialist Alliance were allocated broadcasts in England, Scotland and Wales. The Green Party had broadcasts in England and Wales, while the Scottish Labour Party and the Pro-Life Alliance had their broadcasts shown only in Scotland and Wales respectively. Nevertheless, a large number of small parties contested the 2001 election and did not qualify for broadcasting time, including the Communist Party, as well as the National Front.

There were a number of disputes about the allocation of time in 2001, with concerns being raised by the BNP (denied a broadcast, though it did qualify in 2005) and the Greens (unhappy about the method of allocation). Such disputes have led in the past to unsuccessful judicial proceedings by aggrieved political parties.[33] But the governing principle here is proportionate access not equal access. The large parties have an advantage over the small parties and any advantage that the large parties are to have over each other is to come largely as a result of the quality rather than the number of their broadcasts. The other issue here is that the broadcasters may refuse to carry broadcasts that breach their other duties, such as the duty to maintain taste and decency. This power was used by the BBC in 2001 to refuse to carry the images of an aborted foetus in a Pro-Life

[31] There is also the question of independent candidates who are denied access. See *Huggett v United Kingdom* (1995) 20 EHRR CD105.

[32] Representation of the People Act 1983, Sch 1 (Parliamentary Election Rules, rules 9 and 53).

[33] *Grieve v Douglas Home* 1965 SLT 186 (Communist Party); *Lynch v BBC* [1983] NI 193 (Workers' Party); *R v Broadcasting Complaints Commission, ex p Owen* [1985] QB 1153 (Social Democratic Party); *R v BBC, ex p Referendum Party* [1997] COD 459.

Alliance broadcast.[34] The broadcast was eventually carried without pictures, but with 'a red screen covered with the single word "censored"'.[35] Although the Pro-Life Alliance did not qualify at the 2005 general election, the number of qualifying small parties continues to rise. Apart from the BNP, the other parties qualifying in 2005 were UKIP and the Green Party (GB wide); the Socialist Labour Party (Scotland and Wales); Operation Christian Vote and the Scottish Socialist Party (Scotland only); and Legalise Cannabis Alliance and Forward Wales (Wales only). Two small parties that did not qualify for broadcasts nevertheless each won a seat, namely Respect and the Independent Kidderminster Hospital and Health Concern, as did the late Peter Law who won the Labour stronghold of Blaenau Gwent as an independent.

New Forms of State Support

It is an important feature of the system of State support for the political parties considered so far that the State provides facilities or requires others to provide facilities to ensure that the parties are able to undertake core electoral activity. In other ways, in a variation of this theme, the State has also absorbed some of the costs the parties themselves had to meet, these costs becoming a direct charge on the State. They include the costs of registration of electors (since 1918) and the payment of MPs (since 1911). This particular method of providing support is by no means obsolete, with the State now providing special advisers to government ministers at a cost of £5.9m annually. Either way, the State does not provide cash. In more recent times, however, these strategies of the State (i) providing support for core electoral activity, and (ii) absorbing costs that might otherwise have to be met by the parties, have been supplemented by different strategies. In 1975, an experiment with the tax system was introduced in an apparent attempt to stimulate donations to political parties, and direct cash grants to the parties were introduced for the first time to help with specific parliamentary activities. The latter is the so-called Short scheme after the Leader of the House who introduced it. So here we have the State taking steps to encourage the parties to become more self-sufficient in meeting organisational needs, while also providing direct financial assistance to help them to discharge their duties, in this case of a representational nature.

Inheritance Tax Relief

The first of these initiatives was introduced in the Finance Act 1975, in the form

---

[34] See *R (Pro Life Alliance) v BBC* [2004] 1 AC 185. See A Geddis [2002] PL 615; (2003) 66 MLR 885.

[35] Electoral Commission, *Election 2001*, *supra* n 28, p 60.

of relief from what was then capital transfer tax. That particular tax was replaced with inheritance tax by the Conservatives in the 1980s, and the relief is now to be found in the Inheritance Tax Act 1984. Although shrouded in mystery, the relief seems to have been introduced to stimulate contributions from the estates of the dead. And although introduced by a Labour government, it is hard to believe that it would be the principal beneficiary of such an initiative. But it is not only donations to political parties that qualify for such relief, with donations to a large number of other public and charitable purposes also covered. As originally introduced, the relief applied only to donations to political parties up to £100,000; there is now no limit as to amount so that all gifts to political parties are wholly exempt. But in order to qualify to benefit under the scheme, a party must satisfy one of two conditions. It must show either that it had two members elected to the House of Commons at the immediately preceding general election; or that it had one member elected *and* that its candidates obtained at least 150,000 votes in total. This means that access to this particular benefit is conditional upon being able to demonstrate a significant level of popular support among the electorate.

At the present time only five British parties would benefit from this scheme (Labour, Conservative, Liberal Democrat, SNP and Plaid Cymru), which does not require the party to be registered, and conversely for which registration is not enough to secure access. At least two Northern Ireland parties –the Democratic Unionist Party (DUP) and the Social Democratic and Labour Party (SDLP) – would also qualify, and there is a question mark about a third, namely Sinn Fein, which won a sufficient number of seats to qualify but which has refused to sit at Westminster. It has been pointed out, however, that a party may have representation in the Scottish Parliament, the Welsh Assembly and/or the European Parliament and still not qualify. There are a number of parties that would fall into this position, including UKIP (represented in the European Parliament) and the Scottish Socialist Party (represented in the Scottish Parliament). But it is thought that this is not a great source of income, though the Conservative Party has produced a leaflet drawing the attention of the scheme to its members, pointing out that it is perfectly legal for individuals to reduce the taxable value of their estate by making gifts to a charity or a political party, as these gifts are not subject to inheritance tax. In evidence to the Neill Committee in 1998, however, the Inland Revenue thought that in practice 'little use' is made of this and a similar relief from capital gains tax.

Support for Opposition Parties in Parliament

A week after the Finance Act 1975 was passed, the Leader of the House (Edward Short) announced the introduction of a new scheme of Financial Assistance for Opposition Parties. The scheme was designed to 'enable the Opposition parties more effectively to fulfil their parliamentary duties'.[36] Although it was for the

---

[36] HC Debs, 20 March 1975, col 1869.

parties to decide how they would use the money for this purpose, it was intended that 'the principal areas of expenditure would be research assistance for Front Bench spokesmen, assistance in the Opposition Whips' Offices . . . and for staff for the Leader of the Opposition'.[37] In order to ensure that the money was used only for the purposes intended, the parliamentary parties have been required to submit audited statements confirming that the funds have been used exclusively for parliamentary purposes.[38] There is, however, no funding for the parliamentary work of the party of government, even though there is important work done by the party of government in looking after the needs of its own backbench MPs. This includes servicing a large number of backbench committees, maintaining a resource centre, and dealing with inquiries from the public and the press about parliamentary business.[39] Apart from the fact that the money is not available to the governing party, self-evidently it is not available to all other political parties. It is available only to those with parliamentary representation. Even then, it is available only to those with at least two MPs or with one MP and an aggregate number of 150,000 votes in favour of that party's candidates at the most recent general election. Money is distributed according to a formula based on both seats won by and votes cast in favour of the party in question. Following the recommendations of the Neill Committee, the amount of Short money was increased by a factor of 2.7 in 1999 and a separate sum of £500,000 was introduced to finance the office of the Leader of the Opposition.[40] The Conservative Party now receives £4.3m (including £595,999 for the office of the Leader of the Opposition); and the Liberal Democrats £1.6m, with smaller allocations to each of the other parliamentary parties (the SNP, Plaid Cymru and two Northern Ireland parties).

The large increase in the amount of money available since 1999 has led to some concern that the money was not always being used for strictly parliamentary activities. An investigation by the House of Commons Public Administration Committee revealed lax auditing procedures.[41] This followed complaints that the Conservative Party was using its Short money allocation to 'strengthen the "War Room" of researchers and press officers'.[42] It was also reported that the Conservative Party's auditors were described by 'insiders' as being 'acutely anxious' that 'some expenditure arguably fell outside the strict rules governing the use of the money'.[43] It transpired that (unknown to the other parties who were using their money for purposes within the confines of the Palace of Westminster) the

---

[37] *Ibid.*

[38] Funding for opposition parties in the House of Lords (referred to as Cranborne money after the Leader of the House who introduced it) was introduced (on a much smaller scale) in 1996, and a scheme similar to Short money was introduced for the opposition parties in the Scottish Parliament under the authority of the Scotland Act 1998.

[39] The Labour Party, *Making Government Work*, HC 238–viii (1999–2000), pp 138–39.

[40] Home Office, *The Funding of Political Parties in the United Kingdom*, Cm 4413, 1999, para 6.8.

[41] For the evidence to the Committee, see HC 238–viii (1999–2000).

[42] *The Independent*, 10 August 1999.

[43] *Sunday Telegraph*, 23 April 2000.

Conservative Party had agreed a wide definition of parliamentary activities with the House of Commons Fees' Office to include

> Research associated with front bench duties, developing and communicating alternative policies to those of the Government of the day; and shadowing the government's front bench. It does not include political campaigning and similar partisan activities, political fundraising, membership campaigns or personal or private business of any kind.[44]

In the course of proceedings before the Public Administration Committee, it was quite clear that the money was being used to finance activities at Conservative Central Office, including 'research, communications and policy'.[45] It was also clear that there was some difficulty in distinguishing between communicating alternative policies (permitted under the definition) and campaigning (not permitted under the definition).[46] Indeed the Public Administration Committee concluded that 'the Official Opposition and its auditors were unable to give a categorical assurance that its Short money funding was being used exclusively for parliamentary business'.[47] This led the Committee to conclude that there was 'an urgent need for stricter regulation as to what Short money may be spent on and more transparency as to how it has been spent'.[48] But the episode is important not only because of the weaknesses it exposed. It also revealed that the cash-strapped Conservative Party was dependent on State cash for party activities, despite the same party's opposition to State funding at the time. In the same way, it revealed that public money was now being used informally to pay for the organisational activity of a political party, as well as its representational activity.

Proposals for Additional State Support

There is a now a significant body of State support for political parties that helps to ensure that certain core needs are met. Indeed, in 2003 the Electoral Commission estimated that existing State support was worth £24.47m in a non-election year, and £111.07m in an election year. This means that in a parliamentary cycle of four years, the State's contribution will be £184.48m. The most recent initiatives considered above have seen a change in the nature of State support, with a move from electoral to representational activity, and with a move from providing aid in kind to the provision of cash. The next step would be to increase the amount of funding available to the parties, by following the example of most other parliamentary democracies which make annual subventions to the parties

---

[44] Memorandum by the Head of the Fees Office, HC 238–viii (1999–2000), p 120.
[45] HC 238–viii (1999–2000), Q 669 (Mr David Prior).
[46] *Ibid*, Q685–Q689.
[47] Public Administration Committee, *Special Advisers: Boon or Bane?*, HC 293 (2000–2001), para 50.
[48] *Ibid*, para 51.

to help them with their organisational activities. As already indicated earlier in this chapter, a scheme of this kind was in fact proposed by the Houghton Committee as long ago as 1976. Its recommendations were never implemented, but its analysis is peerless and repays valuable study even thirty years later, combining wisdom, common sense and persuasiveness in equal measure.

The Problems Facing the Parties

The Committee on Financial Aid to Political Parties was appointed by the then Labour government on 8 May 1975 to consider whether provision should be made from public funds to assist political parties in carrying out their functions outside Parliament. Chaired by Lord Houghton of Sowerby (a Labour peer), the Committee included representatives of the three main parties, as well as the SNP. It also included journalists, academics, a businessman and a trade unionist, and it split 8:4 in favour of financial aid for the parties. The Committee was in no doubt about the plight of the parties even then, a conclusion that had been reinforced by their study of the resources available to the parties in the European countries the Committee members had visited:

> By contrast, the evidence we have gathered in this country shows that party organisa-
> tion is in a number of cases weak at national level, and at local level generally exists on
> a pitifully inadequate scale of accommodation, equipment, trained staff and resources.
> Membership fees are low; fund-raising takes up too much time; organisation is fre-
> quently inadequate; and the level of political activity is far below what is needed to gain
> the attention and interest of the general body of the electorate, especially the young.[49]

The 'considered view' of the majority was that 'British political parties frequently operate below the minimum level of efficiency and activity required'. These are judgements that apply with equal if not greater force today, and there is nothing to suggest that a modern-day Houghton would not be forced to the same conclusions.

The majority thought it unlikely that the parties could raise more money from their traditional sources of support (business in the case of the Conservatives and the unions in the case of Labour). But Houghton had reckoned without foreign funding or the large personal donations that have disfigured the political scene in recent years. These, however, have proved to be only a temporary and unwelcome respite, which helped manage the crisis of funding in the 1990s in particular. But in view of the controversy which has been created by private funding on this scale, we are back thirty years later to the same point that Houghton reached: a funding crisis and no obvious way of finding money to enable the parties to perform their constitutional obligations, except from the State itself. If the private sector is unwilling to provide the means, or if the means of providing the money are unacceptable, there is no alternative to State funding. Yet although the

---

[49] Cmnd 6601, 1976, para 9.8.

Houghton Committee argued for State aid, it was aid on a modest scale compared to the practice in other countries. The Committee proposed:

> The amount should provide significant help to the parties, but should not be too high in relation to their other financial resources. It is desirable that the amount of aid given should not discourage voluntary effort or the constituency activity which at the present centres around fund-raising. Above all, no proposal for expenditure at the present time can ignore the country's economic position and the pressure of competing demands on the nation's resources.[50]

The Houghton Proposals

With these considerations in mind, it was proposed that the State should contribute about 20 per cent of the income of the parties at the time (that is, 20 per cent of national and local income). Houghton also proposed that the money should go to help the parties at the centre and in the constituencies, with about £1.5m (about £7.5m at today's values), to be allocated between the parties nationally on the basis of their electoral support. Eligible parties would be entitled to 'a specified sum per vote cast at the previous general election for candidates, whether elected or not, who declared themselves to be standing in the name of the party'.[51] Not all parties would qualify, but only those whose candidates saved their deposits in at least six constituencies, had at least two of their candidates returned as MPs, or had at least one candidate returned and received as a party at least 150,000 votes. Following the 1974 general elections, seven parties would have qualified (Labour, Conservative, Liberal, SNP, Plaid Cymru, Ulster Unionists and the SDLP). So far as support at local level is concerned, it was proposed that this should be by the partial reimbursement to parties of the election expenses of parliamentary and local government candidates. The aim was directly to aid local party funds, though it was also proposed that independent candidates would be eligible, and (assuming a general election every four years) it was expected that this part of the scheme would cost on average £860,000 annually (about £4.5m at current values). The total cost would thus have been £2.3m annually (about £12m at current values).

The Houghton scheme was thus a combination of annual cash grants to the parties nationally and a rebate of election expenses to candidates to help the parties locally. It would be up to the parties to decide how to spend the money in accordance with their own priorities, the Committee expressly rejecting the idea that aid should be given for hypothecated purposes. So although there was 'no reason for questioning the existing aid in kind to candidates and parties', the Committee did not 'consider that a case has been made out for its extension'. In the words of the Committee:

---

[50] *Ibid*, para 9.18.
[51] *Ibid*, para 10.25.

> The needs of the parties differ considerably; whilst one party might want free accommodation and a party newspaper, another might prefer to have free research facilities, and another more staff at regional or constituency level. Such a scheme could therefore . . . only be of selective value to the parties, and its effects might be unfair.[52]

Other schemes considered but rejected included matching aid, rejected because 'the amount of State aid would be in proportion to the fund-raising capacity of the respective parties and not to their needs or to the extent of their electoral support'.[53] Also rejected was the proposal for a flat rate grant to the parties, rejected on the ground that it wrongly assumes 'the existence of comparable basic needs in all parties which the State should meet'.[54] Clearly it would be inappropriate to make equal provision without regard to the size, support for and responsibilities of the parties. Finally, the Committee also rejected a number of proposals for assistance by using the tax system to stimulate donations to political parties.

Reluctance and Resistance to Change

The Houghton proposals were never implemented for a number of reasons. The Conservative Party was opposed, and at the time the Labour Party was split and the government was not confident that it could carry the House of Commons. Since then, the Conservative Party has maintained its opposition, though both Labour and the Liberals have been in favour. The matter resurfaced in the 1990s, but a Conservative-dominated Home Affairs Committee concluded that unless all the parties were in favour, the idea did not make 'practical politics'.[55] As we saw in chapter one, the Committee was not in any event convinced 'that the parties are in such desperate financial straits that they need to support of the taxpayer'. It was also noted that the parties 'have carried on functioning since the Houghton Report very much as they did before', leading the Committee to conclude that 'Houghton's direst warnings have not proved well founded'. Although a time of budgetary restraint was not the time for the 'general extension of State funding', the Committee was nevertheless attracted by the case for helping the Opposition parties with their research work:

> One possibility is a further extension of Short money, allowing it to be used more extensively outside Parliament as well as within. To maintain equality of treatment, this would require the government party also to receive extended Short money outside Parliament, since at the moment that fund provides opposition parties with the wherewithal to obtain assistance on a par with Cabinet Minister's special advisers.[56]

[52] *Ibid*, para 10.9.
[53] *Ibid*, para 10.10.
[54] *Ibid*, para 10.11.
[55] Home Affairs Committee, *Funding of Political Parties*, HC 301 (1993–94), para 56.
[56] *Ibid*, para 57.

This intriguing suggestion has been rather overlooked in the subsequent debates about party funding, and ought to be more fully considered.

The Neill Committee

The Neill Committee also recommended against the introduction of State funding for the political parties. On this occasion, however, most of the political parties were against, or at least not in favour. The Conservative Party repeated a passage from its submission to the Home Affairs Committee in 1993 when it said that

> The Conservative Party is opposed to the direct funding of political parties. State funding would either unduly favour established parties or encourage the formation and growth of extremist parties. It would require state regulation of the organisation and management of political parties, and it would undermine the voluntary activity of political parties.[57]

The Labour Party's position was rather different.[58] Although it recognised that 'there is a case in principle for various forms of State aid', it was also acknowledged that 'at a time of fiscal prudence', the 'needs of the political parties are not the greatest priority in terms of public expenditure'. So although not recommending public funding on the scale of a number of European countries, the Labour Party nevertheless recommended that there should be a 'modest extension of State aid which is focussed solely on enhancing the quality of public representation'.[59] This entailed an extension of the Short scheme, and the introduction of public funding schemes for political education and training by the parties. This change in the position of the Labour Party can be explained on a number of grounds. At the time there may have been a perception that the party did not need the help of the State, able to raise private money in the brief afterglow of the 1997 general election result. But as we have seen, that was to change, and that change was in part caused by the legislation – the PPERA – which the Neill Report helped to generate. For their part, the Liberal Democrats were not so restrained, arguing for an annual subvention to the parties. But even this was modest, it being proposed that qualifying parties would each receive £2m, with another £10m being distributed between the parties based on election results.[60]

Faced with the caution of the main parties, it is unsurprising that the Neill Committee should not reveal any enthusiasm for State funding. The Committee considered the arguments for and against. The arguments in favour were that

---

[57] Committee on Standards in Public Life, *supra* n 23, Appendix V, reproducing the Conservative Party's evidence at pp 237–43.

[58] Committee on Standards in Public Life, *supra* n 23, Appendix V, reproducing the Labour Party's evidence at pp 226–36.

[59] *Ibid*, p 222.

[60] Committee on Standards in Public Life, *supra* n 23, Appendix V, reproducing the Liberal Democrat Party's evidence at pp 244–49.

State funding would help 'purify' the political process by making the parties less reliant on large individual donations, and that it would help the parties to perform their essential functions more fully and effectively. The arguments against increased public funding were the familiar arguments about (i) taxpayers being *compelled* to make a contribution, (ii) the ossification of the party system, (iii) a reduction in grassroots funding activities, (iv) the capture of the parties by the State, and (v) the fact that public funding would be unpopular with the public ('a view unproven but almost certainly true').[61] The Committee apparently thought the latter arguments to be more compelling than the former, but did, however, recognise that the arguments for and against State funding were 'finely balanced' and could 'envisage circumstances in which substantially increased State funding of the political parties – including the funding of their general activities – might become an imperative'.[62] The Committee took the view that to the extent that public funding was supported in response to concerns about donations to the parties, these would be allayed by the disclosure regime it proposed. Although it was not thought that there would be any significant reduction in donations, the Committee's proposed spending limits would 'curb the parties need for ever-increasing financial resources'. The Committee also thought as 'somewhat implausible' the idea that the parties were underfunded, given 'the scale of the parties' spending at the 1997 general election'. According to Neill, the 'truly poor cannot afford to put up so many billboards'.

Policy Development Grants

Although Neill was not in favour of a new system whereby the State should fund the parties, this was subject to an important exception. The Committee was troubled by the fact that the political parties were 'hard pressed to meet the mounting costs of election campaigns and also the mounting costs of their day-to-day activities'. This led them to concentrate resources on campaigning and routine administration at the expense of long-term policy development. In evidence to the Neill Committee, the Labour Party had – as we have seen – proposed that public funding should be made available to the parties to help them to train candidates for public office.[63] But this was rejected by the Committee, which proposed instead that a policy development fund should be established to encourage the parties to 'think long' and to fulfil 'better' one of their 'vital functions'. In the view of the Committee, the 'political parties should be one of the major sources of ideas in British politics', but that they 'were not always so at present'. It was proposed that the fund should be administered by the Electoral Commission and that the annual amount for distribution should be a modest £2m, based on an estimated £1.5m spent by the three main parties on research in

---

[61] Committee on Standards in Public Life, *supra* n 23, paras 7.19–23.
[62] *Ibid*, para 7.24.
[63] Committee on Standards in Public Life, *supra* n 23, Appendix V, p 223.

1997. It was anticipated that proper accounting procedures would be introduced to ensure that the political parties did not spend the money on such objects as routine party administration, electioneering and opinion polling. Not all parties would qualify, with the scheme being applicable only to those parties 'represented in the House of Commons'. This formula would exclude those parties without a great deal of concentrated electoral support. But it would also exclude those like Sinn Fein whose successful candidates refused to take their seats at Westminster.

The government accepted these recommendations, and a scheme for policy development grants was introduced by the PPERA. As such, the scheme is an important leap of principle, with the State now formally accepting a responsibility for party organisation activities as well as electoral and representational activities of the political parties, and is doing so with the transfer of cash. In this sense two important Rubicons have been crossed. Under the Act, the scheme applies only to 'represented registered part[ies]'.[64] For this purpose a party is 'represented' if there are at least two members of the House of Commons belonging to the party, who have sworn the parliamentary oath and who not are disqualified from sitting or voting in the House.[65] This penultimate requirement excludes Sinn Fein, which unsuccessfully challenged the limitation under the Human Rights Act 1998.[66] The rules for the distribution of the money have been developed by the Electoral Commission, which consulted the political parties though was clearly not bound by the views of the parties. The parties in any event each had different interests to promote in the distribution of the money (all wanted as much as possible), with the larger parties in particular seeking a distribution formula that would give them a bigger slice of the pie. The solution adopted by the Electoral Commission is in some respects quite ingenious: recognising that all parties will need a basic allocation sufficient to fund a small policy development team, half of the available £2m is therefore split equally between the eligible parties; the allocation of the other half is based on the share of the vote at parliamentary, assembly and European elections. It does mean, however, that there are different principles and procedures for allocating the two principal cash subsidies made available by The Treasury to the political parties for their representational and organisational activities. These, in turn, are different from the schemes for providing support for the electoral activities of the parties. We have come a long way since the universality of the free postage scheme.

Tax Relief – A False Trail

Although the Neill Committee was thus against public funding for the political parties, it would be a mistake to conclude that it was against all forms of

---

[64] PPERA, s 12(1)(a).
[65] *Ibid*, s 12(1)(b).
[66] *Sinn Fein, Re application for Judicial Review* [2003] NIQB 27.

additional State support for the parties. Apart from the policy development grants, Neill recommended that the Short scheme should be increased threefold, and also recommended the introduction of core funding for referendum campaign groups. In addition, the Committee recommended that income tax relief should be introduced for small donations to political parties, thereby extending in a serious way the system of inheritance tax relief. This is an idea that attracts a lot of support from time to time, though it is not to be overlooked that it is a form of State subsidy, albeit a different form to that proposed by Houghton. It is, however, a form of subsidy that was considered but firmly rejected by Houghton for reasons that seemed convincing and compelling. One objection to this method of distributing State support is that 'it would operate in favour of the parties with better-off members',[67] while another is that the amount of money raised would be 'unpredictable, and there would be no necessary relationship between the amounts raised and the needs of the parties'.[68]

Proposals for Income Tax Relief

There was not a great deal of support for income tax relief for political donations in the written evidence by the main parties to the Neill Committee. The Conservative Party appeared to offer the strongest support, urging the Committee to give 'serious consideration' to the idea of using the tax system to stimulate voluntary donations. In the course of oral evidence, the Liberal Democrats revealed that they would not be against it, if the scheme could be designed in such a way as to stimulate small donations and encourage the parties to build up their membership base. But the Labour Party was strongly opposed, with its Finance Director explaining that

> Tax relief is of value only to people who pay tax and where the donations given are of significant size. It would be of little value to the Labour Party, which has 400,000 members who are paying an average £20 each to the Labour Party's coffers.

Yet despite the lukewarm nature of this support, the Committee was an enthusiastic advocate of tax relief for donations. The scheme proposed was by deduction at source, whereby political donations would be treated in the same way as tax relief for charitable donations. This was explained in the following terms:

> Tax relief on gifts to charities is given for payments made by at least four annual instalments under a deed of covenant (with no minimum payment being required) or for one-off payments of at least £250 under the Gift Aid scheme. A taxpayer who wants to give £500 to a charity, and who is liable to pay tax at or above the basic rate (23 per cent in 1998–99), can achieve that by making a net payment of £385 out of his taxed income. The Inland Revenue treats that as a gross payment of £500 from which £115 has been deducted for basic rate tax, and allows the charity to reclaim the £115. If the

---

[67] Cmnd 6601, 1976, para 10.14.
[68] *Ibid.*

taxpayer pays higher rate tax, the Inland Revenue will also reduce the taxpayer's tax bill by £85, representing the difference between basic rate tax and higher rate tax (at 40 per cent) on the sum of £500.[69]

There were said to be a number of overlapping advantages of such a scheme, relating mainly to the desire to stimulate a large number of small donations, the Committee finding 'widespread support for the view that it is more democratic, and therefore in the public interest, that political parties should be funded by a large number of small donations rather than by a small number of large donations'.[70] Income tax relief on donations would increase their value and make it more worthwhile for the parties to seek eligible donations. It would also 'partially make up for what is likely to be a fall in the amount obtained by way of large donations following the introduction of rules requiring disclosure'.[71] In line with the desire to stimulate small donations, it was proposed that the scheme would apply to donations of less than £500.[72] But this would be confined to those parties that satisfied a test of eligibility similar to that used for the purposes of inheritance tax, for the following reasons:

> We believe that the test for relief from inheritance tax . . . is the correct test for tax relief on donations. We acknowledge that since it requires the election of at least one MP, it would exclude relief on donations to the Green Party and other genuinely active political parties. However, we do not think that it would be right to extend relief to all registered political parties. Registration is intended to be an administrative act which will not require evidence of political activity beyond a declaration that the party intends to have one or more candidates at an election. If tax relief is given to all registered parties, some organisations might register as parties simply to be able to claim tax relief. In our view, the inheritance tax test provides a mechanism for ensuring that a tax relief scheme for political parties is not abused.[73]

The Government's Response

The proposal for income tax relief suffered the same fate as the Houghton Committee's different proposals for State aid some twenty-two years earlier. It was estimated by the Treasury that the scheme proposed by Neill would cost between £4m and £5m annually, and it was rejected by the government as a form of public subsidy which could be better spent on other projects.[74] The arguments of cost will not, of course, appear convincing to supporters of public funding. Indeed, the sums involved look extremely modest, compared to what is provided to political parties in other parts of the world. A more convincing basis for ruling out tax relief as a way of distributing State aid to the political parties are the

---

[69] Committee on Standards in Public Life, *supra* n 23, para 8.4.
[70] *Ibid*, para 8.6.
[71] *Ibid*, para 8.7.
[72] *Ibid*, ch 8.
[73] *Ibid*, para 8.23.
[74] Home Office, *The Funding of Political Parties in the United Kingdom*, *supra* n 40, para 6.3.

reasons provided by Houghton: that it benefits the parties which are supported disproportionately by people with higher incomes and does so in a manner that bears no relationship to the needs of the parties. Indeed, it may be a way of giving money to those who need it least. The Neill Committee anticipated the argument that the scheme would benefit parties 'whose members were already wealthier', but not the others. Curiously, these latter arguments were neither directly addressed, nor answered. But so far as the relative wealth argument is concerned, the principal solution to this was 'a fairly low ceiling on donations qualifying for tax relief'.[75] Yet it is difficult to see how this begins to answer the concern, even if the ceiling is set as 'low' as £500, and even if opponents of the income tax relief scheme 'underestimate . . . the cumulative value of tax relief on small donations'.[76]

Even taking these points fully on board, it remains the case that the Neill scheme would produce greater benefits for higher donations (even with a cap of £500). It would also produce the greatest benefits to those parties that do not necessarily have more members than the others or more donors than the others, but more donors of up to or near the £500 ceiling for the tax benefit. This point was raised during the House of Lords debates on the Political Parties, Elections and Referendums Bill following the Conservative amendment proposing income tax relief for donations. Although Lord Rennard for the Liberal Democrats supported the amendment, in an interesting contribution he did so with 'slight reluctance', and explained that he was not persuaded by the government's concerns about the cost of the scheme, which it was estimated would come to about £4m. In his view

> The Government's objection must simply be that the £4 million would go disproportionately to parties with supporters able and willing to donate up to £500. I understand their legitimate concern that there is already an uneven playing field in our democracy and that this scheme may make the slope steeper in the Labour half of the pitch.[77]

But as Lord Rennard pointed out, there was an 'easy answer' to the problem, which was for the Electoral Commission to distribute the estimated £4m on the basis of the estimated levels of support for the parties. The government's view was that a 'tax relief scheme for political donations' would 'amount to general State aid by another route', and that the case had not been made out for State aid either by way of direct grants to the parties or by tax relief which was said by the minister to be 'another method of securing the same undesirable end'.[78] The refusal to implement this recommendation drew strong criticism from Lord Neill and other members of his committee.[79]

---

[75] Committee on Standards in Public Life, *supra* n 23, para 8.17.
[76] *Ibid.*
[77] HL Debs, 18 October 2000, col 1053.
[78] *Ibid*, col 1054 (Lord Bassam).
[79] HC Debs, 13 March 2000, cols 53–54 (Mr John McGregor); HL Debs, 3 April 2000, cols 1126 (Lord Neill); and 1137–38 (Lord Goodhart).

Conclusion

Public funding for political parties in the United Kingdom is very different from that which exists in many other countries. In Canada, France, Germany, Sweden and France, the State makes generous annual subsidies to the parties, and may also assist with election expenses as well as provide income tax relief for political donations. However, we should not underestimate the extent to which the British political parties are supported or aided by the State: as we have seen, it is estimated that State support may amount to as much as £111.07m in an election year. As we have also seen, the nature of that support is changing as it is becoming gradually more extensive and more important. We have moved from a position in which the State (i) underwrites some of the expenses that would otherwise be incurred by the parties and their candidates, and (ii) has absorbed some of the costs that were previously borne by the parties themselves. The move is now in the direction of direct cash grants to the parties, albeit for hypothecated purposes (parliamentary activities and policy development grants). With this move in the form that State support has taken is a shift in the purposes for which support is provided – a move from the support for the electoral and representational activities of the parties to support for party organisation, albeit so far on a modest scale.

There is a sense of an inexorable move in the direction of more State aid for the political parties, though there is also a great deal of hesitancy about moving in this direction. It is true that since the Houghton Report none of the main political parties has perished, and certainly none has perished for want of funds. But it is nevertheless facetious to claim – as the Home Affairs Committee did in 1994 – that because the parties 'have carried on functioning since the Houghton Report very much as they did before', therefore 'Houghton's direst warnings have not proved well founded'.[80] The truth is that the parties have been able to carry on functioning only by fund-raising practices that have brought discredit upon the British political system and raised a number of questions of constitutional propriety. It is quite clear that Houghton was correct that the parties could not rely on established sources of funding to meet their funding needs. What perhaps Houghton did not – and could not – anticipate is the length to which the parties would go to meet these funding needs in the absence of support from the State. As the funding difficulties of the parties have increased – partly as a result of the PPERA – so the funding needs of the parties have expanded – partly as a result of the wave of constitutional reform introduced since 1997. The failure to attend at the time to Houghton's diagnosis has caused an even more urgent problem, as the parties courted disaster in the irresponsible pursuit of large donors and lenders, domestic and foreign.

It is difficult to resist the conclusion that the State must assume a greater

---

[80] Home Affairs Committee, *supra* n 55, para 56.

responsibility for meeting the reasonable needs of the parties if the parties are to be weaned off their large personal donations. It is quite clear that membership subscriptions together with small donations from members will not generate the money the parties need to fulfill their constitutional obligations. But this is not to deny a huge contradiction. Political parties are in financial difficulty partly because their membership is in steep decline. Why then should the people be coerced into supporting political parties with their taxes when they are not prepared to support them voluntarily with their subscriptions or contributions? It may be argued, of course, that a government that included a provision for the funding of political parties in its election manifesto would then have the authority of a mandate to implement such an initiative. But although the mandate would give the authority, some may question the legitimacy of such a form of coercion where – as at the general election in 2005 – the mandate has the support of only 36 per cent of those voting and 22 per cent of those eligible to vote. Declining electoral turnouts and popular alienation from party politics provides an additional cause for caution on the question of public funding. Nevertheless, it is for those who are simultaneously offended by both large personal donations and public funding to explain how the former are to be staunched without the use of the latter. The real question now is the form that any such funding should take.

9

Lessons from Canada

Introduction

The questions of party funding and campaign financing have given rise to difficulties in a number of different jurisdictions. However, the jurisdiction most like
the United Kingdom in this area is Canada, the similarities being most striking
when comparing the United Kingdom with the Canadian federal system. Canada
inherited a number of features of the Westminster system of government, including parliamentary democracy and responsible government.[1] It has an electoral
system similar to that of the United Kingdom, with single-member constituencies elected by a system of first past the post, and with a system of strong party
government. This is not to say that the two systems are on all fours with each
other. A major difference is federalism in Canada, very different from devolution
in the United Kingdom. The Canadian provinces have much greater powers than
even the Scottish Parliament, and these powers can be altered only by a constitutional amendment.[2] One example of this greater power relates to election law and
party financing arrangements, each province being responsible for the regulation
of elections to its own legislature and for the regulation of the parties competing
at provincial level.

Political Parties in Canada

The organisation of political parties in Canada has undergone some change in
recent years, though there remains a degree of continuity and consistency. New
parties come and go, but only two have formed government since 1867, these
being the Liberals and the Conservatives. There are now three main political
parties operating at national level: the Liberal Party; the Conservative Party and
the much smaller New Democratic Party (NDP). The Liberal Party emerged
shortly after Confederation in 1867, and has been in government for forty-three

[1] See British North America Act 1867, Preamble.
[2] Some may, however, see similarities in the separatist ambitions of a section of the people of
Quebec, and the independence ambitions of the people of Scotland.

of the sixty-one years since the end of the Second World War. Sometimes referred to as the natural party of government in Canada, the Liberal Party won the federal elections in 1993, 1997, 2000 and 2004, but was defeated at the general election in 2006. At these successful elections the party secured 41.24 per cent, 38.46 per cent, 40.85 per cent and 36.7 per cent of the popular vote, though at the election in 2000 the turnout was the lowest ever recorded (61.2 per cent), falling still further to 60.5 per cent in 2004. The Liberal Party of Canada, which has had close links with the business community, was badly damaged by a funding scandal in Quebec, and lost the general election in 2006, with its share of the vote falling to 30.2 per cent on a 64.7 per cent turnout.

The Conservative Party, in contrast, was formed in 2003 as a result of a merger of two parties, the Alliance Party and the Progressive Conservative Party. The latter in fact had a long pedigree, which can also be traced back to Confederation. Under Brian Mulroney, the Progressive Conservatives won successive general elections in 1984 and 1988, though the number of its seats fell from 211 to 169, along with its share of the popular vote from 50.3 per cent to 43.2 per cent. In the general election in 1993, the party was all but wiped out, returning only two MPs, a figure that climbed to twenty in 1997 and then fell back to twelve in 2000. In the process, its share of the vote declined to 16.04 per cent, 18.84 per cent, and 12.19 per cent at the elections in 1993, 1997 and 2000. The decline of the Progressive Conservatives was accompanied by the emergence of the Reform Party, a right-wing populist party based mainly in western Canada, which was established in 1987, changing its name to the Canadian Alliance in 2000. But the Reform Party was able to secure only fifty-two (1993) and sixty (1997) seats while the Alliance was able to secure only sixty-six (2000). The merger of the Progressive Conservatives (which had been squeezed into fifth place) and the Alliance (which was the Official Opposition) is said to have been an attempt to create unity on the right to challenge the dominance of the Liberals.

At the general election in 2004, only four parties had candidates elected, these being the Liberal Party (135 seats), the Conservative Party (99), the Bloc Québécois (54) and the NDP (19).[3] Belying its origins in 1990 as a coalition of Liberal and Conservative MPs from Quebec, the Bloc Québécois is a social democratic party with close links to the labour movement in Quebec. It also has close links to the Parti Québécois, and exists essentially to promote the interests of Quebec at Ottawa. As such it is the largest federal party in Quebec, winning 49 per cent of the popular vote in Quebec at the federal election in 2004 (this accounting for 12.4 per cent of the national vote).[4] The NDP, in contrast, was formed in 1961 as a democratic socialist party with close links to the Labour movement.[5] The party

---

[3] The other seat in the 308-seat House of Commons was held by an independent.

[4] An identical result in 1993 led to the Bloc becoming the Official Opposition, as the second largest party.

[5] A good account of its origins is provided in the decision of the Supreme Court of Canada in *Oil, Chemical and Atomic Workers' International Union v Imperial Oil Company* (1964) 41 DLR (2d) 1 which was concerned with British Columbia legislation introduced in 1961 with the apparent intention of undermining the financial security of the party.

Table 9.1 Canadian federal election 2006

(1) Party	(2) Number of seats	(3) Per cent vote
Conservative Party	124	40.3
Liberal Party	103	33.4
Bloc Québécois	51	16.6
New Democratic Party (NDP)	29	9.4
Independent	1	0.3
Total	308	100

Source: Chief Electoral Officer.

(which does not now organise in Quebec) grew steadily until 1988 when it secured forty-three seats and 20.38 per cent of the vote, in the process supporting a minority Liberal government from 1972 to 1974. But in 1993 the party collapsed at the polls, winning only nine seats and 6.88 per cent of the vote. This was by some way the party's poorest electoral performance, and is one from which it has only slowly made a recovery. Its nineteen seats in 2004 were based on 15.7 per cent of the vote, which made the party the third largest in terms of popular support, though not seats.[6] The position of the parties after the general election in 2006 is shown in Table 9.1.

The Election Expenses Act 1974

The modern legislation in Canada has its origins in the pioneering Election Expenses Act 1974.[7] Introduced by a minority Liberal government with the enthusiastic support of the NDP,[8] the Act was passed at a time when the subject of political funding was a matter of acute political interest elsewhere in Canada. Saskatchewan and Manitoba had joined Quebec and Nova Scotia with party financing legislation, and the Ontario government had set up an inquiry into the subject following a provincial scandal. It was at this time too that Watergate had rocked the United States, and the tremors from that political earthquake were to be experienced as far north as Ottawa. The 1974 Act in fact introduced a range of reforms designed to address a number of core problems associated with the Canadian system of party finance. First, it addressed the question of political contributions. Although no controls were imposed on the sources or the amount

---

[6] Indeed, the NDP won more seats (21) based on a lower percentage of the vote (11.5 per cent).

[7] This section draws freely on K D Ewing, 'The Legal Regulation of Campaign Financing in Canadian Federal Elections' [1988] PL 577.

[8] The immediate origins of the legislation lay in the Report of the Barbeau Committee in 1966. See Ewing, ibid.

BOX 9.1
The NDP and Collective Membership

As a party with close links to the labour movement, the NDP bears many similarities to the Labour Party in Britain, though these should not be exaggerated. Nevertheless, the NDP is like the Labour Party in the sense that it is a mixed party of individual and affiliated members (trade unions and other organisations). This is reflected in the federal constitution of the party (agreed at Winnipeg in 2001) in which it is expressly provided that the party would have individual and affiliated members. Affiliated membership was open to trade unions, farm groups, co-operatives, women's organisations and any other groups or organisations which by official act agree to accept and abide by the constitution and principles of the party and are not associated with any other political party. But although there is thus scope for affiliation by a wide range of bodies, in practice it is only trade unions that enjoy affiliated status. In the United Kingdom, affiliated membership of the Labour Party is limited to national organisations, such as trade unions and socialist societies. In Canada, in contrast, the constitution of the NDP provides for affiliated membership not only by international, national, provincial or regional organisations, but also a provincial or regional section of an international or national organisation, as well as a local or branch of any of these organisations.

Affiliated unions thus paid a per-capita fee for each affiliated member. Under the rules of the party, however, it is expressly provided that a member of an affiliated organisation 'may at any time officially notify their organisation that they do not wish a per capita payment to be made to the party on their behalf, and the organisation shall forthwith cease to make such a payment'.[1] In practice, this is a rather meaningless provision given that unions typically did not affiliate on the basis of all their members, and in view of the fact also that the member was not entitled to a refund of the money that would otherwise go to the party. Nor did these provisions give the member the right to object to other forms of support to the party, such as election donations. Decisions on affiliation were thus taken by union executives, and did not necessarily bear any relationship to the number of members in the union in question. There were, however, reported to be 400,000 trade unionists affiliated to the party in this way, compared to around 100,000 individual members of the party. Although the list of affiliates is not published, the list of donors to the party published by Elections Canada includes Canada's most prominent unions. Apart from affiliation fees, unions supported the NDP by donations at election times, and also provided assistance in kind in terms of an army of officials to work on campaigns.

As with the Labour Party in Britain, organisations affiliated to the NDP have rights of membership corresponding to the level of their affiliation, though affiliated organisations have rights that appear diluted when compared with their British counterparts. Nevertheless, affiliated organisations were entitled to send one delegate for every one thousand affiliated members. Under the NDP Constitution, Article V(2), the Party Convention should meet at least every other year, as the 'supreme governing body of the Party with full authority in all matters of federal policy, program and constitution'. Specific provision is made for affiliated organisations in the procedures for electing the party leader. Here the Constitution provides by Article VII(3)(b) that 25 per cent of the votes should be allocated to trade unions. By Articles VIII and IX, the Constitution also provides for the representation of affiliated organisations on the Executive and Council of the party. The former is the body responsible for setting the goals and objectives of the party, as well as forming the basis of its election planning committee; and the latter is the governing body between Conventions. Affiliated organisations have two places reserved on the Executive and sixteen on the Council, though in both cases this represents trade union representation rather than trade union control.

[1] NDP Constitution (2001), Art IV (3)(3).

of contributions, steps were taken to try to broaden the base of party finances and to require the disclosure of donations. Secondly, steps were taken to regulate access to broadcasting, by requiring the broadcasting authorities to limit the time available to the parties and by ensuring that the time was allocated fairly. And thirdly, the Act introduced a number of measures designed to enhance equality of opportunity in election campaigns. This was done by means of the partial reimbursement of election expenses on the one hand and spending limits on the other.

Disclosure and Tax Credits

The approach to contributions was one that was consistent with the party structure then operating in Canada, in the sense that it respected the different forms of party organisation. Although the parties were free to take large corporate donations, it was also the case that the NDP could continue to receive affiliation fees from trade unions as collective members of the party, without any ceiling being imposed on the level of affiliation by individual organisations. A contribution cap would mean that a trade union could affiliate to the party only up to the amount of the cap, regardless of the number of members. Although some provinces imposed restraints on the size of donations,[9] there was no demand for this at federal level, and it seems unlikely that any such initiative would have been supported by the NDP. The Act did, however, require a greater deal of account-ability for political donations, introducing a system of mandatory disclosure of donations to political parties, which were required to submit an annual report of all donations of more than $100 (now $200) to the Chief Electoral Officer.[10] For this purpose donations were widely defined to include not only money but also the commercial value of any goods and services provided to the party by way of loan, advance, deposit, contribution or gift. The donors were to be named, and the information published by the Chief Electoral Officer, albeit in the fiscal year after the donation was made.[11]

If disclosure was designed to operate as a restraint on large donations to the parties, the income tax credits also introduced by the 1974 Act were designed to broaden the base of political giving by encouraging more individuals to give small donations. An amendment to the Income Tax Act enabled registered polit-ical parties to issue tax receipts to donors, thereby encouraging the parties actively to seek small donations from taxpayers. Under the Act, a donor could deduct the following amounts from tax otherwise payable:

- 75 per cent of the value of the donation, if the donation did not exceed $100;
- $75 plus 50 per cent of the amount by which the donation exceeds $100 but does not exceed $550; and
- $300 plus 33.33 per cent of the amount by which the donation exceeds $550.[12]

The maximum relief permitted in any one year was $500, on a donation of $1,150. In the report of the Neill Committee on *The Funding of Political Parties in the United Kingdom*,[13] it was explained that on receiving a tax credit certificate from a party official for a donation, the taxpayer 'then sends that certificate to the Revenue when he or she receives an income tax demand, and the certificate is treated as [a] payment . . . towards the tax bill'.[14] But such a system can only

---

[9] See K D Ewing, 'The Funding of Political Parties in Ontario' (1989) 27 *Osgoode Hall LJ* 27.

[10] See now Canada Elections Act, 48–49 Eliz II, SC c 9 (2000), s 424(2).

[11] The Canada Elections Act, *ibid*, s 424(2) now requires contributions to be reported on a quarterly basis.

[12] The allowances have since been increased so that in 2003, the tax credit was worth (a) 75 per cent of the total, if the total does not exceed $200, (b) $150 plus 50 per cent of the amount by which the total exceeds $200, if the total exceeds $200 and does not exceed $550, or (c) the lesser of (i) $325 plus 33 1/3 per cent of the amount by which the total exceeds $550, and (ii) $500. See *Figueroa v Canada* [2003] SCR 912, para 5. It was raised further by the 2003 Act: under the new formula the deduction applies '(a) when that total does not exceed $400, 75 per cent of that total, (b) when that total exceeds $400 and does not exceed $750, $300 plus 50 per cent of the amount by which that total exceeds $400, and (c) when that total exceeds $750, the lesser of (i) $650, and (ii) $475 plus 33 1/3 per cent of the amount by which the total exceeds $750'.

[13] Cm 4057–I, 1998.

[14] *Ibid*, para 8.4.

operate effectively in those jurisdictions where (unlike in the United Kingdom) the bulk of taxpayers submit tax returns.[15]

State Support and Spending Limits

These income tax credits were in effect a form of State support for the parties which was based to some extent on the level of their popular support rather than their electoral support. More direct forms of State support were also introduced by the Act, including a reimbursement of election expenses incurred by candidates who polled at least 15 per cent of the votes cast in their respective ridings, the reimbursement being based on the number of electors in the riding. Under a new simplified formula, candidates are entitled to a reimbursement of up to 60 per cent of their total expenses, provided they poll now at least 10 per cent of the valid votes cast.[16] In addition to the reimbursement of candidate expenses, the 1974 Act also reimbursed the parties for their broadcasting expenses. Broadcasters were required by the Act to provide free time to the political parties, and an additional 6.5 hours were to be allocated to the parties based on a formula agreed with the Canadian Radio-Television and Telecommunications Commission (now the Broadcasting Arbitrator appointed by the Chief Electoral Officer). This additional 6.5 hours was paid time, and the parties were entitled to a rebate of up to 50 per cent of the costs incurred in buying such time in accordance with their allocation. In 1983, however, the law was changed so that the parties were entitled to recover 22.5 per cent of all their permitted election expenses rather than 50 per cent of their broadcasting expenses. But the reimbursement would be paid only if the party incurred at least 10 per cent of its maximum permitted expenditure. The law has been changed again: parties are now entitled to a rebate of 50 per cent of their election expenditure provided they secure 2 per cent of the vote nationally or 5 per cent of the vote in ridings where they had candidates.[17]

The reimbursement provisions can be seen as a part of the commitment to electoral fairness, designed to ensure that all credible candidates and parties have an opportunity to get their message out. They may also be seen as part of the commitment to prevent undue influence in the political process, guaranteeing that candidates and parties can operate at a minimum level of efficiency without being unduly dependent on large donors or donations. These commitments are also reflected in the comprehensive spending limits that the Act introduced, and these index-linked provisions apply to both candidates and parties. The limits applying to candidates are based on the number of electors in the riding in question; and the limits on the parties are based on the number of ridings in which

[15] As the Neill Committee explained, only a minority of taxpayers in the United Kingdom submit annual tax returns, with most people paying through the employer-operated PAYE system: *ibid*, para 8.5.

[16] See now Canada Elections Act, *supra* n 10, s 464.

[17] *Ibid*, s 435, as amended in 2003.

the party fields candidates. So the more candidates a party fields, the higher its level of permitted expenditure. At the federal general election in 2004, the main parties with candidates in every riding were permitted to spend up to $17,593,925.32 each. Unlike in the United Kingdom, however, these limits apply only from the issuing of the writ for the election until polling day. In addition to these limits on the candidates and political parties, the 1974 Act also introduced what were to be controversial limits on third-party spending at both riding and national level. As originally introduced, these restrictions effectively prevented any third-party electoral activity.[18] But as a result of several legal challenges the law has been relaxed,[19] though third parties can only spend up to $175,800,[20] which is very low by British standards.

The Parties and their Funds

Some thirty years after the enactment of the 1974 Act, another Liberal government introduced a second radical package of funding reform. The measures were promoted as one of the last acts of Jean Chrétien before standing down to be succeeded as Prime Minister by Paul Martin. Chrétien's proposals were to be found in what was to be become known as Bill C-24, a measure that reflected a concern with the sources of income to the parties, and the apparently continuing dependence on corporate donations and large personal donations. Before considering the new funding regime, it is necessary to deal first with the problems to which it was addressed. This can best be done by a snapshot examination of the financial returns of the political parties shortly before the legislation was introduced. Although the legislation came into force in January 2004, the proposals were announced in January 2003. The best year to examine, then, is 2002 rather than 2003, also because donations were distorted in 2003 by higher than normal corporate and trade union donations in what was to be the last year under the old funding regime. In 2003, company donations were almost doubled in value; trade union donations were up fivefold; and the value of individual donations increased by a quarter. Yet although apparently controversial in Canada, the problems of corporate dependence on the one hand and large donations on the other do not seem as acute as in other countries, even in the inflated circumstances in 2003.

---

[18] See *R v Roach* (1980) 101 DLR (3d) 736.

[19] See *National Citizen's Coalition v Attorney General* [1984] 5 WWR 436; *Somerville v Canada* (1996) 184 AR 241. A more tolerant approach of the Supreme Court is to be found in *Libman v Quebec* [1977] 3 SCR 569 and *Harper v Canada* [2004] SCC 33. For an account, see A Geddis, 'Liberté, Egalité, Argent: Third Party Election Spending and the Charter" (2004) 42 *Alta Law Review* 429.

[20] Canada Elections Act, *supra* n 10, s 350. Of this, no more than $3,516 may be spent in each electoral district supporting or opposing the candidate.

Fund-Raising Before Bill C-24

It would be useful to start with an account of how much money the parties were raising in the period before the law was changed. Table 9.2 provides details of the number of donations to the registered parties, the total donation income of the parties, and the size of the average donation in 2002. It will be seen that there is a great inequality between the main parties, with the Liberals raising almost as much as all the other parties combined.[21] It will also be seen that the Liberals raised almost twice as much as the Alliance, despite having only about a fifth of the number of donors.[22] It will be seen further that the NDP raised only about two-fifths of what the Liberals raised despite having twice as many donors.[23] These inequalities reflect in part the size of the average donation, even though overall these seem relatively small: the total average donation to all parties was only $181 compared to $298 in 2003. Yet although these figures appear very modest, it is nevertheless the case that the average Liberal Party of donation of $741 is about ten times larger than the average Alliance donation of $76, thereby ensuring the financial advantage of the Liberals.[24] These figures thus reveal quite acutely how unregulated donations can undermine ambitions for political equality through funding regimes. For although almost a quarter of all donors donated to the Alliance, the Alliance was nevertheless able to raise only just over a half of the income raised by the Liberals.[25]

Having determined how much the parties were raising before the law was changed, the next issue is to determine from whom they were raising it. Table 9.3 shows that the overwhelming majority of donations were made by individuals, each donating an average of only $100.[26] These individual donations accounted for more than half the value of all donations, and the role of individual donations may be higher still if donations to electoral district associations are taken into account. It is not known officially who contributed at this level, and it is perfectly possible that these electoral district association donations are made up of multiple small donations. It is also the case, however, that a donation to an electoral district association was one way of undermining the disclosure obligations by those who wanted to avoid publicity,[27] and that there is no way of knowing whether all (or indeed any) such donations were made by individuals. But although the overwhelming majority of donations to the parties nationally were

---

[21] The gap between the parties was greater in 2003, with total donations of $48m, of which $24m was donated to the Liberals.

[22] In 2003 the Alliance had more than half the total number of donors but just over a sixth of all donation income and just over a third of the donation income of the Liberals.

[23] In 2003 – a bumper year for the NDP – this did not change as it was also a bumper year for the Liberals. Although the NDP raised $10m, the Liberals raised $24m.

[24] This compares with $100 (Alliance) and $1,106 (Liberals) in 2003.

[25] It is not to be overlooked, however, that the Alliance secured only 3.2 million votes in 2000 compared to the 5.2 million secured by the Liberals out of a total of 12.8 million votes cast.

[26] It was still only $131 in 2003.

[27] See *Toronto Star*, 12 July 2003.

Table 9.2 Summary of contributions by registered political party 2002

(1) Registered political party	(2) No. of contributions	(3) Value of contributions ($)	(4) Average contribution ($)
Bloc Québécois	5,499	896,023	163
Canadian Action Party	592	49,816	84
Canadian Reform/Conservative Alliance	95,531	7,294,757	76
Communist Party of Canada	283	102,027	360
The Green Party of Canada	841	137,286	163
Liberal Party of Canada	17,891	13,262,644	741
Marijuana Party	53	25,828	487
Marxist-Leninist Party of Canada	47	33,644	716
Natural Law Party of Canada	65	21,185	326
New Democratic Party	35,614	5,258,883	148
Progressive Conservative Party of Canada	11,555	3,358,232	291
Total	167,971	30,440,325	181

Source: Chief Electoral Officer (except for column 4).

provided by individuals, the value of these donations nevertheless accounted for just over a half of total contributions to the political parties in 2002. This is because of the much higher value of the average corporate contribution, which combined with other businesses and organisations accounted for almost one third of contribution income. Even so, the average corporate contribution is relatively modest, and even more so when compared to the average trade union contribution, though the trade union contribution is the collective fees of thousands of individuals.[28]

An Exaggerated Case for Change?

These data do not reveal a compelling case for change. They show a system that had a large number of individuals paying on average quite small sums of money. They also show a system that was balanced in terms of its funding base: if the electoral district associations are put to one side, the data show that individuals were contributing about two-thirds by way of small donations and that organisations were providing the other third. What these data conceal, however, is the

[28] In 2003 the number of business contributions increased to 5,996, amounting to $13.5m in total with an average of $2,257. In the same year trade union contributions increased sharply to $5.3m, averaging $18,705 per donation.

Table 9.3 Source of contributions to political parties 2002

(1) Source of contribution	(2) No. of contributions	(3) Value of contributions ($)	(4) Average contribution ($)
Individuals	162,694	16,337,515	100
Businesses, commercial organisations	4,467	7,498,374	1,679
Governments	9	4,637	515
Trade unions	179	1,089,795	6,088
Corporations without share capital	2	314	157
Unincorporated organisations or associations	226	305,992	1,354
Electoral district association	394	5,203,698	13,207
Total	167,971	30,440,325	181

Source: Chief Electoral Officer (except for column 4).

pattern of distribution of donations between the parties. In particular more than half of the business donations were made to the Liberal Party, amounting to $5,144,528 in total. This far outstripped 'the fund raising in business circles by all other political parties combined',[29] with only $1.1m being donated by businesses to the Alliance, $1m to the Progressive Conservatives, $95,269 to the NDP and $88,350 to the Bloc Québécois.[30] Such data would appear to provide some support for the view of one commentator that 'the old style political financing system almost always tilts the balance of funding towards the governing party, even when it has lost favour with most of the public. That's because corporate money tends to gravitate to power.'[31] Yet although there was a great deal of criticism of the Liberal Party's reliance on 'Corporate Canada', it remains the case that corporations were providing less than half of the party's known sources of income, and that the average corporate contribution was only $1,995.

It is true that the size of the average contribution masks great variations in the size of individual donations. But this too is not to be exaggerated, even if some exceptionally high donations were received in 2003.[32] Returning to 2002, the largest donation to any party was the $250,450 donated by Ontario Public Service Employees Union (OPSEU) to the NDP. Indeed trade union donations to the NDP accounted for five of the top ten donations in 2002, with a personal

[29] *Toronto Star*, 3 July 2002.
[30] In 2003, $10.8m of the business contributions of $13.5m were donated to the Liberal Party.
[31] See *supra* n 29.
[32] Mainly as a result of a remarkable and unprecedented donation of over $2.9m from a controversial and shadowy company called KKKKK Inc.

donation in excess of $100,000 to the NDP also being among the ten largest. Paradoxically, six of the eight donations in excess of $75,000 were paid to the NDP, including $109,680 from the United Steel Workers of America (USWA) District 6 and another $83,000 from USWA National Headquarters. Only one donation to the Liberals exceeded $100,000, this being $142,329 from Bombardier Inc, and only another six were between $51,000 and $100,000 (from such as the Bank of Montreal, the Bank of Nova Scotia and CIBC); with another sixteen between $25,000 and $50,000 (including the Toronto Dominion Bank and Price-WaterhouseCoopers). Seventy-seven of the top hundred donations to the Liberals were thus in the range from $10,000 to $25,000, with the largest personal donation being for just over $15,000. Although some of Canada's largest companies (notably the banks) were also donating to the opposition parties, these donations too were quite modest. The Alliance and the Progressive Conservatives picked up only ten corporate donations in excess of $25,000, the largest being $50,000 by the Power Corporation of Canada to the Tories.

Bill C-24, Political Donations and State Funding

But although these contributions appear modest by current British standards, they were merely part of a culture in which the Liberal Party mixed business with politics. Another symptom of this culture was to be found in press reports that Paul Martin had raised millions from Corporate Canada to fund his campaign to succeed Chrétien, with the unused balance being donated to the Party.[33] So although it is important to assess the financial state of the parties before 2004, it is also important to acknowledge that this may not provide the whole explanation for the new wave of legislation. As the Prime Minister acknowledged in the Second Reading debate of the Bill, 'there is a perception that corporate and union contributions buy influence',[34] though given the role of the NDP this seems like hyperbole on stilts. But as if to reinforce the perception about business and politics, the government's reform proposals were published just as another funding scandal was about to break. This was associated with a government sponsorship programme in Quebec in which $100m had been paid to Quebec-based advertising companies sympathetic to the Liberal Party for work that in some cases was never done. The scandal engulfed the government at the highest levels and

---

[33] *Toronto Star*, 12 July 2003; 23 December 2003.

[34] House of Commons Debates, 11 February 2003, col 1541. See also the remarks of the Chief Electoral Officer in a lecture to an IPSA gathering in Montreal in 2003 where he said that 'public expectations of the electoral and political processes have evolved considerably since 1974. Whereas at that time, controlling election spending was seen to be the primary objective, today controlling political contributions is also a major concern. For example, the 2000 Canadian Election Study found that 63 per cent of Canadians believed there should be a limit on how much people can give to candidates and parties. Of particular concern is the perception of undue influence that large political donations might bring.'

was the subject of investigation by a retired Quebec judge, Mr Justice Gomery.[35] Some of the public's money that had been misused in the sponsorship scandal is said to have made its way back to the Liberal Party in the form of donations.[36]

Proposals for Reform

The plans for further legislation were published on 29 January 2003. At that point the proposal was for a ban on company and trade union contributions to political parties and an annual contribution cap of $10,000 by individuals. In place of private contributions there would be greater public funding to the parties of $1.50 for every vote secured by the parties at the immediately preceding general election. It was thought as a result that taxpayer support for political parties in the forthcoming election would double to about $80m, a sum based on election spending rebates, income tax receipts for donations and the new allowances for the parties.[37] A potentially controversial issue related to the qualifying conditions for public funding, which required a registered party to have secured at least 2 per cent of the national vote or 5 per cent of the vote in ridings where the party had a candidate. It is hardly surprising that the Communist Party – said to be 'the only registered federal party to oppose the Bill in principle' – should be outraged by the eligibility requirements for public funding. If these discriminatory rules were removed, claimed the party, 'the allowances for all six smaller parties combined – based on the past two general elections – would amount to a trifling 1.5 per cent of the total subsidies paid out annually, while the "big five" would scoop up the remaining 98.5 per cent'.[38] Nevertheless, these requirements were not altered, though they were the subject of a legal challenge alleging a breach of the Canadian Charter of Rights and Freedoms.

The government's proposals were warmly endorsed by the Bloc Québécois and by the NDP, as well as by the Canadian Labour Congress and leading trade unions. But they encountered opposition mainly from the Alliance, though there was also some resistance from Progressive Conservatives. The former was concerned in particular about the nature of the burden that the Bill would impose on party activists (for reasons that will become clearer),[39] while the latter were

---

[35] The legislation might otherwise appear to reflect a very high standards of propriety on the part of Prime Minister Chrétien who bequeathed the legislation as one of the last acts of his administration. It also might otherwise reflect an act of extraordinary generosity on the part of the Prime Minister, for as we shall see, one effect of the legislation is that the governing Liberal Party would lose quite a remarkable fiscal advantage enjoyed over the other parties.

[36] *Globe and Mail*, 1 October 2004.

[37] *Toronto Star*, 30 January 2003.

[38] *People's Voice*, 16–31 May 2003.

[39] The Alliance leader also attacked the Bill in Second Reading as being concerned to address the problems of the Liberal Party of Canada rather than address the wider public interest: 'the appearance of this legislation at this time is too driven by internal Liberal politics and needs: the need of the Prime Minister to whitewash various scandals from his record before he retires; the need to deal with his leadership rival within the Liberal Party; and, as stated by the Prime Minister's own principal adviser to

concerned that it would favour incumbent parties by banning private funding and tie State support to previous election results:

> The first flaw is that it proposes that future funding be determined by past results. In fact it goes far to defining the financial future of a party by looking to its past. In other words, if the financial side of an election campaign were a 100-yard dash, I can hear the starter now – 'Tories, you go to the starting line. NDP, take 15 steps behind. Alliance, start at the 25-yard line. Liberals, start at the 50-yard line. And by the way, you all have the same finish line!'[40]

The government also encountered resistance elsewhere, with some opposition within the Liberal Party, embarrassed by the fact that the government had miscalculated the Bill's effect on its own party. 'Howls of outrage' were said to have been heard from some Liberal backbenchers 'who complained it would cramp their fund-raising activities and that they had not been consulted by the government in advance on the bill'.[41] Top Liberal Party officials told a House of Commons Committee that the Bill would leave the party with a $1.3m annual shortfall, and that it should be amended to allow corporations and unions to make annual donations of up to $10,000 to parties.[42] The same officials also argued that the implementation of the Bill should be delayed 'to allow parties to adjust the way they raise money, and to train their volunteers to work within the new rules'.[43]

Adjusting the Proposals for Reform

But the Prime Minister was determined to have the new regime in place for the forthcoming general election which was held in 2004. He did, however, dilute his original proposals in the face of opposition, and did so in two ways. First, the amount of public subsidy was increased from the proposed $1.50 a vote to $1.75 a vote,[44] with election rebates also increased from 50 per cent to 60 per cent of expenditure (though for the 2004 election only); and secondly, the legislation reduced the ceiling on donations from the proposed $10,000 to $5,000 annually.[45] These amendments seemed to be enough to persuade the bulk of critics within the Liberal caucus,[46] though the party president was reportedly 'unhappy with the amount for which taxpayers will be on the hook',[47] albeit satisfied the

his caucus, the need to deal with the bank debts of the Liberal Party itself': House of Commons Debates, 11 February 2003, col 1555.

[40] House of Commons, Standing Committee on Procedure and House Affairs, 30 April 2003.
[41] *Ibid.*
[42] *Toronto Star*, 30 May 2003.
[43] *Ibid.*
[44] An Act to amend the Canada Elections Act and the Income Tax Act (political financing), 51–52 Eliz II, SC c 19 (2003), s 40, adding a new Canada Elections Act, above s 435.01–435.47.
[45] An Act to amend the Canada Elections Act, *supra* n 10, s 25, replacing Canada Elections Act, *ibid*, s 405.
[46] *Toronto Star*, 5 June 2003.
[47] *Ibid.*

party would no longer be facing a shortfall of $1.3m. Mr LeDrew's other concern was that the amendments 'do nothing to encourage parties to raise money on their own as opposed to being now on the public dole'.[48] These concerns were not without foundation, it being estimated by the government that the amendments would add another $10m to the estimated annual cost of $23.3m–37.2m.[49] Similar concerns were expressed beyond the Liberal Party, with a spokesman for Democracy Watch ('an independent advocacy group for democratic reform') claiming that the level of public financing was now too high:

> Political fundraising reform should encourage the parties to broaden their base of support. When you have this kind of guaranteed annual income that's so high, there's little incentive to do that.[50]

These criticisms were echoed by a leading columnist, concerned that the legislation would 'weaken the grass roots of a system that is unduly dominated by a professional political elite'. This would be done by making riding associations 'beholden to the political centre' and, by 'relieving parties of much of the hard work of soliciting citizen support'.[51]

Bill C-24 came into force on 1 January 2004. So far as political contributions are concerned, it prohibits contributions from corporations, trade unions or other associations,[52] to the evident chagrin of at least one prominent businessman.[53] He was heard to complain that the law 'prohibits him from supporting

---

[48] *Ibid.*

[49] *Ibid.*

[50] *Toronto Star*, 11 June 2003.

[51] J Travers, 'Take this Bill to the Electorate', *Toronto Star*, 12 June 2003.

[52] Thus it is provided that 'No person or entity other than an individual who is a citizen or permanent resident as defined in subsection 2(1) of the *Immigration and Refugee Protection Act* shall make a contribution to a registered party, a registered association, a candidate, a leadership contestant or a nomination contestant': An Act to amend the Canada Elections Act, *supra* n 44, s 24, amending new Canada Elections Act, *supra* n 10, s 404.

[53] But the business community generally was not against controls, though it did appear to be against a ban on donations. According to Mr. David Stewart-Patterson (Senior Vice-President, Policy and Communications, Canadian Council of Chief Executives) in evidence to the House of Commons House Affairs Committee on 1 May 2003: 'By a margin of four to one, the council's members opposed both an outright ban on corporate donations and any exemption for smaller business from a general ban. By a two to one margin, though, they did support caps on both corporate and individual donations at a reasonable amount, which we defined in our survey question as between $1,000 and $10,000 a year. This leads me to what may be the most important question for this committee to consider. There is clearly considerable support in principle within the business community for a reasonable limit on corporate donations. The responses from our members, however, suggest that the limit imposed in Bill C-24 may be unduly restrictive. My sense is that even among business leaders who support a cap in principle, there is genuine concern that too small a limit could unfairly restrict the ability of a company even to participate in the democratic process at the riding level. For a company that operates in just a single riding the $1,000 limit may be perfectly reasonable, but for a company that operates in every riding from coast to coast it drops to a little more than $3 per riding. Since corporate donors are more likely than individuals to support more than one party, this could effectively drop the annual limit per party in each riding to less than $1. To illustrate the potential absurdity, it could become illegal for the representative of a major employer in a community to buy each of the local candidates in an election a cup of coffee, much less attend the local member of Parliament's summer barbecue.'

the candidates and parties he wants to support while sending public money to parties he opposes.[54] The same individual found this 'absolutely offensive', claiming to have 'the right to support' whoever he wanted to support, a right that 'has been taken away'.[55] This restriction is, however, subject to a qualification in the sense that contributions may be made by a corporation or a trade union that do not exceed $1,000 in total in any calendar year 'to the registered associations, nomination contestants and candidates of a particular registered party'.[56] For these purposes a donation is defined to mean both monetary and in-kind donations. Alongside the ban on contributions, Bill C-24 introduced a State subsidy for the political parties based on the outcome of the most recent general election. Each party that qualifies for the subsidy (and as we have seen not all registered parties do qualify) is entitled to a payment of $1.75 (index linked) for every vote cast in its favour at the most recent general election. The money is paid on a quarterly basis, and according to the Communist Party constituted 'a massive and obscene transfer of public wealth to the large, established parties, amounting to almost $80 million over a four year period'.[57]

The Impact of Bill C-24

At the time of writing, Bill C-24 had been in operation for only thirty months. It is thus premature to reach definitive conclusions about its impact, and indeed the contribution caps are about to be lowered still further by Bill C-2 introduced by the new Conservative government in 2006.[58] It is, however, possible to draw a number of initial comparisons between life just before and life just after the legislation was introduced. It is also possible to conclude that the Bill has not fully overcome concerns about political funding in Canada. The Liberal Party in particular was evidently ill-equipped for the legislation for which its government was responsible, being too heavily dependent on corporate money and not having as good a base of individual donors as the other parties. In the first year of the new legislation, the Liberals had fewer donors than either the Conservatives or the NDP, and raised less than half in donations than the Conservatives and only slightly more than the NDP. Thus the Liberals had 17,501 donors in 2004, the Conservatives 68,000 and the NDP 30,097, these contributing $5.2m, $10.9m and $5.1m respectively.[59] Further evidence that the Liberals were having

---

[54] *Toronto Star*, 13 June 2004.

[55] *Ibid.*

[56] Similarly, contributions may be made by a corporation or a trade union of up to $1,000 in total to an independent candidate. See An Act to amend the Canada Elections Act, *supra* n 44, s 24, adding a new Canada Elections Act, *supra* n 10, s 404(1).

[57] *Ibid.*

[58] This will prohibit all trade union and company donations and reduce to $1,000 the amount that may be given annually by an individual to a national party, with another $1,000 in aggregate being permitted to riding associations and candidates.

[59] *Globe and Mail*, 5 July 2005.

difficulty building up their fund-raising base was provided by a press report about 'secretive, $5,000-a-head private fundraisers with Prime Minister Paul Martin'.[60] It is reported that a cocktail party in Calgary helped to draw in forty–fifty people who donated $5,000 each, this amounting to a $200,000-plus bonanza that made up a big chunk of the Liberal's fund-raising efforts in the second quarter of 2005.[61] The decision by Mr Martin to meet contributors was said to be due to the Liberal's poor fund-raising performance and was criticised on the ground that such cocktail parties 'amount to selling access to the Prime Minister'.[62]

Quarterly Allowances

The first quarterly allowances were paid in 2004, as shown in Table 9.4. In accordance with the provisions of Bill C-24, the four payments in the first year were made in advance at the beginning of 2004. They were based on the results of the thirty-seventh general election (held in 2000) and were adjusted later to take account of the general election in the middle of 2004 (the thirty-eighth general election). Paradoxically, the election which was thus the benchmark for State funding of the political parties was the election in which the parties attracted what was then the lowest electoral turnout in Canadian history at 61.2 per cent (compared to 67 per cent in 1997, 69.6 per cent in 1993 and 75.3 per cent in 1988). At the general election in 2000, a total of just over 12.8 million votes were cast, with 5.2 million being cast in favour of the Liberal Party, 3.2 million for the Alliance, 1.2 million for the Progressive Conservative Party, 1.1 million for the NDP and 1.3 million for the Bloc Québécois. The rest were cast for an array of small parties and for independent candidates. In 2004 the number of votes cast increased to 13.5 million (although turnout continued to fall – to 60.5 per cent). But the Liberal vote fell to 4.9 million, the Conservative vote fell to 4 million, while both the NDP and the Bloc Québécois vote increased to 2.1 and 1.6 million respectively. All parties winning seats at these two general elections met the eligibility requirement of 2 per cent of the national vote or 5 per cent of the valid votes cast in the electoral districts where the party had an endorsed candidate. In 2005, the payments were made on a quarterly basis as anticipated by Bill C-24, but again an adjustment was made to take account of the election result and payments already made. The payments made in 2005 are shown in Table 9.5.

Tables 9.4 and 9.5 both reveal and conceal a number of points of interest. The first is that payments are made to parties other than the parliamentary parties – although not all registered parties qualify, it is also the case that registered parties may qualify even though they do not win any seats. This is true of the Green

---

[60] *Globe and Mail*, 6 August 2005.
[61] *Ibid*. This followed an earlier private cocktail party held in March 2005 at the home of a prominent businessman.
[62] *Ibid*.

Table 9.4 Quarterly allowances to the registered political parties 2004

(1) Registered political party	(2) Advance paid in Jan 2004 (1 Jan– 31 Dec, 2004) ($)	(3) 3rd quarter (Jul–Sep 2004) payable or (receivable) ($)	(4) 4th quarter (Oct–Dec 2004) ($)
Bloc Québécois	2,411,022	0	322,846
New Democratic Party (NDP)	1,914,269	12,958	956,692
Green Party of Canada	0	261,847	261,847
Liberal Party of Canada	9,191,054	(49,646)	0
Conservative Party of Canada	8,476,872	(563,360)	0
Total for year			23,809,407 (613,006)

Source: Chief Electoral Officer.

Table 9.5 Quarterly allowances to the registered political parties 2005

(1) Registered political party	(2) 1st quarter (Jan–Mar 2005) (with inflation adjustment as of 1 Apr 2004 – based on the 38th general election) ($)	(3) 2nd quarter (Apr–Jun 2005) (with inflation adjustment as of 1 Apr 2005 – based on the 38th general election) ($)	(4) Total for the year (including 3rd and 4th quarters calculated on same basis as 2nd quarter) ($)
Bloc Québécois	755,740	769,708	3,064,864
New Democratic Party (NDP)	956,692	974,375	3,879,817
Green Party of Canada	261,847	266,686	1,061,905
Liberal Party of Canada	2,240,772	2,282,187	9,087,333
Conservative Party of Canada	1,807,734	1,841,146	7,331,172
Total for year			24,425,091

Source: Chief Electoral Officer.

Party of Canada, which qualified on the basis of 5 per cent of the vote in areas where it had candidates. The Greens were in fact fairly phlegmatic about the eligibility criteria when they gave evidence to the House of Commons House Affairs Committee, even though their share of the national vote at the time stood at only 0.8 per cent:

> given that the government has chosen to impose a threshold, we are at least relieved that it is a realistic threshold, and not 5 per cent or 10 per cent. We think 2 per cent is a target that a party could set out to compete for and would have a real shot at. I wonder if there has ever been a party that has run anything like a full slate across the country and has not received 2 per cent of the vote. We think it is something our party can reach for. At this point, you would not have our support for a 10 per cent threshold, but 2 per cent is something I think we can live with.[63]

It is notable that the Green's qualified despite securing only 4.3 per cent of the national vote in 2004, whereas the other small registered parties secured only between 0.00 per cent and 0.03 per cent and did not qualify. The second point to note is in response to the concerns that public funding favours incumbents. On the contrary, public funding on this model rewards strength of electoral support and ensures that money is distributed on an equitable basis. Thus although the Liberals got the largest slice of the pie, it was still not as much as half. Corresponding to votes won at the previous general election, the Liberals received 39 per cent, the Conservatives 34 per cent and the other parties the balance. This compares with the position before 2004 when, say, corporate money went disproportionately to the Liberal Party and when the Liberal Party enjoyed a slightly larger slice of the pie provided to the parties by private funding.

The Flow of Private Funds

Turning from the quarterly allowances to the legislation in general, it would appear at this stage to have provided contestable benefits for the party that introduced it. This is surely one of the 'unintended consequences' to which Mr Chrétien referred in the course of his Second Reading speech.[64] At one level the Act had a fairly stable impact on the Liberals, and perhaps even a beneficial one in the sense that, at least initially, it enabled the party to maintain income levels compared to 2002. One effect of the legislation was that the party lost its $4.7m from businesses and its $51,214 from trade unions.[65] Another effect of the legislation was to wipe out personal donations in excess of $5,000, though in practice this may not have been such a huge blow, with only twenty-eight personal donations in excess of $5,000 being made in 2002. These amounted in total to

---

[63] House of Commons, Standing Committee on Procedure and House Affairs, 30 April 2003.

[64] House of Commons Debates, 11 February 2003, col 1550.

[65] It was not only the NDP that benefited from trade union donations, with the Liberals receiving ten such donations in 2002, including from the Canadian Marine Pilots' Association, the BC Council of Film Unions, and the International Union of Marine and Shipbuilding Workers.

Table 9.6 Total election expenses and reimbursements in the Canadian general election 2004

Registered political party	Total paid election expenses ($)	Authorised limit of election expenses ($)	Reimbursement ($)
Bloc Québécois	4,507,531.12	4,591,747.38	2,704,518.67
Conservative Party of Canada	17,284,256.91	17,593,925.32	10,370,554.15
Green Party of Canada	498,179.39	17,593,925.32	298,907.63
Liberal Party of Canada	16,604,528.20	17,593,925.32	9,962,716.92
New Democratic Party (NDP)	12,018,931.25	17,593,925.32	7,211,358.75
Total			30,548,056.12

Note 1: The reimbursement for 2004 was based on 60 per cent of expenses incurred, as part of the transition to the new regime. The reimbursement before 2004 was 50 per cent and will revert to 50 per cent for the 2006 election, the details of which were not available at the time of writing.

Note 2: Seven other registered parties contested the 2004 election but did not qualify for an election expenses rebate because they did not attract a sufficient level of support. The parties in question are the Canadian Action Party, the Christian Heritage Party, the Communist Party of Canada, the Libertarian Party, the Marijuana Party, the Marxist-Leninist Party of Canada and the Progressive Canadian Party. These parties are challenging their exclusion in legal proceedings which had not concluded at the time of writing, the Communist Party of Canada having succeeded in an earlier challenge to a previously high threshold for party registration: *Figueroa v Canada* [2003] SCR 912.

Source: Chief Electoral Officer.

$247,402 with the surplus in excess of $5,000 × 28 being only $107, 402, which would be the extent of the revenue lost under the new regime. The other impact of the new law would be in relation to internal party transfers, which although still permitted are unlikely to yield as much as in the past, partly because of new transparency requirements, and partly because of restrictions on what may now be moved by way of internal party transfer. The contribution and transfer income of the party in 2004 thus fell from $13.2m in 2002 to $5.2m in 2004, even though the number of donors remained fairly stable at 17,429 in 2004 (compared to 17,891 in 2002). With the public subsidy, however, the total income of the party increased from $13.2m in 2002 to $14.3m in 2004. Unlike the Conservatives and the NDP, however, the Liberals now relied on the State for more than half their income, with Table 9.6 showing additional funding being provided by way of the election expenses rebate.

Although the income of the Liberal Party was thus stable between 2002 and 2004, the Liberals have lost the comparative advantage that they had over the other parties. In 2002, the Alliance and the Progressive Conservatives combined raised $10.5m, while the NDP raised $5.2m and the Bloc Québécois $0.9m. This gave the Liberal Party a lead over each of the other parliamentary parties, and an income which at $13.2m was about 80 per cent of the combined income of all the other parties together. By 2004, this had changed, with the Conservative Party having a donation and transfer income of $10.9m, the NDP $5.1m and the Bloc Québécois $0.9m. The Liberals were thus raising less donation income than the Conservatives and about the same as the NDP, though, as already pointed out, having fewer donors than either of them. It is thus only the public subsidy that allowed the Liberals to maintain their financial advantage over the NDP. But even with the quarterly allowance, the Liberals lost their financial advantage over the Conservatives, which in 2004 had a combined public and private income of $18.9m compared to the Liberals' $14.2m. The Liberals also lost their comparative advantage over the NDP which now had an annual income of more than rather than less than half of that of the Liberals. Indeed, having raised an income that was almost 80 per cent of that of all the other parliamentary parties combined in 2002, by 2004 the Liberals had an income at a level which represented less than 50 per cent of the combined income of these parties.

Bill C-24 and Party Structure

It is not only the Liberal Party that has been affected by the legislation, which was calculated to have a different – but potentially more dramatic – impact on the NDP. Here, however, the impact was not simply one of funding but one which went to the very structure and organisation of the party, as it would no longer be possible for a union to make a collective affiliation fee. An affiliation fee paid by a union would constitute a contribution, and as such is forbidden under Bill C-24, thereby threatening the whole concept of collective membership. The other problem for the NDP–trade union relationship is that trade unions could no longer second staff to work in election campaigns. This would constitute a donation, which under the old regime would have to be disclosed but which under the new regime would be prohibited. Trade union officials would be required to take vacation time to work in a campaign. The rest would have to be paid for by the party, presumably by the party paying the union. Yet despite these and other drawbacks, the NDP strongly supported the legislation. According to NDP spokesman Dick Proctor, during the Second Reading debate 'the only people who should be allowed to contribute to political parties are those who are actually eligible to vote at election time. That would exclude organizations, corporations and trade unions.'[66] Related to this was the perceived need to eliminate the influence of 'Corporate Canada' on the other parties and on the Liberal Party in particular. This was seen to be especially important in light of the incoming Liberal Party leader's close connections with corporate interests.

[66] House of Commons Debates, 11 February 2003, col 1645.

NDP and the Trade Unions

Although the NDP supported the legislation, it also vigorously defended its links with the trade union movement:

> Our political enemies always take every opportunity to point out that the New Democratic Party is overwhelmingly supported by the trade union movement. We are proud of the special and unique partnership with the labour movement. That was how the New Democratic Party was founded back in the early 1960s. We are and remain full partners with the labour movement, and, yes, unions do support us, but to a far lesser extent than most people believe. About 30 per cent of our donations come from the trade union movement but the overwhelming amount, 60 per cent, comes from individual donors.[67]

These remarks gave rise to two concerns. First, what did the unions feel about being excluded from making contributions and expenditures; and secondly what form of relationship could survive Bill C-24? Perhaps surprisingly, the unions also supported the legislation for broadly similar reasons as the NDP. As one union official explained:

> Broadly speaking, for some time there has been a body of opinion in the labour movement and in the NDP supporting the position that banning corporate donations to political parties was an urgent enough priority that it was worth accepting a parallel ban on union donations. The opposing view was that this ban would disrupt the link between NDP and labour, founded as it was on affiliation dues, leading in turn to convention delegates, etc. Over time, the position in favour of the ban appeared to win a narrow majority, at least within the Canadian Labour Congress, which took that position officially.
>
> The debate within the left was pre-empted, in a sense, when Liberal Prime Minister Jean Chrétien decided to drop C-24 on the country as a legacy gesture on his way out the door. In this context, the most stalwart defenders of union financing of the NDP saw the political disadvantage of opposing the bill, especially considering its fairly generous substitution of public financing of the parties. As a result the positions taken by unions and others once C-24 was introduced did not necessarily reflect their long-standing positions.[68]

Indeed, not only did the unions support the legislation, but they argued that as originally drafted it did not go far enough. Thus the Canadian Labour Congress argued for a total ban on corporate and trade union contributions:

> Democracy in Canada will be strengthened if it is passed into law, it thought that the Bill did not go far enough, and proposed a total ban on trade union and business contributions as well as tight controls on third party spending.[69]

These political concerns were articulated along two lines of argument. One was the argument that reform was necessary to restore faith in Canadian democracy,

---

[67] *Ibid*, col 1650.
[68] Private correspondence.
[69] House of Commons, Standing Committee on Procedure and House Affairs, 1 May 2003.

in the words of the Canadian Auto Workers Union (CAW) 'to temper the hugely distorting influence of big money in our system'. To this end, the legislation was seen as 'one important step towards re-engaging Canadians in the political process'.[70] Related to this was the perceived need to remove the influence of corporate money from the political process. This is a point made forcefully by the CAW in evidence to the House of Commons Standing Committee

> The current system is undermining democracy. Political financing reform is vital to getting things back on track. Poll after poll suggests that a majority of Canadians support an activist government and strong social programs. And yet what we get is an economic liberalization agenda scripted by the Business Council on National Issues. The huge influence of corporate money on the political process at all levels is impossible to ignore. According to Elections Canada, overall 3 percent of party donors account for 45 percent of the money donated. In the last federal election year, 2000, the Liberals received $12 million in corporate donations and the Canadian Alliance took in $7 million. The amount that Canadian workers contributed through their unions was dwarfed by these figures. . . . Banning corporate donations to political parties is an important and necessary step.

In order to achieve this, the unions were prepared to give up their own political voice as expressed in contributions and expenditures, which were 'a very small measure of counterbalance to the kinds of influence and donations that, for example, [the business community] are able to contribute'.[71] According to the CAW:

> It is understood that a similar ban on union donations is politically requisite to achieve this end. There should be no illusion, however, that union donations in any way match the power of corporate donations to bend and distort the political process. There is simply no comparison to the resources that can be marshaled by corporate interests. There is no 'level playing field'. This huge disparity in resources defines the reality that our members face. This is why politics for the CAW must be about much more than elections and political parties. It is about educating and organizing ourselves to fight for the interests of our members and their families every day of the year.[72]

But not everyone was sanguine about the legislation successfully controlling the influence of big business, though it was left to the tiny Communist Party of Canada (CPC) to articulate these concerns. The CPC claimed that similar measures introduced in Quebec many years ago 'have had little impact on the way corporations influence the election process'.[73] So while business would find other ways to strut its stuff in election times (notably through the constitutionally

---

[70] CAW, Submission to the Standing Committee on Procedure and House Affairs re Bill C-24 (May 2003).

[71] House of Commons, Standing Committee on Procedure and House Affairs, 1 May 2003.

[72] CAW, Submission to the Standing Committee on Procedure and House Affairs re Bill C-24 (May 2003).

[73] *People's Voice*, 16–31 May 2003. But others were more positive about the Quebec system. One commentator addressed a number of concerns by comparing the experience of Quebec where similar legislation had operated since 1980. Thus it was claimed that levels of voter apathy and cynicism were lower in Quebec than elsewhere in Canada, with higher electoral participation in both provincial and

protected corporate press), the labour movement would be effectively disenfranchised.

Transforming the Trade Union Relationship

But although the unions were prepared to give up their right to make contributions, it did not follow that the link with the NDP would be ended. It would, however, have to be changed, and the party constitution rewritten to reflect the new legal restrictions. Thus it was proposed that the principle of affiliated membership would continue but on a different basis. So rather than affiliate on the basis of total membership, trade unions would now affiliate on the basis of full party members. But in a sense this is a rather contrived arrangement, as there will be no financial transfer to the party to the union as a basis for continued affiliation. This will lead to a huge fall in the number of trade unionists affiliated to the party, given that there were said to be approximately 400,000 trade unionists affiliated to the party before the legislation was introduced and approximately 100,000 individual members. Henceforward, unions will have to find out which of their members are also members of the NDP, having joined the party as individual members. The rule changes will allow these people to be counted twice – once as riding association members and once as union members. The right of the union to affiliate on the basis of the aggregate number of members of the union who are also full individual members of the party is thus a device to keep some notion of affiliated membership alive, and with it representation at the party convention and on the management bodies of the party. But the trade union role has been transformed: they are at best vicarious or virtual members whose role and status is diminished as a result. The third-party limits on election spending of $175,800 for each organisation means that these are also tight restraints on the ability of unions to engage in significant independent campaigns on behalf of the party.

It would, however, be a mistake to see Bill C-24 as bringing an end to the relationship between the trade unions and the NDP. Before the Bill was passed, the unions helped the party in a number of ways, including donations of $3.5m in

federal elections. It was also pointed out that in the Quebec system parties had not become 'empty shells' which had 'come to rely on the public purse rather than on their own devices to raise money' (C Hebert, 'Quebec's Healthy Election Process', *Toronto Star*, 3 February 2003). On the contrary: while the federal Liberal Party had not convened for more than three years, the Quebec parties were said to gather the rank and file several times a year and to engage in other forms of membership activity. This was thought to explain why 'on average, Quebec parties have tended to boast more members than most federal parties'. Nor had State funding in Quebec prevented the advent of new parties. Again the contrary appeared to be true, as reflected by the emergence and growth of the ADQ: 'Until last year, the ADQ had never managed to get anyone except its leader, Mario Dumont, elected to the 125 seat National Assembly. But under Quebec's financing system, it has received a yearly subsidy in tune with its share of the votes in the last [Provincial] election (11 per cent). Far from stunting the ADQ, the financing structure of the Quebec system has nurtured it by making up for its fund raising growing pains with public funds' (*ibid*).

total from the trade union movement to enable the party 'to buy mortgage-free an office building in downtown Ottawa that it can use secure bank loans to finance election campaigns'.[74] The largest donors were reported to be the CAW, the United Steelworkers, the United Food and Chemical Workers, and the Communications, Energy and Paperworkers' Union, who each gave $500,000. In the past the unions had guaranteed the loans, but this would no longer be possible under the new legislation. Now that the Bill has been enacted, it is anticipated that the unions will help in other ways. The first is by grass-roots activity, it being anticipated that the unions will be active in the workplace to promote the cause of the party, and that union officials in the workplace will be encouraged to recruit full members to the party. Although the unions will have an incentive in recruiting party members, it may not be only the sceptical who will have doubts about whether an initiative of this kind will yield lasting results. The other proposed form of union support is by independent political campaigns on progressive issues. Although there are third party spending limits during election campaigns, there are no restraints outside the short election period, when unions are free to spend with relative impunity. It is also the case that union money may continue to flow into the provincial wings of the NDP for use in provincial elections, in those provinces where such donations are permissible.[75]

Conclusion

What lessons can be learned about recent Canadian experience? The first is that contribution limits and State funding do not create a perfect equality between the parties. The public funding formula adopted in Bill C-24 means that different sums go to the parties in accordance with their electoral support, which until the general election in 2006 meant that the Liberal Party received more than the other parties, and which since the 2006 general election means that the Conservative Party receives more than the others. But although parties with a greater intensity of support can bridge the funding gap by encouraging more people to make small donations to them, private money does not flow to the parties on an equitable basis, even when it moves in small amounts. The Conservative advantage in recent years was maintained in 2005, with annual financial returns showing the Conservatives with 106,000 donors generating $18m. This contrasted with the $9m generated by 23,000 Liberal donors, the $5.1m generated by 27,000 NDP donors,[76] and the $819,407 generated by 7,773 Bloc Québécois

---

[74] *Toronto Star*, 20 December 2003.

[75] H Jansen and L Young, 'Solidarity Forever? The NDP, Organised Labour, and the Changing Face of Party Finance in Canada' (CPSA, 2005).

[76] These figures do not make such good news for the NDP, and tend to show the difficulties of contribution caps for parties of the Left. Despite having more donors than the Liberals, these donors produce almost half the total donation income produced by Liberal donors. The average NDP

donors. The Conservatives are thus raising more than the other parties combined from more than twice as many donors, and are now receiving more in State funding. Yet although this threatens to create serious funding inequality, it is hard to deny that this is a better inequality than the inequality that existed before the legislation was introduced. It is better because it is based on levels of grass-roots support, it is an inequality that is not accounted for by large donations from sources of doubtful legitimacy, and it is an inequality based on numbers of small donations.

The second lesson from the Canadian experience is that a cap on contributions does in fact have major implications for party structure, in the sense that it has compelled the NDP to rethink the nature of its relationship with organised labour. The principle of collective membership by the traditional method of organisational affiliation is no longer possible, and the current constitutional structure of the party is unlikely to be sustainable. Although the compromise reached by the NDP and the unions could be copied in the United Kingdom if the reformers got their way, it is not yet certain how far this will weaken the trade union role. Much may depend on the ability of the unions to recruit party members, and it is not certain how realistic it is to expect trade union officials to act as recruiting sergeants for a political party in the workplace. What is certain, however, is that a reform with such a dramatic impact could only take place with the consent of the party which would be most directly affected by it. Admittedly Bill C-24 was passed against the wishes of the Conservative Party in Canada. But their demand to be able to continue to receive business donations is a demand of a qualitatively different order from the position of a party which is being told by the State who its members may be and the permissible forms which that membership might take. It is true that the NDP and the unions agreed to Bill C-24 largely for tactical reasons. But in a system (such as the British) where the labour-based party is the governing party, it is not clear why trade unions would or should agree to this weakening of their political voice. The need to neutralise their own political voice in order to neutralise the even louder political voice of the business community is a much less attractive and much less persuasive argument.

A third lesson is that legislation of this kind is unlikely to drive money from the system. Although the legislation was welcomed across the political spectrum (with notable exceptions), there were few illusions about future problems. In a thoughtful contribution Joe Clark (an elder statesman, from the Conservative side) said that

> Our political system has changed. The weight of private interests has grown. The sense of public interest has declined. That is why the lobbying industry, which virtually did not exist in Canada 30 years ago, is so powerful today. The reality now is that in this capital city good lobbyists have much more influence than good members of Parlia-

donation amounted to $188 compared to the average Liberal donation of $391 and the average Conservative donation of $169.

ment. That raises a very serious question for the Canadian political system. Special interests, by definition, fracture community. They put particular interests ahead of the whole. Historically in Canada, two institutions performed the function of knitting together different claims and putting the public interest first. Government itself was one of those institutions. The other was political parties, particularly political parties that were national in their reach and in their ambition. It is not healthy for the public interest to have the role of parties decline and the role of lobbyists and special interests fill the vacuum. That is a large issue of which this question of party funding is one important element, because the present situation allows the enfeeblement of political parties. It makes it much more difficult for them to perform their task of drawing together the interests of the whole community.[77]

The ban on corporate and trade union contributions is likely to be met by increased political expenditures by both.[78] But while a ban on third-party spending during the election period will go a long way to meet this concern, it will not go all the way. Although the legislation bans corporate and trade union donations to political parties it also regulates rather than bans third-party spending at elections. It will still be possible for groups to spend money on national campaigns and indeed if they want to engage at election time this will be the only route they will be permitted to travel. There is no limit on how much can be spent outside the election period, and the reason why this is more relevant in Canada than in the United Kingdom is because of the short period under federal law (from the issue of the writ) during which the regulated period operates. Outside the period of an election, there is nothing to prevent third parties (and others) engaging in large-scale expenditure, unlike in the United Kingdom where the regulated period at national level operates for twelve months before polling day.[79]

---

[77] House of Commons Debates, 11 February 2003, col 1725.

[78] See the concerns by the chief fund-raiser of the Progressive Conservatives: 'even with this legislation, corporations will not stop being interested in politics. The reality is that severe limits or the elimination of corporate giving will drive this funding to other places, often less transparent than donations to political parties. Third-party advertising, now before the Supreme Court, political action committees (PACs) or other so-called underground activities are all foreseeable and will put a new meaning on the opening of Pandora's box. In America, corporations have not been allowed to donate to federal political campaigns for many years, but can anyone say with a straight face that corporate funding does not influence Washington? The deeper you drive it down, the more the head it raises is ugly' (House of Commons, Standing Committee on Procedure and House Affairs, 30 April 2003). Nevertheless, the Conservative government elected in 2006 has no plans to restore corporate giving and indeed Bill C-2 proposes that all corporate donations should be prohibited.

[79] The problem would be more acute in the United Kingdom than in Canada by virtue of the fact that unions collect money for political purposes by a separate political levy which is paid into a separate political fund which can be used only for political purposes. That is not the case in Canada where union political contributions were paid from the general funds of the unions. The concern in the United Kingdom is that if unions were prevented by law from paying affiliation fees and making donations to the Labour Party, they would have a pot of money that could be used only for political purposes, and for which other uses would have to be found. In the context of the United Kingdom this is not something which the political parties could view with equanimity given the high spending limit of about £1m for third parties in campaigns.

10

Building on PPERA

Introduction

On 23 August 2006, the Electoral Commission published the latest donation reports of the UK's political parties. It also published details of loans under the voluntary code brokered with the same organisations.[1] The figures made grim reading for Labour, showing loans to the tune of £28m and a donation income in the second quarter of 2006 of only £3.4m. According to one leader column, 'if Labour were a private company it would be bankrupt',[2] an extraordinary position for a party of government. Although the Conservative Party was raising much more (£5.9m) and showing loans of only £2.8m, undisclosed loans in 2006 were said by one newspaper to amount to a hard to believe £35m,[3] the party having reported to the Electoral Commission only those loans secured in the second quarter of 2006 (unlike Labour which had reported all outstanding loans). But although the Conservatives appear now to be doing much better financially (and certainly much better than the Labour Party), it was not so long ago that the party's auditors refused to sign off its accounts 'because they fear it is no longer a going concern'.[4]

The Next Step – Regulatory Objectives

What is to be done about this sorry mess? The only thing that is clear is the fog ahead – there is no simple or permanent solution to the problem of party funding. There is, however, an inexorable drive in the direction of more and more regulation throughout the world,[5] as each jurisdiction seeks its own solution to

---

[1] The legal obligation to report loans to the Electoral Commission under the Electoral Administration Act 2006 (on which see pp 140–142 above) did not commence until 11 September 2006.

[2] *The Guardian*, 24 August 2006.

[3] *The Times*, 24 August 2006. This is said to arise from £16m owed to private individuals, 'a similar amount owed to banks', £4.5m owed to Conservative associations and clubs. According *The Guardian* on the same day, the 'current cumulative total' of Conservative loans was £15.9m.

[4] *The Times*, 29 May 2003.

[5] See K D Ewing and S Issacharoff (eds), *Party Funding and Campaign Financing in Comparative Perspective* (2006), ch 1.

its own problems. The most successful regulation is likely to be that which runs with the grain of existing political institutions and legal structures, which in Britain means building on the framework confirmed by the Representation of the People Act 1983 and developed by the Political Parties, Elections and Referendums Act 2000 (PPERA). The current problem presented by the loans affair, however, suggests that the next stage of reform in the United Kingdom should be driven first by a need to *reduce the dependence of the parties on large personal donations*, paradoxical though that may seem in the light of the current financial problems of the parties described above. Large donations cause concern throughout the world – from Alaska to Australia,[6] from where it has been claimed that, 'Whether real or perceived, influence peddling has done much to weaken public faith in our system of government.'[7] But while it is easy to identify the need to control donations in order to advance objectives outlined in chapter 2, identifying an appropriate solution to meet this need is much more elusive.

A second regulatory objective in the current round of reform is *to ensure that the parties have enough money or other resources to carry out their activities in an environment of fair electoral competition*. This invites consideration of what might be referred to as both demand- and supply-side initiatives, which means measures that both reduce the demand for money on the one hand, and ensure an adequate supply of money or resources on the other. Reducing the demand for money means reducing the capacity to spend it. This requires an examination of the spending limits which were introduced in 2001, and a consideration of some of the problems identified in chapter 7, where the limits were shown to be simultaneously too high and too porous. Ensuring an adequate supply of funding or resources requires in turn an examination of whether there is scope for the State to provide additional support or funding for the parties, particularly in a regime in which large personal donations are forbidden or discouraged. Additional State support of the kind identified in chapter 8 would have the added benefit of reducing the demand for money, if the need was being met by the State. Another benefit of such funding or support is that it would provide an opportunity to meet a third regulatory objective, which is to *encourage higher levels of popular support for political parties, and higher levels of participation within political parties*.

This last objective invites different kinds of responses. One is to desist from regulatory measures that discourage citizens from taking part in the affairs of political parties, whether as members or donors. This objective is, however, not without limitations in the sense that there are certain forms of participation or a

---

[6] According to the US Court of Appeals for the 9th Circuit, 'a failure to regulate the arena of campaign finance allows the influence of wealthy individuals and corporations to drown out the voices of ordinary citizens'. There was thus a danger of big money producing a 'political system unresponsive to the needs and desires of the public, and causing the public to become disillusioned with and mistrustful of the political system': *Jacobus v Alaska*, 338 F 3d 1095 (2003), at p 1061 (rejecting a challenge to Alaska's campaign finance reforms).

[7] *Sydney Morning Herald*, 5 February 2003, referring to John Boyle O'Reilly, a Fenian escapee and writer of note who urged us to 'take gifts with a sigh; most men give to be paid'.

certain intensity of participation that might be seen to compromise other regulatory objectives. Thus, for example, it would not be undesirable to discourage donations given in the hope of a benefit in return. But it would not necessarily be desirable in the absence of a compelling public interest to discourage forms of engagement that draw large numbers of people into the political process, with small financial contributions. A good example of the latter is the process by which trade unions affiliate to the Labour Party on the basis of the number of members who pay the political levy. At a time of creeping democratic elitism and popular disengagement, it would be remarkable to contemplate cutting adrift what remains in this country the greatest commitment of working people to political parties. However, this third objective also requires more positive responses, to encourage the parties to recruit and retain members, and measures that ensure party members have full opportunities to participate in the decisions of their parties. The issue here is whether such incentives and/or requirements can and/or should be tied to State aid or public funding.

The Problems with Contribution Limits

There is a strong case – based on arguments drawn from liberal principle – for the imposition of further legal restraints on political donations.[8] But there is an equally compelling case the other way, based on arguments of party autonomy and freedom of association, and the ability of political parties to determine their own constitutions and rules.[9] As we have seen from Canada,[10] the existence of what Duverger refers to as mixed parties is not an obstacle to donation reform.[11] But the Canadian experience also shows that it is perhaps an inevitable consequence of donation reform that it will have a big impact on such parties. This is because a collective membership fee will inevitably come to be seen as a donation and be treated in the same way as other institutional donations. In Canada, these changes were introduced with the full and active support of the New Democratic Party (NDP) and the trade unions, for reasons discussed in chapter 9. However, neither the trade unions nor the Labour Party in Britain see the same tactical advantage in the former disengaging from the latter.[12] But even if they did, the issue of principle here is bigger than the Labour Party and the trade unions – it is still not clear why interest groups should not be free to form political parties and

---

[8] See pp 45–49 above.
[9] See further, K D Ewing, *Trade Unions, the Labour Party and Political Funding* (2002), ch 3.
[10] See ch 9 above.
[11] M Duverger, *Political Parties* (1959), p 7.
[12] A second major difference between Britain and Canada is that the Labour Party is a party of government whereas the NDP never has been a party of government at federal level. Although there may have been tactical or opportunistic reasons for the Canadian unions (supporting a party in permanent opposition) to seek State rather than trade union funding, there is no reason why the British trade unions (supporting a party of government) should want to do the same.

present candidates for election to political office. Party structure is a matter for the electorate, not the existing political parties or the State. There are, in any event, other problems to overcome with a contribution cap.

The Problem of Electoral Competition

Notwithstanding its potential impact on party structure, for reasons explained in chapter 3, a contribution cap nevertheless would appear at first sight to have equalising tendencies, in the sense that it would allow individual citizens to have similar levels of participation and influence. Every citizen would be free to give the same as his or her neighbour, and his or her wealthy neighbour could not secure greater access or influence by giving more. It would also appear to have equalising tendencies between parties, in the sense that it would prevent a party of the wealthy from amassing a large number of large donations, with a capacity thereby to drown out its competitors. But as is often the case, the first sight is an optical illusion, though much may depend on the level at which a contribution cap is set, and the jurisdiction in which it operates. In the British context where the debate is about a contribution cap of £50,000,[13] any such notion of an equalising tendency is facetious. Given income levels, only a small number of people could contemplate donating at this level, thereby undermining the idea of equality between citizens. Given the nature of the support for the political parties, there is also a danger that such a cap would give the Conservative Party a significant benefit, thereby undermining the idea of equality between parties. For reasons that are perhaps too obvious to restate, the Conservative Party receives more reported individual donations than the other parties, remembering that for this purpose a donation is a payment in excess of £5,000 nationally or £1,000 locally.[14]

The capacity of a donation cap to create inequality is not simply a matter of speculation. Data on the Electoral Commission website reveal that that if there was to be a contribution cap of £50,000, as some have proposed, this would disproportionately damage the Labour Party if the cap were to include income from trade unions. This is because in the reporting periods from 2001 to 2006:

- The Labour Party received 226 cash donations (predominantly from trade unions) in excess of £50,000, amounting to £59m in total, in contrast to the Conservative Party which received 137 cash donations in excess of £50,000, amounting to £33m.
- The Conservative Party received 2,359 cash or in kind donations from individuals of £50,000 or less, amounting to £15.6m, in contrast to the Labour Party which received 765 such donations, amounting to £4.3m.

[13] See A Tyrie, *Clean Politics* (2006).
[14] PPERA, s 62.

- The Conservative Party received 1,068 cash or in kind donations from companies (public and private) of £50,000 or less, amounting to £9m, in contrast to the Labour Party which received 528 such donations, amounting to £2.8m.

The average individual donation of less than £50,000 to the Conservative Party is thus £6,644, in contrast to the average Labour Party donation of £5,707; while the average such Conservative corporate donation is £8,426, in contrast to Labour's £5,303. The Conservatives thus had in excess of three times more individual donations of £50,000 or less and twice as many such corporate donations than Labour, with each Conservative donation being significantly larger than its Labour counterpart.

The Problem of Enforcement and Evasion

Two concerns about contribution caps of the kind being proposed in the United Kingdom thus relate first to their impact on freedom of association, and secondly to their impact on fairness and balance between the main parties. But there is a third concern identified powerfully by the Neill Committee, namely the more practical one of enforcement.[15] There are in fact three such problems with contribution limits, as follows:

- *Money can be disaggregated.* Rather than make a single one-off contribution, the donor can make a commitment to give a fixed sum by standing order over a number of years. Members of the donor's family can each be encouraged to do the same. A limit of £50,000 annually could lead to £500,000 in a parliamentary cycle. In the case of companies, or law firms, or accountants, each of the directors, partners or senior executives can be encouraged to make a donation which looks like a series of donations by individuals but which *de facto* is a single donation over the limit.[16]
- *Money can be spread around.* If an individual is restricted as to how much money can be given to a party, the money can be redirected to other causes with the knowledge of the party or with a view to secure influence with the party. Donations can be given to constituency parties, candidates and MPs to help with constituency development, election expenses and office accommodation. Although the donations would all have to be disclosed and although they all might also be subject to an annual limit as to amount, these considerations alone would not stop them being made.

---

[15] Committee on Standards in Public Life, Fifth Report, *The Funding of Political Parties in the United Kingdom*, vol 1, Cm 4057–I, para 6.10.

[16] For an account of this problem in Quebec, see Y Boisvert, 'The Hypocrisy of Political Finance Law', *Toronto Star*, 1 July 2006. See also L Massicotte, 'Financing Parties at the Grass-Roots Level: The Quebec Experience', in Ewing and Issacharoff, *supra* n 5, ch 8.

- *Money can be moved to unregulated recipients.* Money can be given to third parties, the interest groups that may campaign on particular causes in an election,
  whether it be the countryside, the single European currency, or voting reform. If
  those with money to spend on political causes are unable by virtue of legal
  restraints to give as much as they would like to a political party, they will always
  be able to give indirectly by sponsoring a cause (such as State funding for political parties), a think-tank or an interest group that is close to the heart of a
  political party or its leadership.[17]

In the view of the Neill Committee, there would be a 'strong temptation' to avoid
any cap, which would require a 'panoply of rules and bureaucracy' to enforce,
which in turn 'would not be justified by the purposes of the cap'.[18] Nothing has
happened since the Committee's report in 1998 to suggest that this judgement is
flawed.

Donations – Let the Members Decide

Although there is thus a strong case against a statutory contribution cap, this is
not to deny that there is also a strong case for a statutory response to the donations problem that has been revealed since 2001. As we have seen, however, one
of the main obstacles for the regulator is the asymmetrical nature of our political parties. Although they have common objects (the election of candidates to
representative bodies), British political parties are radically different: they have
different origins, represent different interests, and as a result have different
organisational forms and membership arrangements. In searching for a solution
to the problem of contributions, we cannot proceed on the basis that all parties
are the same, with the same structure as the Conservative Party, or the same
structure as the Labour Party. Nor can we proceed on the basis that our political
parties are the same as political parties in the United States where the parties
appear to have evolved from the same mould. Party funding reform should
reflect party structure and should not be used as a vehicle to change that structure, or to impose an officially approved form of party organisation.

Asymmetrical Political Parties and the Inflexibility of Legislation

Given the nature of the asymmetrical party structure in Britain, it is difficult to
see how a contribution cap imposed by statute could operate in a way that would
respect concerns about freedom of association without also giving one party a
partisan advantage over the others, assuming that problems of enforcement

---

[17] These points are drawn from Ewing, *supra* n 9, pp 27–28.
[18] Committee on Standards in Public Life, Fifth Report, *supra* n 15, para 6.10.

could be overcome. A statutory cap of £50,000 annually from any donor, individual or organisation would not meet these concerns. It would undermine the structure of the Labour Party and it would give the Conservative Party a partisan advantage over Labour, for reasons already explained. There is no reason why that would be acceptable to the Labour Party, or why the Labour Party should be thought unreasonable in rejecting any such proposal. It is sometimes thought that one way round this problem is to have a more flexible contribution cap that somehow 'ring-fenced' trade union affiliation fees to the Labour Party and any other organisational fee to Labour (such as that paid by the Co-operative Party), and other parties. This could be done by having a cap for individual donations and a separate cap for organisations based on the number of members in the organisation in question. As we saw in chapter 2, the Power Commission made a proposal of this kind in 2006, but as we also saw this may not work either.

The reason why such a proposal – or any variation thereof – would not work is that it would secure the Labour Party an advantage over the Conservatives, given that so much of its money comes from trade union affiliation fees and donations.[19] Thus from 2001 to June 2006, the Labour Party received about £39m from trade unions in the form of donations (including affiliation fees) of £50,001 or more, with another £12.9m or so in donations of £50,000 or less. This would mean that while the Labour Party could accept multimillion-pound cheques from affiliated trade unions, the Conservative Party and the Liberal Democrats would be limited to £50,000 cheques from individuals and companies.[20] There is no reason why that should be acceptable to the Conservative Party or the Liberal Democrats, or why they should be thought unreasonable in opposing it. Nor are the Conservatives in particular likely to accept the logical corollary of a contribution cap at national level, namely the very close scrutiny of local activity, and a very low and tight contribution cap on donations to local parties in order to level the playing-field at local level.[21] This is unlikely to be attractive, given that so much of the activity of the Conservative Party is focused on constituency associations, very many of which do not rely on the monies of Bearwood Corporate Services Ltd, the Midlands Industrial Council or other such bodies.

A Statutory Donations Policy

The only practical solution to the problem of contributions, given the constraints identified above, is for a system of what might be referred to as supervised self-regulation, which allows party members rather than the State to set the cap for their party. The system would be flexible in the sense that each party could set a different cap, reflecting its different forms and structures. The Conservatives

---

[19] See Power Commission, *Power to the People* (2006), p 211 (Recommendation 19); p 49 above.
[20] Unless companies could also giver large donations based on the number of shareholders. But the last thing that is needed is to reawaken large donations by public companies.
[21] See K D Ewing, *The Funding of Political Parties – The Trade Union Case for Reform* (2006), ch 8.

would have to accept that the Labour Party is funded by trade unions, and the Labour Party would have to accept that the Conservative Party receives larger donations from personal or corporate supporters. Under such an arrangement, each registered party would be required *by law* to have a donations policy determined by the party in consultation with its members, either directly or at its policy-making forum. The donations policy would form part of the financial scheme that each registered party is required to lodge with the Electoral Commission, and as such would form part of 'the arrangements for regulating the financial affairs of the party'.[22] By this amendment to the financial scheme, a party would be required to specify the maximum amount it was prepared to accept from each of the categories of donors and affiliates falling within the definition of a permissible donor in the PPERA, section 54(2).[23]

Once party members had decided what the donation limits were in their party, and once registered with the Commission, steps would need to be taken to prevent the policy being changed at will to accommodate a prospective act of unanticipated generosity. Steps would also need to be taken to ensure that a party could not breach the policy approved by the members with impunity. So far as the first of these issues is concerned, it would be possible to say that once a donations policy was registered with the Commission, donations could only be accepted in accordance with the registered procedure and not otherwise, and that the policy could be changed only with the approval of party members, and only after any changes are registered with the Commission. It would be possible, further, to provide that any change could be made only on an annual, biennial or triennial basis, as required. So far as breach of the policy is concerned, the policy would create legally binding obligations with which a party would have to comply. It could be enforced either as a civil matter at the suit of aggrieved members, or in the criminal courts (if necessary against the donor and the recipient for giving and receiving a donation in breach of a party's donations policy) following an investigation by the Electoral Commission, in either case with the full amount of any donation to be forfeited.

A Focus on Spending

It would be a mistake to think that controlling contributions would be a solution to the problem of party funding. There will be no solution until the parties are subject to tighter constraints about what they can spend. Although we have comprehensive spending controls under the existing law, they are not low enough and an important apparent loophole in the legislation has been identified in

---

[22] PPERA, s 26. See pp 79–80 above.

[23] In the case of individuals and companies that would be straightforward, with the donations policy setting out how much each donor could give. In the case of trade unions or other affiliated bodies it would be possible to indicate how much could be given per affiliated member.

chapter 7 above.[24] Spending limits are important because they reduce the demand for money by reducing the ability to spend it. The lesson of the loans affair is that parties will spend what they can, and will take whatever steps they can to raise the money to ensure that these spending opportunities are realised.[25] The lesson of the Bearwood Corporate Services Ltd and Midlands Industrial Council donations is that money will be redirected to areas where it can be spent without being subject to regulation. As a contribution to the donations problem, and in order to maintain the integrity of spending limits themselves as instruments of electoral equality and fair electoral competition, these limits need to be comprehensive, low and tight. There are two ways by which the existing spending limits could be developed.

Campaign Spending Limits

The most straightforward solution would be to revise the existing limits to take account of the failings identified in chapter 7, with a view to making the limits more comprehensive. So far as the national spending limit is concerned, there are three steps that could be taken. The first would be to review the matters currently counted as campaign expenditure for the purposes of PPERA, Schedule 8. The obvious issue here is staffing costs, including staff hired specifically for the campaign. There is an inconsistency in the sense that candidates must account for staff (on a much smaller budget) while parties need not (on a much larger budget).[26] The second would be to increase the time to which the campaign period applies, currently one year in the case of a parliamentary election. This allows for campaigning to take place outside this time without any regulatory consequences. There would be a case for saying that the regulated period should be two years, and a case also for a more radical step whereby a limit on campaign expenses applies to an entire parliamentary cycle.[27] The third and final revision relates to the amount of permitted expenditure, it being widely held that the current limit of over £18m is too high, though care needs to be taken in driving permitted spending levels down too far. The extent to which this should be reduced would be determined in part by the length of the campaign period and the extended list of items which it would be expected to cover.

So far as local spending is concerned, reform appears to be equally urgent with the great inflation in spending by local parties in marginal seats in the pre-election period, fuelled by carefully targeted donations.[28] The current spending limits

[24] See pp 166–168 above.
[25] See pp 133–141 above.
[26] Compare PPERA, Sch 8, para 2(d) with RPA, s 90A. See pp 151–152 and 147–148 above.
[27] In this case a party would have a spending limit for an entire parliamentary cycle which would cover not only European but also Westminster and devolved body elections. The spending limit would have to be adjusted to take account of the fact that it was to cover four or five (including local government and London) elections. It would also have to be calculated on the basis of the number of seats being contested by the party in these elections.
[28] See pp 166–168 above, on local spending generally.

BOX 10.1
Spending Limits

Although there is a case for lower spending limits, there is also a case for not reducing them by too much. This is because parties must have an opportunity to get their message out, and should not be wholly dependent on commercially owned media outlets in doing so. The less the parties spend, the greater will be the influence of the press in particular. If a limit of £5,000 was introduced for constituency parties, this would allow these parties to spend £3.1m in total, though it is likely that some such parties would not spend their full amount. If at the same time the limit for the national parties were to be reduced by a third to £12 million, this would produce a combined national and local party limit of £15 million.

---

apply to national spending, as well as to candidate spending. As the law is now drafted, any local expenditure promoting a candidate before the dissolution of Parliament may in some circumstances have to be included in the national party return.[29] But it is not clear how effective this provision is in practice, and there appears to be a case for tighter regulation of local spending as a result. There are, however, a number of factors to be taken into account before extending spending limits to local parties. While there is a clear need for such limits on the one hand, there is an equally clear need to avoid any chilling of general political activity at local level on the other. With this in mind, the most appropriate solution would be to impose a cap of £5,000 on the expenditure of constituency parties directed specifically to the election of their candidate, to apply over the same period as the national spending limit. If such a limit were to be introduced, however, it would open up another loophole whereby money could be directed to candidates rather than local parties. As a result, the existing candidate limit would also have to be changed – not in amount, but to apply before as well as after the dissolution of Parliament.

Annualised Spending Limits

A more radical approach still to spending limits would be to move from the regulation of election spending limits to the regulation of all-party spending, by the imposition of an annual cap on party spending. There are certain attractions about this idea, which is based on the assumption that (a) parties are effectively election machines, (b) that everything they do is directed towards winning

---

[29] PPERA, s 72. See pp 152–153 above.

elections, and (c) that we live in an era of the perpetual campaign, reinforced by the frequency of elections. The idea is attractive also for administrative reasons in the sense that it would be much easier to enforce a total spending limit applicable to overall party spending, rather than a segmental limit applicable only to a portion of a party's spending. In the case of the former, the only question is whether the money was spent by the party, whereas in the case of the latter the question is whether it was spent (a) by the party and (b) for campaign purposes. There is also the problem of two elections running simultaneously (say European and parliamentary), and of having to allocate a portion of spending to one, and a portion to the other, in order to stay on the right side of the law.[30]

But although there are attractions with annualised limits, there are also formidable obstacles to be overcome. First, to whom would the restrictions apply? An annual spending cap on the parties would lead to a redirection of money to constituency parties with the result that there would have to be a limit there too. This in turn might lead to a redirection of money to individual politicians with the result that there would have to be an additional limit on spending at this level as well. There is also the question of third parties, which might find themselves the recipients of political money that cannot be spent elsewhere. Except in the case of the third party which is the obvious *alter ego* of a political party (of which we currently have few, if any, examples), it is difficult to see how these bodies could meaningfully be regulated, except in relation to campaign spending, as currently defined in the PPERA. But having identified to whom the spending limits would apply and the steps that would be necessary to prevent avoidance and evasion, it would then be necessary to identify how much the limit or limits would be. It would be necessary to set a limit for national parties as well as for constituency parties. The latter in particular would be difficult to fix, in view of the great disparity of income of constituency parties,[31] and the different ways in which the parties are organised. It would make a huge difference if the figure is to be fixed according to the practice of Conservative Associations on the one hand or Constituency Labour Parties on the other. These difficulties suggest that, at least for the time being, the most sensible way forward would be tightening up the existing campaign spending limits, along the lines proposed above – a smaller limit, extending over a longer period, applying to a wider range of activity.

State Aid: Building on the British Model?

Apart from donation and spending limits, the other issue on the agenda for reform is State aid or public funding. This would compensate for the loss of the large private donations and would reduce the need to seek such money. Caution

---

[30] On the current position, see PPERA, Sch 9, Part III.
[31] See pp 84–85 above.

BOX 10.2
Annualised Spending Limits

Apart from issues considered in the text, there are a number of problems with annualised limits that would need to be addressed:

- Should the spending limit be a flat-rate limit, which applies regardless of the number of members of the party, or should it be based on a formula relating to membership? A flat-rate limit would not provide an incentive to recruit members once a party had reached a level of membership that guaranteed that its spending needs for the year would be met. On the other hand, spending according to membership levels would be difficult effectively to enforce.
- Should the spending limit be the same every year, or should there be variations according to whether there is an election in the year in question? If so, should the election premium be higher in the year of an election to the European Parliament than to the devolved bodies, and higher still in the year of a general election? Should the election premium be based on the number of seats contested so that it would be different for each party?
- Should the limit apply to matters such as property maintenance in the case of those parties which own their own premises (and which may be commercially let), or to other commercial expenditure? If the answer is no, are we saying that only some expenditure is to be regulated, thereby breaching the principle of annual limits?If the answer is yes, would this give rise to serious problems of fairness, if a party was to be required to divert resources which other parties would be free to devote to general campaigning?

---

about public funding has, however, led some to look for a compromise position. This is based on the existing British model of State support discussed in chapter 8, the State absorbing costs incurred by the parties on the one hand, and providing funding for hypothecated purposes on the other. This would not relieve the parties of the need to raise money. But it would mean that core work would continue to be undertaken, and that funds would be needed for a smaller range of activities. One of the attractions of this approach is that it would allow the State to continue to support the parties without at the same time giving public money for the purposes of party political campaigning. This appears to be one of the major objections to public funding in Britain, though paradoxically in other countries campaigning is the reason why money is given in the first place, to ensure that the parties' message reaches the electorate, in the interests of fair electoral competition. It is also the case that one of the most expensive items of

State support in this country is the free postage at elections which is used unmistakably for campaigning, and that the most important forms of State support include party election broadcasts.[32]

Short Money as a Template

One basis for further reform would be to use the Short money scheme as a template for supporting the parties outside Parliament. The Short scheme is designed to support the work of the Opposition parties in Parliament, and is designed to meet the research costs of the Opposition front bench in particular.[33] These needs would normally take three forms: accommodation, office equipment and information technology, and staff. Similar needs exist for the parties outside Parliament. Everything they do requires them to have dedicated office space, information technology and other office equipment, and staff. One way by which the State could support the parties without handing over money for campaigning would be to underwrite some of these *infrastructure costs*. As we saw in chapter 8, this is a matter that was raised by the Home Affairs Committee in 1994,[34] and it has been revived on a number of occasions since.[35] Accommodation costs would contribute to the rent or mortgage repayments of a party, information technology costs would enable the parties to maintain up-to-date information technology systems, while staff costs would enable the parties to recruit and retain enough employees to ensure that essential activities were carried out.

Closely related to the foregoing is *political training*, for which public support could also be provided under a modified Short scheme. This too is part of the work of political parties, and it takes a number of forms relating mainly to the training of candidates for political office, as well as the training of party activists. One of the key roles of political parties is the recruitment of people to government at all levels, from membership of the European Parliament to local government. But members of political parties serve their communities in other ways: as school governors, magistrates and on NHS bodies. There are clearly important training needs for the skills required to perform these many different roles. The training needs take several forms: politicians need communications skills, which some have more than others; they need to know how to work with the media, both printed and electronic; and they need to know about effective campaigning, as well as aspects of electoral law. Once elected to office, these needs will continue, but others arise: these include ethics training about conflicts of interest; office management and relationships with electors; and the nature and responsibilities of the office to which the individual has been elected.[36]

---

[32] See pp 183–185 above.
[33] See pp 188–189 above.
[34] Home Affairs Committee, *Funding of Political Parties*, HC 301 (1993–94), para 57.
[35] See Ewing, *supra* n 9, p 32.
[36] In its submission to the Neill Committee, the Labour Party proposed that public funding should be available to finance education and training conducted by political parties, which was designed to

Policy Development Grant as a Template

The Short scheme provides a template for core funding for core activities. The policy development grant scheme provides a template for the State to underwrite under-developed activities of the parties. Particularly important, but rather neglected, is *political education*. In the same way that money is given to policy development, it would be possible to give similar funding to the parties for this latter purpose. The importance of political education has been recognised by governments of both parties in the United Kingdom, with the Conservative government creating the Westminster Foundation for Democracy in 1992. This provides assistance in building pluralistic institutions overseas, and although it is fully independent, the three main parties are represented on the Board of Governors. There are also representatives from the business world, trade unions, the academic community and NGOs. We thus have a scheme for the disbursement of State funds for citizenship education for people abroad, Foundation programmes being delivered partly by the British political parties, which make applications to the Foundation to fund educational work with sister parties in the developing world and in eastern Europe. But although the parties are funded by the State to perform this work overseas, there is no equivalent funding for work in this country, though with declining electoral turnout it can hardly be said that there is no need.[37]

In other countries, public funding is made available for political education of a varied kind. In Germany, the government funds programmes of citizenship education provided by the political foundations attached to the political parties. Although there are close links between the foundations and the political parties, the former are at least formally independent of the latter. In other countries such as Austria, autonomy on this scale does not appear to be so formally recognised. Although it may not now be possible to contemplate anything so elaborate as the German foundations, in this country there is work for the political parties to do in political education, particularly at community level. This is work that could be done by the parties alone, in conjunction with each other, or in conjunction with other bodies responsible for providing education, such as trade unions, schools and colleges, and universities. As in the case of the policy development grants,

include 'the provision of training courses for prospective and existing holders of public office, for example local councillors', and 'training for party workers (who are lay volunteers) on subjects such as electoral law and other relevant legislation'. Curiously the Committee did not even address this proposal, though it did recommend the introduction of the policy development grants, on which the existing legislation was based. The grants were designed 'to enable the parties represented in the House of Commons to fulfil better what is, after all, one of their most vital functions', the costs of which they were 'hard pressed to meet' because of the 'mounting costs of election campaigns and also the mounting costs of their day to day activities. But there is little point in political parties being encouraged to be 'one of the major sources of ideas in British politics' if they are unable to communicate these ideas to a wide audience or be represented by candidates who are trained to implement them'.

[37] For details, see www.wfd.org.uk. The Foundation currently receives just over £4m from the Foreign Office for these purposes.

any funding for political education would have to be used only for this purpose, with the proper scrutiny of accounts to ensure that the money was not used for other purposes. This would help to overcome the problems that beset the Political Education Fund introduced in New South Wales in 1993. Despite assurances given by the Liberal government at the time the scheme was introduced,[38] reports from Sydney suggest that the scheme is now being used by the State parties to finance their administration, office management and staff.[39]

Making a Fresh Start – Back to Houghton

Does the foregoing form the basis of a distinctively British way to the funding of political parties? This would mean a continuation of the existing strategy of supporting the parties by funding an open-ended and expanding body of specific projects or activities rather than by handing over cash without any limitation as to its use. In this way, it would be necessary to establish two new funds. The first would be *an infrastructure and training fund*, and the second *a political education fund*. The first of these proposed funds would be used for office, administrative support and training needs of the parties, as well as staff; while the purposes of the second are self-evident. In terms of the distribution of the money, the same principles that currently apply to the allocation of the policy development grants could apply to both of the proposed funds, though provision would have to be made for their application to non-parliamentary parties. On this basis, there would thus be five funds (at national level) for allocation to the parties. In addition to the policy development fund and the two funds proposed here, there are also the funds currently used to fund the Opposition parties in Parliament, which could be extended to ensure that there is core funding for the parliamentary activities of all parliamentary parties.[40]

State Direction or Party Autonomy?

Such an approach might address some of the concerns of those who are opposed to State funding of political parties. But even if it did, the approach outlined above is not without difficulties of its own, which might well lead to unfavourable comparisons being made with the public funding regimes in Sweden and Germany,[41] where the parties are free to spend the money on the priorities of their choice, as had been recommended by the Houghton Committee in 1976.[42]

---

[38] Election Funding (Amendment) Act 1993 (NSW).
[39] *The Sun-Herald* (Sydney), 25 May 2003. The Act expressly excludes funding for travelling and accommodation.
[40] See pp 183–185 above.
[41] For an account of the Swedish and German models, see Appendices 4 and 5.
[42] Cmnd 6061, 1976, paras 10.19–10.37. See pp 186–188 above.

The first problem is a problem of principle, and in particular the principle of party autonomy. This suggests that it should be for the parties themselves to spend their money on the projects of their choice and to allocate funds between these projects as they see fit. So although most parties would be expected to spend some money on office accommodation, training and education, and regional infrastructure, it would be for each party to decide how much to devote to these different activities. To this extent, it might be complained that a sophisticated scheme of hypothecated funding would be coercive, in the sense that the State is determining what it is that political parties should do, and encouraging them by financial inducements to do those things that have State approval. There is also the additional danger that any system of hypothecated funding would be devised to meet the needs or vision of the party of government (the party that drafts the legislation) rather than all the parties, which may have different visions, needs and priorities.

Related to the foregoing is a very practical problem: the needs of parties for which hypothecated funding is available may already be adequately met. What happens if the State creates an infrastructure and training fund to be used for accommodation, but one party already owns significant property? Does this mean that it would not qualify for this benefit, or that it would be able to expand its property portfolio by using State money to purchase property that it does not need? Would the party then be free to treat this windfall as an investment and rent the property for additional income, while also able to liquidate the capital to pay for an election? Similar questions arise in relation to the party that already has a good supply of fixtures and fittings or a newly installed IT system. There is also the position of the party that may employ few full-time staff because it relies on an army of unpaid volunteers. In these cases the State is not meeting need, and at best may be meeting needs that not all parties have, with the result that hypothecated funding may encourage public expenditure for the sake of it. This is a problem identified by Houghton which saw proposals of this kind as an extension of the existing aid in kind. Although the Committee saw no reason to question the existing provision, it made a pointed case against extension in a persuasive passage to which reference has already been made.[43]

The 'Illusion' of Hypothecation

But these are not the only concerns. One of the reasons for hypothecated funding of the kind described above is to sidestep the current reluctance for the State to be seen to be subsidising the campaign costs of the parties. However, it is unclear why the State should not have such a role. In the first place, electioneering is a legitimate function, and it is a function like other functions for which the parties need support. As we saw in relation to Canada in chapter 9, public funding has

---

[43] *Ibid*, para 10.6. See p 188 above.

been introduced to ensure that minimum needs in relation to campaigning are met.[44] It is also the case that in Britain the State has intervened in a number of ways to ensure that candidates and parties can communicate with the electorate. Secondly, State support of this kind serves important regulatory goals, addressing concerns about equality of electoral opportunity as well as reducing the pressure during campaigns to take money from controversial sources. On this matter, it is instructive that before and during the last two general elections the parties found it necessary to seek large donations and loans, some of which have contributed to the political problems of party funding under which we now labour. Thirdly, it is surely disingenuous to say that hypothecation avoids this problem of State-subsidised elections. As was persuasively pointed out by the Institute for Public Policy Research (IPPR), 'hypothecated State funding is an illusory subsidy for planned party expenditure, simply freeing up more money for parties to spend on other areas'.[45]

But it is not only that hypothecation would be disingenuous if designed to stop State money being used for electioneering purposes. Hypothecation is open to objection on the additional ground that it is likely to be excessively bureaucratic as well as intrusive if it is to be administered in such a way as to ensure that public funding was spent only for the purpose for which it was authorised. It would inevitably create fresh drama as one or more parties were alleged to have used money for purposes for which it was not intended: the controversy in 2000 over the Conservative Party's use of Short money should be a salutary warning.[46] Proper accounting for the use of public money is, of course, perfectly proper, even if in Sweden the principle of party autonomy is taken to such lengths as to discourage such intrusion by the State.[47] But in the United Kingdom the culture is such that even a payment of an annual grant to the parties for unspecified general purposes along the lines proposed by Houghton would have to be properly audited as having been spent on party activities. Yet although proper accounting is to be encouraged, it seems unnecessary to require the parties to keep a series of separately audited accounts for the purpose of different expenditure underwritten by the State. This in turn would entail an obligation to justify every item of expenditure as having been spent not only on the purposes of the party, but on a specific purpose of the party. It may well be that the additional costs that this would entail for the parties on the one hand and the National Audit Office on the other would be better spent meeting the needs of the former.

---

[44] Similarly for Australia, see G Orr, 'The Currency of Democracy: Campaign Finance Law in Australia' (2003) 26 *New South Wales Law Journal* 1.

[45] IPPR, *Keeping it Clean* (2002), p 17.

[46] HC 238–viii (1999–2000); HC 293 (2000–01). So too should the experience of the New South Wales Political Education Fund, which is allegedly used for a wide range of party purposes, though the permitted purposes for which the fund may be used are in fact very wide. See Election Funding Authority of New South Wales, *Political Education Fund Determinations*.

[47] See K Ewing, *The Funding of Political Parties in Britain* (1987), ch 7.

Qualifying Conditions for State Support

For the foregoing reasons, there is a case for repudiating the continuation of the current piecemeal approach of rigid hypothecated funding. The alternative would be a scheme of non-hypothecated funding on the Canadian model, whereby an annual cash grant is made to qualifying political parties to be used for purposes of their choosing. In view of the concerns about not directly subsidising campaign costs, it could be provided that the fund was not to be used for election purposes, with appropriate auditing. One justification for this is that the State already makes adequate provision for the parties at election time. Such a scheme would be in addition to the support already provided, and discussed in chapter 7, with two modifications. First, the Short scheme and related schemes would be extended to assist with modest needs of the governing party in Parliament. And secondly, the policy development fund would be wound up and subsumed under the proposed party-funding scheme, with the parties free to use party funding for policy development or not as they see fit. So far as the administration of such a scheme is concerned, a number of questions would have to be addressed. To which parties would it apply apply? How much funding would be provided? How would any funding be allocated?

Eligible Parties

The first question that arises is whether all parties would qualify under a wider-ranging scheme: at the time of writing there are several hundred parties registered with the Electoral Commission. It would be inappropriate that registration alone should be a qualification for funding when the conditions for registration are so informal. Registration is simply a mark of purpose, not an indication of support or seriousness. So while registration may be a requirement of eligibility, it ought not to be the only requirement. Although the free postal facility is made available to all parliamentary candidates of all parties, the other major schemes of State support currently in operation are typically limited to parties of significant standing. Party political broadcasts (not party election broadcasts), policy development grants and Opposition funding are all available only to parliamentary parties, while party election broadcasting is available only to those parties that present a minimum number of candidates at an election.[48] It would be perfectly consistent with existing aid to say that proposed party funding would be limited to parliamentary parties, though it is not clear whether the definition in the PPERA is suitable.[49] The requirement of representation at Westminster as a condition of eligibility for policy development grants is an indefensible

---

[48] See pp 179–182 above.
[49] PPERA, s 12. This applies only to those parties which have at least two members of the House of Commons who have 'made and subscribed' the parliamentary oath.

restriction in an era when other political parties are represented in the European Parliament, the Scottish Parliament and the devolved assemblies.[50]

The current definition of a parliamentary party in the PPERA is significantly narrower than what was proposed by the Houghton Committee for the distribution of State support. Here there were three eligibility criteria: one was that the party had two members elected to the House of Commons; the second was that it had one MP and a total of at 150,000 votes at the immediately preceding general election; and the third was that it had saved the deposits of its candidates in at least six constituencies.[51] The last two of these criteria are important for addressing concerns that State support should not operate against the interests of small parties or prevent the emergence of new parties. These proposals would allow any new party that demonstrated sufficient electoral support to qualify for an appropriate level of funding. So apart from a definition of eligibility that looks beyond representation at Westminster, there is also a need for a definition that includes parties that have no formal representation.[52] But in developing such a system for the allocation of party funding, it would be well to have regard to French experience where very lax eligibility rules have seen 'a large number of people' create 'their own parties just to get public subsidies'.[53] While public funding should not be used to encourage and maintain political cartels, equally it ought not to encourage the development of spurious parties.[54]

Funding and its Distribution

The question which arises now is this: how much should be provided? One response is that the amount provided ought to reflect the amount the parties receive in large personal donations, being designed to compensate for the loss of such donations. But the cost of displacing donations and loans in excess of £250,000 alone would be in the region of £5m–7m annually for each of the two large parties, and it would be even higher if the aim were to displace donations and loans of a lesser amount, though slightly less in both cases if reduced levels of permitted election expenditure were to be taken into account. Reduced spending could amount to more than £6m at a general election, reducing income demands by the equivalent more than £1m annually over a parliamentary cycle. This would lead to a figure of £4m–6m annually to the two largest parties, a figure not far removed from the Houghton proposal that State aid should not exceed 20 per cent of the funds of the parties.[55] However, as Houghton also recognised, a fund

[50] See also Electoral Commission, *The Funding of Political Parties* (2004), para 6.43 (in relation to the policy development grants).

[51] Cmnd 6601, 1976, para 10.22.

[52] See for example the Canadian scheme, considered at pp 209–215 above.

[53] Y-M Doublet, 'Party Funding in France', in K D Ewing (ed), *The Funding of Political Parties: Europe and Beyond* (1999), p 72.

[54] For a discussion of the issue of thresholds, see *Figueroa v Canada* [2003] 1 SCR 912.

[55] Cmnd 6601, 1976, paras 9.17–9.18. See also Ewing, *supra* n 9, p 33.

that allowed for payments of this kind to the two main parties would also have to make provision for what is now the Liberal Democrats and for the smaller parties as well, for whom the fund would provide a significant additional source of support. On the assumption that these smaller parties would benefit on a pro rata basis with the two larger parties, party funding would be likely to cost a minimum of between £12m and £18m per annum in total.

The question then arises as to the allocation of the money. It ought to be part of any scheme for public funding that the parties are given incentives, not only to encourage people to vote, but also to recruit and retain members. Such a scheme operates in Germany, following a lengthy exchange between the Bundestag and the Constitutional Court.[56] If such a scheme were to be adopted in Britain, a formula would have to be developed for party funding whereby

- half the money was allocated to the parties in accordance with votes at the most recent general election and intervening European and devolved body elections; and
- half the money was allocated to the parties in accordance with the number of members of the party, a member for this purpose being an individual rather than an affiliated member.

The Houghton Committee concluded that money should be allocated on the former basis only and that to allocate money on the basis of membership would give rise to difficulties on the ground that in some parties 'membership is not closely defined', and would be difficult to 'audit and control'.[57] But although these problems are formidable, it seems inconceivable today that public money would be handed over without the parties themselves having to earn it, and indeed without having to meet other conditions of the kind proposed below.

Promoting Democracy: A Quid Pro Quo

If the State is to support the parties in these ways, is the community entitled to expect something even more in return? In particular, if public money is being used to support political parties because political parties play an indispensable role in the democratic process, is the public not entitled to expect that the bodies that spend its money themselves meet some basic democratic criteria, in the form of 'stipulations designed to guarantee a democratic organisation of political parties'?[58] Is it enough for the State to encourage people to join and vote for political parties without also encouraging them to take part in the activities of the party? At the present time there is very little regulation of the internal affairs

---

[56] On which see D P Currie, *The Constitution of the Federal Republic of Germany* (1998), pp 207–15.
[57] Cmnd 6601, 1976, para 10.12.
[58] H Kelsen, *General Theory of Law and State* (1949), p 295.

of political parties,[59] in contrast to the position in Germany where the *Grund-gesetz* or Basic Law provides that although parties 'may be freely established', nevertheless their 'internal organisation must conform to democratic principles'.[60] It is also provided that parties which 'by reason of their aims or the behaviour of their adherents, seek to impair or abolish the free democratic basic order or to endanger the existence of the Federal Republic of Germany, shall be unconstitutional'.[61] The content of this constitutional obligation is fleshed out in the *Law on Political Parties of 1967*.[62]

An Australian Precedent

But it is not only in Germany that the State has intervened to regulate the internal affairs of political parties in order to promote open, transparent and democratic government. Also important – though on a much smaller scale – is the initiative taken by the Australian State of Queensland where the Electoral and other Acts Amendment Act 2002 intrudes further into the internal procedures of political parties than is typical in common law jurisdictions.[63] A new condition of registration of a party is that it must have what is referred to as a complying constitution.[64] This is defined to mean one that contains a number of requirements, including the party's objects, one of which must be the promotion of candidates for election to the Legislative Assembly. A second requirement is the procedure for amending the constitution, and a third is the rules for membership of the party. The latter must include the rules for accepting a person into membership, the procedure for ending a person's membership, and a rule prohibiting a person from being or remaining a member if convicted in the previous ten years

[59] See ch 4 above.

[60] *Grundgesetz*, Art 21(1). So far as Spain is concerned, see Spanish Constitution, Art 6 (internal structure and operation of political parties must be democratic).

[61] *Grundgesetz*, Art 21(2).

[62] Although the *Law on Political Parties of 1967* gives the parties great scope to determine the content of these statutes and programmes, it also provides that the 'regional structure of the party must be developed to a sufficient degree to enable individual members to participate to a suitable extent in the forming of political opinions within the party', and that 'the party convention decides on programmes, statutes, subscriptions, arbitration procedure, dissolution of the party and merging with other parties'. It also deals with matters such as members' rights, the election and composition of the executive committee, and the composition of delegates' assemblies.

[63] For proposals that similar measures be introduced at federal level, see Senator A Murray and M Rock, 'The Dangerous Art of Giving', *Australian Quarterly*, June–July 2000, p 29, where concern is expressed about the fact that political parties are subject to little if any real control as to the propriety of their conduct and the fairness of their internal processes (p 32). It was said that as political parties are extensively and intimately involved in public life in every way, this lack of regulation is not in the public interest, and that it was essential that a comprehensive regulatory system be put in place. These points were developed in Senator A Murray, 'Why There Is Still Lax Regulation of Political Parties', Electoral Law Conference, Coogee Bay Conference Centre, Sydney, 6 December 2002, where a scheme similar to that operating in Queensland was proposed with the additional recommendation that the Australian Electoral Commission should be empowered to investigate any allegations of a serious breach of a party constitution, and apply an administrative penalty.

[64] Electoral Act 1992, s 73A(1), inserted by Electoral and other Acts Amendment Act 2002, s 11.

of prescribed electoral offences. A fourth requirement is the inclusion of a statement about how the party manages its internal affairs, including a statement about party structure and the management of dispute resolution. Fifthly, there must be rules for selecting office holders in the party, and the selection of candidates for local government and Legislative Assembly elections.

The 2002 amendments also deal with pre-selection ballots, which are those internal party ballots to select a candidate for local government or Legislative Assembly elections.[65] It is a condition of registration that party rules on pre-selection ballots satisfy the general principles of free and democratic elections. These principles are said to be eight in number:[66] only party members who are electors may vote; only those members who are eligible under the constitution may vote; each member may have only one vote; voting must be by secret ballot; members must not be improperly influenced in voting; a ballot paper must be counted if the member's intention is clear; votes must be counted accurately; and candidates in the pre-selection ballot must be allowed to attend the counting of the votes. Further amendments introduced in 2002 provide for the oversight of pre-selection ballots by the Electoral Commission, which has the responsibility to draft model procedures for the conduct of such ballots.[67] The Commission must be given seven days' notice of the ballot by the registered officer of the party who must also give the candidates a copy of the model procedures.[68] The Commission is also empowered to investigate complaints that a pre-selection ballot has not been conducted in accordance with the model procedures and the party's own rules.[69] Otherwise the Commission must also conduct random audits of pre-selection ballots.[70] It is expressly provided that a pre-selection irregularity does not invalidate a subsequent election to public office.[71]

A Charter of Members' Rights

The constitutional arrangements within British political parties are rarely questioned to determine whether they conform to democratic principles. But this is not to say that problems do not periodically arise about the extent to which these principles are acknowledged or how they operate in any particular case. There were complaints in the 1990s from Conservative Party activists about the lack of financial transparency,[72] and it is still the case that members of political parties have no right to financial information in their capacity as members of the

---

[65] *Ibid.*
[66] Electoral Act 1992, s 73A(2), inserted by Electoral and other Acts Amendment Act 2002, s 11.
[67] Electoral Act 1992, s 148H, inserted by Electoral and other Acts Amendment Act 2002, s 17.
[68] *Ibid*, s 148I.
[69] *Ibid*, s 148J.
[70] *Ibid*, s 148M.
[71] *Ibid*, s 148O.
[72] HC 726 (1992–93) (Memorandums 10 and 11 by the Charter Movement and Mr Eric Chalker respectively).

party.[73] More recently, there have been complaints about the selection of candidates in the Labour Party in particular (including the selection of the candidate for London mayor) and the election of office-holders in the Labour Party (including the leader of the party in Wales). There have also been reports of measures being taken to prevent Labour Party National Executive Committee (NEC) members from speaking to the press about NEC issues with possible disciplinary action under the rules of the party being taken against those in breach.[74] The more aid given, the greater the claim of the State to supervise the internal affairs of the parties. It would thus be possible to have a number of requirements in legislation which would have to be satisfied by any party before it received the various forms of State support, whether currently in existence or proposed above.[75] These requirements would constitute a Charter of Members' Rights, non-derogable rights of every member of a political party. The nearest equivalent form of regulation in British law would be the comprehensive statutory rights of trade union members, which were introduced in the 1980s and 1990s.[76]

It would appear to be particularly appropriate that the institutions of popular government should have open membership rules, in the sense of being open to all who support the principles and policies of the party and are not members or supporters of another party (subject to the right to exclude or expel those who break the rules).[77] There ought also to be transparency to the members on financial matters (which curiously is not currently required, the duty being one to the public at large), as well as right of the members to determine the donations policy of the organisation.[78] This means that parties should have a rule determined by the members indicating from whom they are prepared to accept donations and the limits on the amount of any donation that may be accepted. (The rule should also indicate the procedures that the party has adopted to avoid any improper conduct by those who give and those who receive donations.) By compelling the parties to consider publicly how much they are prepared to accept and to require these decisions to be taken by the members, it is anticipated that restraint would be shown in terms of the donations that would be considered acceptable. Otherwise, political parties would be expected to have democratic

---

[73] The introduction of such a right was proposed by the Labour Party in its evidence to the Neill Committee.

[74] *The Guardian*, 13 November 1998.

[75] See further K D Ewing and N S Ghaleigh, 'The Funding of Political Parties', Submission to the Constitutional Affairs Committee, 10 April 2006.

[76] See Trade Union and Labour Relations (Consolidation) Act 1992 which imposes duties of fiscal transparency to members; requires trade unions to have five-yearly ballots for the election of general secretary and executive committee; and regulates the circumstances in which workers may be excluded or expelled from membership.

[77] This does not mean having to accept into membership individuals who are hostile to the interests of the party: see *Eu v San Francisco Democratic Committee*, 489 US 214 (1989). Compare, however, the position of trade unions in British law: J Hendy QC and K D Ewing, 'Trade Unions, Human Rights and the BNP' (2005) 34 *ILJ* 197.

[78] See pp 230–232 above.

procedures for policy-making and the selection of the party leader; open and inclusive procedures for the selection of parliamentary and other candidates; internal party elections for all nominations to the House of Lords (so long as seats are to be filled by the nomination of party leaders); and fair disciplinary rules and procedures for those who offend against the party rules and practices. It is tempting to think that if such simple procedures had been in place, there would have been no loans for peerages affair.

Conclusion

Despite the enactment of the PPERA in 2000, there is clearly a need for a further round of party funding reform in the light of not only the loans affair but also to address the role of the very large donors. In taking the next step on the road to reform, there is a role for all four of the regulatory strategies identified in chapter 3, namely transparency, contribution limits, spending limits, and State support or public funding. So far as transparency is concerned, the main issue here relates to loans, which were outside the scope of the regulatory framework introduced by the PPERA. But although that loophole has been closed by the Electoral Administration Act 2006, there remains a transparency loophole in the form of donations made by private companies and unincorporated associations. It is not easy to tell who is behind these bodies or who is supplying money which is then passed on to political parties. Some of these organisations have a long pedigree and probably do not exist only or mainly for the purpose of raising money for political parties. But where the principal purposes of a private company or unincorporated association include the raising of funds for a registered party or a registered third party, there should be an obligation on the part of the company or association to reveal the identity of members and subscribers at the time a donation is made.

So far as contributions are concerned, it has been argued that the problems of a flat-rate statutory contribution cap are formidable: it would undermine party structure, it could not operate without giving one party a partisan advantage, and it would be difficult to enforce. The only solution lies in requiring the parties to impose their own limits, which would be legally binding and subject to supervision by the Electoral Commission. This would allow for flexibility in the setting of a cap, and it is likely to operate as a restraint on large donations, particularly if the Electoral Commission were to be empowered to require a party to lower its donation limits in the interests of fair electoral competition. A further step in addressing the party-funding problem would be tighter spending limits to reduce the need for large donations. These spending limits should apply to national party spending, local party spending and candidate spending, as well as third-party spending. Here the need is to reduce the amount that the parties can spend, extend the period over which it may be spent and increase the range of items that fall within the spending limit. There is also a need to close the loophole that sees money flowing to constituencies to fuel campaigns by local parties. These spending limits are necessary to respond to regulatory objectives identified in chapter 2 above, including the need for fair electoral competition.

Finally, there is the vexed question of State aid and public funding. This is an urgent question for two reasons. The first is the impact that transparency is having on the willingness of individuals to make donations, and its implications for party funds. The second is the desire to prohibit or discourage these same large private donations to the parties. A reduction in donations for whatever reason will continue to create a funding or a resources gap, which will need to be filled. There are compelling reasons why the State has some responsibility to fill at least part of that gap, being partly responsible by legislation for its emergence and growth.[79] It has been argued that in filling this gap, the State can do so by one of two routes. The first is by continuing the traditional British approach of State aid, by providing funding for hypothecated purposes. The second is by the Canadian approach of public funding, with the parties free to spend the money on their own needs and priorities. But whichever method is adopted, additional State aid or public funding should be limited in amount, it should be tied to incentives to encourage the parties to recruit and retain members, and it should be subject to the condition that parties accept a Charter of Members' Rights to guarantee a minimum level of openness and participation in the affairs of political parties. Quite how Labour is to repay loans of £28m (at the time of writing) is, however, another matter altogether.

---

[79] See pp 173–176 above.

Appendices

Appendix 1: Exchange of Letters between the Labour Party and Sir Patrick Neill QC

The Labour Party

John Smith House
150 Walworth Road
London SE17 1JT

Telephone (0171) 701 1234
Facsimile (0171) 277 3300
E mail LABOUR PARTY
@ GEO2POPTH ORG UK

Direct lines
Telephone.
Facsimile

7 November 1997

Sir Patrick Neill QC
Chairman Designate of the Committee on Standards in Public Life
Horseguards Road
London SW1P 3AL

Dear Sir Patrick

    After discussion with the Prime Minister, I am writing to seek your urgent advice on a matter of interest to us, and we believe, the public interest.

    It concerns gifts to political parties.

    The facts arise out of a recent government decision on tobacco sponsorship, which you have probably seen covered in the press. The specific issue comes about in this way.

    The Labour Party accepted a substantial personal donation in January this year from Bernie Ecclestone (who is Vice President of the FIA), for the general election campaign. This was one of a number of similar donations from businessmen during the course of the campaign. The Labour Party makes all donations over £5,000 public at the time of the Party Conference – this donation will be listed in our 1997 accounts to be presented to the Conference in October 1998.

    It was made clear to Mr. Ecclestone at the time of his gift, as it is made clear to all donors, that no donation could or would be accepted if the donor had

Labour

- 2 -

any expectation of influence over policy and no policies could be changed as a result of any such donation. Nor did Mr. Ecclestone make any such suggestion.

In the Manifesto, the Labour Party said it would ban tobacco advertising. Though limited to advertising, this was generally understood to cover at least some aspects of a sponsorship. Tobacco companies advertise widely in magazines, on bill boards and through direct mail. In addition they sponsor events, in particular sporting events.

The Government announced through its Health Secretary, Frank Dobson, on 19 May that we wanted a complete ban on sports advertising and sponsorship, though in doing so we recognised the need to protect the future of sport. This could be achieved by national policies similar to those adopted in other countries.

After the election, this Government also became involved in discussions with other European countries about the possibility of an EU-wide directive banning or limiting such advertising and sponsorship. Discussions on this are continuing.

After careful consideration, we concluded that to ban such sponsorship completely Europe-wide from Formula 1 would result in Britain losing its Grand Prix and the race going elsewhere; and if there was a total ban in Europe then Europe could be vacated as a venue and the races moved to Asia where a number of countries are pressing strongly to host such races. They, of course, have no advertising or sponsorship restrictions and their races would be broadcast in the UK with tobacco advertising in place. The Grand Prix races attract vast numbers of people and are huge money earners for the countries concerned.

In addition, Britain, as the original home of the Formula 1 industry, makes 80 per cent of the cars and employs roughly 50,000 people in connected industries. To lose any significant part of the industry would be disastrous. The sponsorship for Formula 1 is far more weighted to tobacco than any other sport. Sponsorship could not realistically be changed except over a long time frame.

Exemptions for Formula 1 are commonplace in other countries for these reasons. For example, Australia, which has some of the toughest anti-sponsorship and advertising laws, expressly exempts Formula 1. A number of other countries, including Germany, Portugal and Austria, have laws banning tobacco advertising but make special arrangements for Formula 1.

On this basis, we decided we had to ensure that whilst holding to the general policy of a ban, we could not agree – along with several other Member

- 3 -

States – to a ban on Formula 1. We therefore, in line with the others, proposed that the Directive should exempt Formula 1.

We are continuing, however, to reduce advertising and sponsorship at the British Grand Prix in conjunction with the race organisers. What's more, we are proposing a worldwide voluntary agreement with Formula 1 to reduce, and ultimately phase out, tobacco sponsorship worldwide, but giving them time to adjust to new sponsorship. Such an agreement, which the FIA have themselves proposed, would have the effect of reducing exposure to tobacco sponsorship on a world-wide basis.

These decisions were not, of course, in any way influenced by Mr. Ecclestone's contribution some months before. Indeed, the policy was hardened in the Manifesto and in the Health Secretary's announcement, both of which came after the gift.

In addition, of course, since the fact of the donation will be made public, there is no possible concealment of the gift.

Mr. Ecclestone has, since the election, offered a further donation. The Prime Minister has decided that in the light of our approach to the Directive and to avoid any possible appearance of a conflict of interest we should consult you on whether it may properly be accepted. The position which we have adopted thus far has been to refuse this further donation, but we wish to be advised whether this is a position, which we need to maintain. This approach distinguished between a pre-election donation which, of course, was not a factor in the government's decision, which was taken exclusively in the national interest as the government judged it, and the receipt of post election donations where an appearance of a conflict of interest might be thought to arise.

However, clearly, the case raises difficult questions for us. The gift or offer of it did not and could not influence our approach to the EU Directive. But to what extent are we unable to receive gifts, as a Party, from people in business whose business may at any point come across the desk of Government. In truth, most businesses are involved with Government in some degree or other. What are the rules and principles which should apply?

If a situation like this arises:

(a)   can we carry on as a party to accept a gift from business, provided there is no question of any agreement, explicit or implicit, of favours by government, and

- 4 -

(b)   when subsequently a business that has made a gift comes into contact with Government, what should, if anything, happen to the original gift?

It seems to us that this is a crucial set of issues. We want to ensure that we have your clear guidance both – if this is possible – in respect of the particular case and we are happy to provide any additional details you wish; and in respect of the matter of general principle.

I look forward to hearing from you. We are of course happy to abide by whatever ruling you give.

Tom Sawyer
General Secretary

Committee on Standards
in Public Life

Chairman:
Sir Patrick Neill QC

Horse Guards Road
London SW1P 3AL
E-mail
Neill@gtnet.gov.uk
Telephone
0171 270 5875
Direct line
0171 270 1966

Tom Sawyer Esq   **URGENT**
General Secretary
The Labour Party
John Smith House
150 Walworth Road
London SE17 1JT   10 November 1997

Dear Mr. Sawyer,

Thank you for your letter of 7 November. You asked for urgent advice.

My Committee has not yet received the precise terms of its remit in respect of party funding, and I do not think it would be sensible for me, in advance of that remit or our study, to endeavour to formulate the sort of general principles about the receipt or refusal of donations which you seek towards the end of your letter. I can assure you that we will address these problems as part of our study.

I have however considered the particular donation and the prospective donation carefully in the light of the principles which the Committee has already published in previous Reports. I have also consulted the Code of Conduct and Guidance on Procedures for Ministers (Cabinet Office, July 1997).

One principle which emerges clearly from the Reports and from the Code is that the conduct of those in public positions must be judged not only by the reality but also by the appearance.

In addition this Committee has established seven Principles of Public Life. Two of them, Integrity and Openness, appear to me to be relevant in the present context. I quote:

INTEGRITY
Holders of public office should not place themselves under any financial or other obligation to outside individuals or organisations that might seek to influence them in the performance of their official duties.

Members: *Sir Clifford Boulton GCB, Sir Martin Jacomb, Professor Anthony King, The Rt Hon Tom King CH MP, The Rt Hon The Lord Shore of Stepney, Sir William Utting CB, The Rt Hon The Lord Thomson of Monifieth KT DL, Diana Warwick, Dame Anne Warburton DCVO CMG* **Secretary:** *Richard Hortman*

OPENNESS

Holders of public office should be as open as possible about all the decisions and actions that they take. They should give reasons for their decisions and restrict information only when the wider public interest clearly demands.

In the light of these principles it seem clear to me that you are right to declare the first donation from Mr Ecclestone. I understand that your normal procedures would cause you to list this donation in your 1997 accounts to be presented to the Annual Conference in October 1998. I do not, however, believe that in the present circumstances it would be right to delay announcing this donation until October 1998. Questions are already being publicly asked about this gift, and delay in announcing it could carry the implication, which you would be the first to repudiate, that receipt of the gift was in some way questionable. As the Committee said in its first Report, whatever the true picture, 'much of the public anxiety about standards of conduct in public life is based on perceptions and beliefs...The erosion of public confidence in the holders of public office is a serious matter'.

It is my view that you should announce the donation as swiftly as possible. In view of the shortage of time I have not had the opportunity to consult my colleagues on the Committee about this matter, but I am sure that they would concur.

As to the second proposed donation, you tell me that you have until now refused to accept it. You wish to be advised whether that is a position which you need to maintain. My advice is that it is.

Your question (b) at the top of page 4 of your letter, when applied in relation to the first donation, raises the issue as to whether this donation can be retained or should be returned. This I regard as a more difficult question and one on which I would have welcomed the views of the Committee. My own opinion is that, while no criticism can fairly be made of the receipt of the first donation, in the light of the way in which Government policy has developed, Ministers could well conclude that, in the special circumstances of this case, their freedom of action would be, and would be seen to be, enhanced, if the donation were to be returned.

It is not clear to me whether you wish this advice to be made public. However, I should say that, if I am asked, in line with my Committee's principle of Openness, I would want to confirm that I have submitted this advice.

I note that you have discussed this matter with the Prime Minister, to whom I am therefore copying this letter.

Yours sincerely,

Patrick Neill

Sir Patrick Neill QC

Appendix 2: Annual Accounts of the Political Parties

Conservative Party 2004

The Conservative Central Office
Consolidated Income and Expenditure Account
For the year ended 31 December 2004

	Note	2004 £'000	2003 £'000
Income			
Donations and fundraising		13,911	7,647
Membership fees and subscriptions	1a	814	814
Grants	1b	4,160	4,144
Investment income	1c	58	96
Notional income	1d	1,098	918
		20,041	13,619
Expenditure			
Costs of fundraising		551	550
Depreciation		711	334
Campaign expenditure		6,702	436
Running costs		16,228	13,572
Net interest payable	4	317	117
Notional expenditure		1,098	918
Conferences		631	107
		26,238	16,034
Deficit for the year before taxation	3	(6,197)	(2,415)
Taxation	5	(30)	-
Deficit for the year	13	(6,227)	(2,415)

All amounts relate to continuing activities.

Conservative Party 2005

The Conservative Central Office
Consolidated Income and Expenditure Account
For the year ended 31 December 2005

	Note	2005	2004 as restated
		£'000	£'000
Income			
Donation income		13,574	13,336
Membership fees	1a	843	814
Income from fundraising activities		239	604
Income from commercial activities		2,388	762
Income from legacies		705	162
Investment income	1b	88	72
Grant income	1c	4,586	4,160
Income from conferences		46	64
Notional income	1d	823	1,098
Other income		935	1,192
Total income		24,227	22,264
Expenditure			
Cost of fundraising activities		421	551
Cost of commercial activities		2,295	182
Notional expenditure		823	1,098
Staff costs		9,413	8,959
Management and administration expenses		7,372	7,212
Depreciation and amortisation		907	711
Campaign expenditure		15,678	6,702
Interest payable	4	1,111	331
Conference expenditure		548	631
Other expenditure		638	978
Total expenditure		39,206	27,355
Deficit before taxation	3	(14,979)	(5,091)
Taxation	5	(20)	(30)
Deficit for the year	13	(14,999)	(5,121)

All amounts relate to continuing activities.

Labour Party 2004

Consolidated Income and Expenditure Account of the Labour Party
For the year ended 31 December 2004

	2004	2003
	£'000	£'000
Income		
Donations	8,958	9,058
Membership	3,492	3,452
Affiliations	7,559	6,762
Fundraising	922	858
Commercial income	3,615	3,130
Legacies	278	571
Interest receivable	39	71
Government grants	440	439
Notional income	600	264
Other income	3,409	2,335
Total income	29,312	26,940
Expenditure		
Costs of fundraising	(744)	(647)
Costs of commercial activity	(3,644)	(2,279)
Notional expenditure	(462)	(239)
Running costs	(22,467)	(17,300)
Campaign expenditure	(1,707)	(982)
Interest payable	(768)	(803)
Grants and payments to CLPs	(1,120)	(1,142)
Other	(1,197)	(889)
Total expenditure	(32,109)	(24,281)
(Deficit)/ surplus from Party activities before taxation	(2,797)	2,659
Taxation	-	(22)
(Deficit)/ surplus for the year	(2,797)	2,637

Labour Party 2005

Consolidated Income and Expenditure Account of the Labour Party
For the year ended 31 December 2005

		As Restated
	2005	2004
	£'000	£'000
Income		
Donations	13,900	8,958
Membership	3,685	3,492
Affiliations	8,009	7,559
Fundraising	877	922
Commercial income	3,385	3,615
Legacies	203	278
Interest receivable (restated, note 29)	274	298
Government grants	440	440
Notional income	1,415	600
Other income	3,116	3,409
Total income	35,304	29,571
Expenditure		
Costs of fundraising	(2,065)	(744)
Costs of commercial activity	(2,797)	(3,644)
Notional expenditure	(345)	(462)
Running costs (restated, note 29)	(23,815)	(20,004)
Campaign expenditure (restated, note 29)	(15,166)	(4,230)
Interest payable	(1,349)	(768)
Grants and payments to CLPs	(1,070)	(1,120)
Other	(3,197)	(1,197)
Total expenditure	(49,804)	(32,169)
Deficit from Party activities before taxation	(14,500)	(2,598)
Taxation	-	-
Deficit for the year	(14,500)	(2,598)

Liberal Democrats 2004

The Liberal Democrats (The Federal Party)
Income and Expenditure Account
For the year ended 31 December 2004

	Note	General fund £	Campaign fund £	Total 2004 £	Total 2003 £
Income					
Donations		811,828	1,287,990	2,099,818	1,406,176
Membership and subscription fees		709,539	-	709,539	680,170
Newspaper income	11	143,727	-	143,727	138,833
Affinity income		50,536	-	50,536	47,988
Grants	5	427,804	-	427,804	445,317
Conference income	10	784,241	-	784,241	660,491
Investment income	6	1,601	12,770	14,371	4,171
Notional income	7	50,583	-	50,583	27,150
Recharges to party bodies	12	663,329	-	663,329	598,679
Other	8	116,173	-	116,173	87,305
		3,759,361	1,300,760	5,060,121	4,096,280
Expenditure					
Conference expenditure	10	319,275	-	319,275	332,494
Newspaper expenditure	11	106,396	-	106,396	103,969
Fund raising expenses		109,483	2,231	111,714	62,874
Depreciation and amortisation	4	46,435	7,000	53,435	32,291
Campaign expenditure		165,000	891,774	1,056,774	667,569
Staff costs	2	1,596,917	-	1,596,917	1,605,341
Premises & office costs		646,710	9,249	655,959	548,073
Interest payable and bank charges	9	20,814	370	21,184	22,429
Notional expenditure	7	50,583	-	50,583	27,150
Grants to party bodies and rechargeable expenditure	13	489,156	-	489,156	467,615
Audit fees	4	13,000	4,748	17,748	11,422
Bad debt provision		30,126	-	30,126	-
Other		105,151	-	105,151	123,922
		3,699,046	915,372	4,614,418	4,005,149
Surplus before taxation		60,315	385,388	445,703	91,131
Taxation	14	(116)	(922)	(1,038)	613
Surplus for the year		60,199	384,466	444,665	91,744

Liberal Democrats 2005

The Liberal Democrats (The Federal Party)
Income and Expenditure Account
For the year ended 31 December 2005

	Note	General fund £	Campaign fund £	Total 2005 £	Restated Total 2004 £
Income					
Donations		672,073	4,770,963	5,443,036	2,099,818
Membership and subscription fees		768,450	-	768,450	709,539
Newspaper income	11	131,719	-	131,719	143,727
Affinity income		47,081	11,130	58,211	50,536
Grants	5	422,050	-	422,050	427,804
Conference income	10	809,720	-	809,720	784,241
Investment income	6	1,706	31,882	33,588	14,371
Notional income	7	50,171	90,205	140,376	50,583
Recharges to party bodies	12	613,575	9,575	623,150	663,329
Other	8	104,652	47,083	151,735	116,173
		3,621,197	4,960,838	8,582,035	5,060,121
Expenditure					
Conference expenditure	10	413,681	-	413,681	319,275
Newspaper expenditure	11	95,516	-	95,516	106,396
Fund raising expenses		33,512	261,857	295,369	111,714
Depreciation and amortisation	4	52,100	10,785	62,885	53,435
Campaign expenditure		210,000	4,662,465	4,872,465	1,056,774
Staff costs	2	1,545,493	4,672	1,550,165	1,505,832
Premises & office costs		669,086	149,494	818,580	655,959
Interest payable and bank charges	9	22,891	7,687	30,578	21,184
Notional expenditure	7	50,171	90,205	140,376	50,583
Grants to party bodies and rechargeable expenditure	13	411,184	-	411,184	489,156
Audit fees	4	12,000	6,169	18,169	17,748
Bad debt provision		16,287	-	16,287	30,126
Other finance charges		5,000	-	5,000	9,000
Other		53,230	-	53,230	105,151
		3,590,151	5,193,334	8,783,485	4,523,333
(Deficit)/surplus before taxation		31,046	(232,496)	(201,450)	527,788
Taxation	14	(285)	(5,317)	(5,602)	(1,038)
(Deficit)/surplus for the year		30,761	(237,813)	(207,052)	526,750

Appendix 3: The Structure of the Labour Party

The British Labour Party is one of a family of democratic socialist/social democratic parties found in most Western countries. Some (such as the Australian Labor Party) are organised on the same basis as the Labour Party with individual and affiliated members. Some (such as the Social Democratic Party in Germany) are organised on different principles with individual members only. Organisational form reflects historical development: in some countries trade unions were established before the party and helped to give birth to the party. In other countries, the party was formed before the trade unions and it was the party that helped to give birth to the unions. But in all cases the same common theme runs through these different organisations sheltering under the banner of the Socialist International, that common theme being the close relationship that exists between the political and industrial wings of the organised Labour movement.[1]

Trade Unions and Labour Party Structure

The Labour Party is unique among the major British political parties in the sense that it is an organisation of individuals and organisations. The former are arranged in Constituency Labour Parties (CLPs), while the latter are affiliated trade unions, socialist societies and political parties. Although organisations affiliate to the party on the basis of the number of relevant members of the organisation, nevertheless it is the organisation (and not its individual members) that is the member of the party. It is thus the organisation that is admitted to the party, may resign from the party and may be expelled from the party. Each affiliated trade union has taken a democratic decision to join the Labour Party, based upon a majority vote of the representative delegates at the union's national conference. These decisions are subject to challenge, so unions frequently have to vote to maintain the affiliation, and again a majority decision is required. There are now seventeen trade unions affiliated to the Labour Party, which is many fewer than in the past, reflecting the tendency of trade unions to merge in recent years.

The level of affiliation to the Labour Party at national level is decided by the affiliated member, but is limited by the number of union members who contribute to the political fund. Affiliation costs £3 per year per member. Trade union regions and local branches also affiliate to the Labour Party at regional and CLP levels respectively. At a regional level, and in Scotland and Wales, unions send delegates to regional Labour Party conferences and elect representatives on the Regional Board of the Labour Party. At constituency level, local union branches affiliate to CLPs at a rate of £6 per 100 members per year. This entitles the union branch to send a delegate to the CLP's General Committee, to submit

---

[1] For a fuller examination of the issues in this appendix, see K D Ewing, *Trade Unions, the Labour Party and Political Funding* (2002).

resolutions, and to make nominations for candidates for the Parliamentary candidacy of that constituency. Members of affiliated organisations may also join the Party in their individual capacity, and individual members of the Party are encouraged to join an appropriate trade union if they have not already done so.

Constitutional Integration

Under the federal structure of the Labour Party, trade unions – as affiliated members – are constitutionally integrated into all aspects of party organisation. Trade unions are directly represented on the National Executive Committee (NEC) of the party, the body responsible for providing its strategic direction. In addition to the twelve seats formally held by trade unionists, other positions on the NEC – such as Party Treasurer – may also be held by a trade unionist. Policy-making in the Party is now conducted by a rolling programme of consultation through policy forums, policy commissions and the National Policy Forum. Trade unions have an opportunity to participate in all of these processes and are guaranteed thirty of the 183 places on the National Policy Forum, a body that meets to consider and agree policy documents before presentation to the Labour Party Conference, the sovereign body within the party. Affiliated organisations have 50 per cent of the votes at Conference, allocated on the basis of affiliation levels, with larger unions affiliating more members and having more votes than smaller unions with fewer members.

In addition to the foregoing, trade unions are a key element in the electoral college arrangements for the election of party leader and deputy leader, along with the CLPs and the Parliamentary Labour Party. Under the current arrangements for election of the party leader and deputy leader, the Parliamentary Labour Party, CLPs and affiliated organisations each have one-third of the votes. In these elections, affiliated trade unions have to conduct a postal ballot of all their members in the relevant area in order to decide the proportions in which their votes are cast. If one union's members decide by 60 per cent to back one candidate, that candidate receives 60 per cent of that union's vote, ensuring that all levy-paying union members can participate and that each individual member's vote counts. In this way the Labour Party constitution ensures that members of affiliated organisations have the right to participate in a major decision affecting the party, provided they pay the political levy of their union. It is not necessary for this purpose for the trade unionist to be a member of the Labour Party in his or her own right.

Trade Unions and Labour Party Liaison Organisation

Trade unions are not just embedded in the structure of the Labour Party: trade union members are also work with the party. Much of this work is now co-ordinated by the Trade Union and Labour Party Liaison Organisation (TULO), established in 1994. TULO is distinguished from several forerunner organisations as a more formal body, while it also serves the dual purposes of not only co-ordinating trade union support for the Labour Party at election time, but also of acting as an ongoing channel of communication between the party and its union members. Every affiliated union automatically becomes a member of the National TULO, and its General Secretary is entitled to sit on the National TULO Committee, if he or she is an individual member of the Labour Party. The Committee is jointly chaired by a member from the union side and the Labour Party Chair. The other members of TULO include the Leader, Deputy Leader and General Secretary of the Labour Party, the Chair of the Labour Party NEC, and representatives of the Trade Union Groups of Labour MPs and MEPs. TULO is registered under the PPERA as a Labour Party accounting unit.

Appendix 4: From Election Funding to Political Funding in Germany

State funding of political parties in Germany is the outcome of a complex and fascinating struggle between the legislature and the Federal Constitutional Court in the search for a fair system. There have in fact been several major decisions, leading one commentator to observe that there can be few countries in the world where the courts have played such an important part in shaping the content of the party-funding rules. A study of the US experience may cause him to revise his assessment. It remains the case, nevertheless, that the current provisions for public funding and tax relief are the product of what commentators in other countries refer to as a 'dialogue' between judges and politicians, in which the Court has been driven to find a system that is compatible with the principle of equality underpinning the German Basic Law, a provision from which the Federal Constitutional Court has inferred 'a doctrine of equal electoral opportunity'.[1] The Basic Law also deals with the political parties, and as such secures their constitutional recognition. But although providing that they should be freely established, that they must be governed in accordance with democratic principles, and publicly account for their funding, there is no provision in the constitution that authorises or requires public funds to be used to sustain the political parties.

The current arrangements (as recently modified) were introduced following a decision of the Federal Constitutional Court in 1992. This decision reversed the earlier rulings of the Court that public funding should be confined only to meet the electoral activities of the parties, the Court holding that the State should be free to meet the other expenses incurred by political parties in the performance of the duty imposed upon them by the Basic Law, namely the formation of the political will of the people. This opened the way for State funding of the general activities of the parties, though the Court also said that public funding must not exceed the income raised by the parties from other sources: this means that no party may receive more than half of its income from the State. It was also held that the eligibility of a party to public funds should be based on its representativeness as well as its membership: representativeness is to be determined by reference to electoral support, the number of donors and the number of members of the party. One additional ruling of the Court was that the annual budget for distribution by the State to the parties must not exceed a legally prescribed maximum, which means that there may not be enough money to meet the entitlements of the parties based on their representativeness. This would have the effect of imposing a cap on the amount of State funding to a party which was unduly successful.

Following the 1992 decision of the Federal Constitutional Court, new legislation was introduced in 1994. This now provides that the total amount of public

---

[1] D P Currie, *The Constitution of the Federal Republic of Germany* (1998), p 208.

funds available for distribution to the political parties may not exceed €133m. Each party is entitled to a fixed sum each year based on the average of votes received at the last three elections. Each party is also entitled to a fixed sum based on the revenue raised by way of membership fees or donations raised. In this latter case, only donations by natural persons count, and they count only up to a maximum of €3,300. Not all parties are eligible for funding, which is limited to those parties receiving a minimum of 0.5 per cent of all the valid votes received at the relevant national or European elections, or 1 per cent of the votes received at the relevant *Land* elections. The 1992 decision of the Constitutional Court also addressed the system of income tax relief for political donations in Germany, and held that tax deductions for political donations should be set at a level at which the majority of taxpayers could make use of the allowance in an equal manner, and that only natural and not also legal persons should qualify for relief. In principle, donations to all parties qualify for tax relief: there is no exclusion of small parties directly or indirectly through high registration thresholds. However, donations of up to only €3,300 qualify for tax relief. Although higher donations may be made, they are not tax deductible.[2]

The State funding of political parties in Germany seems fantastic by British standards. At today's values, €133m is approximately £94m, though as one commentator wrote in 2004, it is the equivalent of €1.66 for every German citizen (or at the then value of the euro, only £1.10 per German citizen). An equivalent sum in Britain (assuming a population of around 60 million) would be £66m, to be distributed to the parties on an annual basis, which is well below what even the most fervent supporter of State funding could realistically contemplate. This level of support for political parties in Germany is justified by the Friedrich Ebert Foundation on the ground that it is the equivalent to less than a cup of coffee for each citizen, and a cost to the national economy of less than the subsidies given to support tobacco growing in Germany. Under the scheme, the main parties received the following amounts in 2004: Christian Democrats, €55.8m; Social Democrats, €43.77m; Liberals, €9.8m; Green Party, €9.55m; and the Left Party €8.52m. (At the time, this was equivalent to £38.7m, £30.3m, £6.7m, £6.6m and £5.9m respectively.) Even then, these generous sums accounted for less than half the annual income of the parties, as the law requires. It is estimated that in 2001, the public subsidies to the parties accounted for an average of only 31 per cent of their income.[3]

[2] E Hillebrand, *State Funding for Political Parties in Germany* (2006).
[3] *Ibid*, on which this paragraph heavily relies.

Appendix 5: State Funding in Sweden – Party Autonomy and Public Funding

Public funding is typically introduced for two principal purposes: the reimburse-ment of all or some of the election expenses incurred by candidates and parties, on the one hand; and meeting the operational costs of the political parties, on the other. The Swedish system falls firmly into the latter category, though the entitle-ment of the parties to public funds is determined on the basis of electoral results.[1] The freedom of political parties is in fact jealously safeguarded in Sweden, where it is recognised that 'independent parties, free press and news media and the free formation of opinion are fundamental elements of democ-racy'. In terms of the role of political parties, echoing the German Basic Law, it is said in official propaganda issued by the Riksdag that political parties mould public opinion, and 'fulfil an essential task in society, especially at general elec-tions. They provide the voters with alternatives and information as well as the opportunity of exerting an influence on society, participating and taking full responsibility.' This at least tells us what it is expected of the parties, even if it does not tell us whether they fulfil these expectations.

The position of political parties in Sweden is underpinned by two comple-mentary principles: autonomy from the State; and support by the State. Like most of the rest of the EU, there is constitutional protection in Sweden for freedom of association, though, unlike Germany, there is no specific guarantee relating to political parties as such. But there is constitutional recognition of the parties in the election procedures to be found in the constitution; this pro-vides that 'seats are distributed between parties', a term defined to mean 'any association or group of voters which appears in an election under a specific designation'. In line with the Swedish views about the independence of the parties, there is no legal obligation for the parties to disclose their accounts or to reveal the identity or amounts of donations. Party accounts are made public as a result of an agreement between the parties, and not as a matter of obligation imposed by the State.[2] And as in Germany, there are no contribution or election spending limits. But any omission here is more than adequately compensated for the fact that a diverse press is sustained by the public subsidies, though it is of course the case that this does not provide the means to reach voters other than party supporters. Nor is there any provision in Sweden for tax allowances to the political parties.

---

[1] Sweden is divided into twenty-eight multi-member constituencies, with seats distributed within each constituency 'in proportion to the number of those entitled to vote'. The seats are then dis-tributed among the parties 'according to the number of votes cast in the constituency'. The 310 constituencies are supplemented by what are referred to as thirty-nine adjustment seats which are allocated to the parties 'in such a way that the distribution of all the seats in the Riksdag . . . is proportionate to the total number of votes respectively for the participating parties in the whole of the country'. Elections are held at fixed intervals every three years.

[2] See K D Ewing, *The Funding of Political Parties in Britain* (1987), ch 7.

For the discharge of their responsibilities the parties receive generous funding from both central and local government. This is considered to be 'of great importance to democracy', and specifically 'gives all parties which have acquired a certain number of votes the opportunity of pursuing their political activities on a long-term basis, without being dependent on various contributors'. The scheme was introduced in the 1960s, and support for the parties from central government and the Riksdag amounts to SEK360m annually, which is approximately £28m. This is made up of two major parts: the first is to support the general activities of the parties, and the second is to support the activities of the members of the Riksdag and the party groups in the Riksdag. The former stands at SEK164m, and the latter SEK172m, or approximately £12.6m and £13.2m respectively. The support for the general activities of the parties is thus proportionately higher than the position in Germany, on the basis that the equivalent of roughly £1.40 per person (not all of whom would be either taxpayers or voters) is allocated from public funds for use by the political parties. An equivalent sum in the United Kingdom would be about £84m annually.

Support for the general activities outside the Riksdag (the allocation of SEK164m) is in turn divided into two parts: one is for *party assistance*, and the other is for *office assistance*. Party assistance is based on the number of seats that each party holds in the Riksdag, and is based on SEK333,300 per seat. Office assistance is paid to each party which received at least 4 per cent of the votes in the most recent Riksdag election. The basic contribution of SEK5.8m is paid to all parties, with a supplementary contribution being paid to the parties according to the number of seats held. In the case of the government party or parties this amounts to SEK16,350 per seat, and in the case of the opposition parties it amounts to SEK24,300 per seat. Before the general election in September 2006, seven parties qualified for both party assistance and office assistance: in the year before the election, the Social Democratic Party received SEK55.49m; the Moderate Party received SEK27.14m; the Left Party received SEK17.20m; the Christian Democrats received SEK18.27m; the Centre Party received SEK13.34m; the Liberal Party received SEK21.30m; and the Green Party received SEK11.88m. Each of these parties also received support for Riksdag members and party groups in the Riksdag, and funding is provided for parties without seats that poll at least 2.5 per cent of the vote.

Index

273